Starved Stuff

Starved Stuff

Feeding the 7 Basic Needs of Healthy Relationships

Matt Townsend

Second Edition

Designed by Scott Eggers, sedslc.com

Manufactured in the United States of America

ISBN
978-0-615-35170-4

To my wife, Mardi,
For her constant feeding of
Safety, Trust, Appreciation, Respect, Validation,
Encouragement, and Dedication,

and

To my children,
Sarah, Jacob, Tanner, Britton, Spencer, and Josh.
I love being your dad!

I love you all!

Acknowledgments

Just as a journey of a thousand miles must begin with a single step, the journey of this book did begin with a single step taken many years ago. And with one step taken, I felt lifted by hundreds of others along the way who have carried me, pushed me, prodded, pulled, and shuttled me to the finish line. In the end, this book is a monumental group effort and there are many people to thank.

Thank you, Tammy Rigby, my most trusted assistant, for having my back and for caring at times even more than I did. Your selfless support, commitment, hard work and focus on the minutia cannot be understated. This book would not have happened without your work.

Thank you, Bettyanne Bruin, for your gifted synthesizing, editing and writing ability. It was your positive energy that pushed this book project forward, and without your direction, people would still be asking, "When is your book going to be out?"

To my wife, Mardi, and my children, Sarah, Jake, Tanner, Britton, Spencer and Josh, thank you for your endless love and support. You have helped me learn the lessons contained in this book and I appreciate your willingness to share our stories with the world.

Thank you to my mom and dad, Carolyn and Martin Townsend, who have both contributed greatly to the success of this book and its author. Mom, thanks for always being my biggest cheerleader and providing the runway to succeed in life. And Dad, thanks for the invaluable gift of humor, which has provided me access to the hearts of so many who desperately need to be fed.

Thank you to my parents-in-law, Mike and Merrilee Preece, and grandparents-in-law, Bill and Margaret Preece, for exemplifying healthy relationships.

Thank you to all of my clients, workshop participants and "guinea pigs" that have helped me sculpt this content while working on their issues. There truly is no doubt in my mind that I learned much more from all of you than you could have ever learned from me. Your hands are all through this material and you need to know that the lessons learned during some of your lowest times together are now lifting others.

Thank you to those associates and colleagues, both past and present, who have selflessly strengthened my voice and enabled this mission of helping to feed relationships. In particular, thanks to Steve Helland, Abraham Shreve, Mike and Amy Bohn, Teresa and Ryne Hazen, Dave and Gerry Fairbanks, Harry Nelson, Jill McIntyre, Peter Brooks, Brint Driggs, and John and Jane Covey

Thank you to my biggest cheerleaders who constantly push me to be better and help me believe in myself: Martianne and Perry White, Jackie and Randy Jolly, Mary and Allan McNichol, Paige Preece, Katie and Adam Jacobsmeyer, Camryn and James Stewart, Mike and Jennie Preece, Stephen and Jenny Preece, Margene McFarland, Joel Wolfgang, Bart Summerhays, Sylvia Brunisholz, Kent and Kristena Eden, and Victor and Lois Cline.

A gifted book team converged on this project and turned a distant dream into a reality. Thank you to Scott Eggers, Jennifer Grillone, Justin Workman, Jeff Bagley, Mardi Townsend, Ann Hoole, Jen Romney, Karen Rozsa, Judy and Lauren Ball, Jyl Pattee, Annie Oswald, and special thanks to Rebecca Merrill for her invaluable thoughts and direction.

Finally, thank you to everyone else not mentioned here whose examples I have followed, whose words have lifted me, and whose positive actions have helped me believe that this could all happen. Thank you! Thank you! Thank you!

PREFACE 1

THE GOAL: Healthy and Enduring Relationships

The Three Stages of Love: Yearning, Earning, and Enduring 11

THE CHALLENGE: The STARVED Stuff

Focusing on the Smoke, Not the Fire 35

Feeding the 7 Basic Needs of Healthy Relationships 51

The STARVED Spiral 79

THE SOLUTION: Four Courses to Feed the Healthy Relationship

Let the Feeding Begin 105

THE COURSE ON CHARACTER

Defining Character 125

The Choice to Keep Your Head in the Game 149

The Choice to be an Empowered Communicator 171

The Choice to Take the High Road 185

THE COURSE ON COMMUNICATION

Checking Your Partner's Vital Signs 215

Getting REAL Communication (Part 1) 229

Getting REAL Communication (Part 2) 255

THE COURSE ON COMPANIONSHIP

Holding the Love You Are Given 283

Pouring the Love Your Partner Wants 311

THE COURSE ON COMMITMENT

The Commitment to Learn and Change 349

Becoming the Change You Seek in Others 377

Preface

As a child of divorced parents, I quite naturally became interested in the dynamics of human relationships at a fairly young age. Whenever I played at a friend's house, I paid close attention to how my friend's parents communicated. For most of my life, for whatever reason, I seemed to be the one other people would approach to discuss their relationship problems. When dating my wife, I studied both her parents' and grandparents' interactions with curiosity. In my own explorations, both educationally and professionally with couples, corporations, and communities, relationships have always fascinated me. Over the years, I have seen very powerful and predictable patterns emerge within all of these relationships I have observed. Even though each relationship is as individual as a snowflake that falls from the sky, I found predictable similarities among relationships, in how they form, how they bind together, and the issues that threaten their longevity and livelihood.

My learning was deepened as I used my communication and conflict resolution skills working as a divorce mediator, trying to help couples who had lost all hope in their relationship and thought the most painless way to get through it was to divorce. In that work, I found nearly one-third of all the people who came to use my services didn't actually want to divorce, but didn't know what else to do; they could no longer live together and felt as though they had tried everything they could to preserve the marriage. They had been to therapy, read the suggested books, and yet nothing seemed to change the pain they continued to inflict upon each other. This was when it dawned on me that often couples just don't have the tools to make a relationship work. From this point on, I changed my course of action from trying to help couples end marriages peacefully, to instead trying to help couples save their relationship courageously. My desire became to share all of the skills and tools I had accumulated over a decade and combine them with the latest research in marriage and family in hopes of preventing other couples from going through the same difficulties.

Research shows that more than 90 percent of people in the world, both male and female, will marry in their lifetime, with roughly 50 percent of marriages in the United States ending in divorce. How can it be that so many people seek the goal of a healthy relationship and yet a healthy relationship remains so elusive?

After working with literally thousands of couples, ranging from newly engaged to nearly divorced, I believe strongly that most couples want the exact same thing when it comes to their relationships: for them to be healthy, happy, and to be able to endure the test of time. Simply put, they want their relationship to last. This book is my attempt to encapsulate the principles I have found that create healthy and enduring relationships. These are the principles taught in my six-week "Feeding the STARVED Relationship" workshop. Just as I help couples set their **Goals**, overcome **Challenges,** and find **Solutions** in my relationship-coaching practice, I have chosen to break down this book into three sections:

The Goal — Creating Healthy and Enduring Relationships
The Challenges — STARVED Stuff: Feeding the 7 Basic Needs of Healthy and Enduring Relationships
The Solutions — The Four Courses That Feed the STARVED Relationship

As a relationship coach, my goal is to help you and your partner create positive change. To help you do this, I've included a page at the end of each chapter for you to record what you have learned and what you feel compelled to change in your relationship. If you fill out "My Feeding Plan" after every chapter, by the time you get to the end of the book, you will have a complete plan for how to create a healthy and enduring relationship.

In **The Goal** section of this book, we will examine one of the most critical yet confusing concepts to creating healthy and enduring relationships, namely the concept we call "love." In order to understand **The Goal**, one must learn how to navigate through each of the Three Stages of Love. These stages include the "hot and heavy" Yearning Love, where we will learn about the chemistry that heats up and blinds a couple during the initial stage of a relationship. Then there's the more monotonous and grueling Earning Love, where we learn about the "smoke" that chokes out marriages and may make us want to end the lifelong journey prematurely. Finally, we will explore the rewarding summit or goal of Enduring Love so we have a crystal clear example of how love is earned and maintained in healthy and enduring partnerships.

The second section of this book is **The Challenge**, or the primary reasons we don't achieve **The Goal**. In this section, we will go in-depth about the endless forms of "smoke" that tend to suck the life out of our relationships. And, everyone knows that wherever there is smoke, there has got to be fire, so in this section we will learn how to cut through all of the hazy smoke of our relationships and get right down to the actual "fire" (the real burning needs) that tends to cause all of the problems. We will also learn to recognize the 7 Basic Needs critical to all healthy and enduring relationships, and the acronym we use to depict those seven needs:

Safety

Trust

Appreciation

Respect

Validation

Encouragement

Dedication

When these seven needs are met, we feel loved and fed. On the other hand, when our most basic relational needs are not being met, we begin to feel STARVED. The number one challenge of healthy and enduring relationships is starvation. In this book, we will be taught how to feed our relationship, whether we are feeling STARVED or whether our relationship is simply suffering from "the munchies."

The final section, and largest section of the book, is called **The Solutions**. This section is where the real feeding begins. In this section, we will be introduced to four complete courses that will help us begin to feed even the most troubled relationship. Each course contains tools designed to help us not only feed our partners, but ourselves as well. The four courses we will review are

1. The Course on Character
2. The Course on Communication
3. The Course on Companionship
4. The Course on Commitment

To see what's on the menu of each course, we'll break them down a little further:

Course 1 — Character: How to Build Mutual Trust

In this foundational course, we will be taught the first principle upon which all enduring relationships are built, namely character. Character is the ability to stick to a decision long after the emotion of the decision has passed. This builds mutual trust.

Course 2 — Communication: How to Build Mutual Understanding

This course on communication will ensure that we are both more skilled and more able to create mutual understanding. We'll learn to get to the heart of important issues and share what's in our hearts.

Course 3 — Companionship: How to Build Mutual Benefit

Enduring relationships require that both partners in the relationship benefit mutually. That means that both parties learn how to give and receive love in the relationship.

Course 4 — Commitment: How to Build Mutual Growth

In this final course on feeding, we will learn how to pull ourselves out of the ruts of relating to create long-term, mutual growth in the relationship. All growth is based in both learning and changing.

It has been said that if we do the same thing over and over again, we will get the same results. If you're tired of getting the same ineffective results with each other, then this book is for you. My experience is that couples, or even just individuals, who want to make a change in their relationship, can make that change. In order to effectively create the change you're looking for, you must have four things, all of which are contained in this book:

- A set **Goal** you want to achieve
- A clear understanding of the **Challenges** you face
- A realistic set of **Solutions** and the tools needed to get the job done
- Consistent and dedicated action on each solution to meet the goal

All of the tools you need are in this book, but maybe more important than that are the principles to follow to create your own tools. They have been handed down from thousands of couples and people over many, many years of coaching. Take advantage of their examples, learn all you can, and commit to start feeding your relationship right now!

The Goal:

Healthy and Enduring Relationships

Chapter 1

The Three Stages of Love: Yearning, Earning and Enduring

Who doesn't want a happy and enduring relationship? You would probably not be reading this book right now if you did not desire to have healthy relationships in your life. It has taken me many years to figure out what it takes to create this kind of relationship. Is it easy? No! Is it worth it? Yes!

After the hundredth couple came into my office complaining that they had "fallen out of love" with each other, it finally dawned on me that we just don't get it! The bottom line is that most people just don't understand love. As a culture, we have accepted the Hollywood definition of love and, because of this, our expectations have become unrealistic to the point that we no longer understand what really comprises true love.

Unlike other languages, the English language has only one word to describe all of the various meanings and usages of love: we love chocolate, a book, and a spouse. We love being able to pay our bills on time, helping another person, or even smoking. We love a lot of things, yet even if we clearly understand that all of these things are loved differently, we still have only one word to describe how we feel towards each of these very diverse targets of our affection.

Most people who have experienced the sensation of love recognize that there is a vast difference between the feelings a young teenage couple experiences while kissing in a movie theater and the loving feelings shared by an older couple who has weathered the storms of life over a sixty-year period. In order to help us understand these differences, I want to introduce a new vision and a new vocabulary to describe what I call the three stages of love: Yearning Love, Earning Love, and Enduring Love.

Yearning Love

The first stage, Yearning Love, is the love that I believe gets the most attention when it comes to our most intimate relationships. For many, this is what "love" is really all about. This type of love is the chemical stage of love—this stage is all about hormones. Yearning Love comprises those initial and very important feelings that propel us towards each other. These powerful feelings are what drove us to our first kiss and our first everything.

Virtually all it took to "get this engine revving" was a breathing male and a breathing female standing next to each other, followed by some superficial chitchat, a little "badda boom, badda bing," and then, "bam!"—the charging chemicals and intense attraction began. These chemicals drove us to be excited and happy when we were with each other, and they are what generated all of the stimulants that helped us stay up talking late into the night.

YEARNING

HIGH CHEMICALS
LOW CLARITY
COMMITMENT UNTESTED

This very important yearning stage of love is actually nature's way of ensuring that males and females hook up, get married, and reproduce. This love is such a strong force it can actually strengthen our stamina and our ability to go without sleep. It can occupy our attention so much that we can hardly think of anything else. This type of love can embolden us to act in ways we wouldn't normally act and can even give us "super human strength."

An excellent example of this superhero behavior might be seen in the reaction of a typical male who, while in the yearning stage, shows up at his female date's apartment and she apologizes profusely for the fact that she is running a little bit behind schedule for the date. In the fog of yearning, the interchange would go something like this:

"Hey, babe, I'm so sorry I'm running late, but I was talking to Jill and lost track of time. Let me change my clothes and put on some makeup and we'll only be a few minutes late."

To this the partner would then reply in his love-induced coma, "Hey, no problem. I'll wait as long as I need to just to be with you, and by the way, your face is perfect just the way it is. You don't need any makeup!"

Love is blind.
—Geoffrey Chaucer

This super heroic demonstration of control on his part is a great sign that someone is under the influence of yearning. In any other stage of love that was not chemically induced, the man probably would have an entirely different response. For example, he might be sitting in his car in front of her apartment, aggressively honking his horn, shaking his head in frustration, and muttering incomplete sentences to himself about how selfish his partner was.

I like to call Yearning Love the chemical stage of love because when two young lovebirds walk around like this, they are nothing short of a well-stocked virtual pharmacy, filled to the brim with measurably different levels of hormones and natural chemicals than they would normally have—chemicals and hormones that make them ignorant to reality. Some experts believe this form of "blind love," with its accompanied elevated chemistry, lasts for about two to three years for most couples.

Certain hormones are elevated during the Yearning stage of love:

Estrogen is thought to be responsible for a person's healthy libido, as well a core enabler of a woman's more nurturing side, with sensitivity to both verbal and emotional communication.

Testosterone is secreted in both men and women, and plays a key role in health, well-being, energy and sexual function. On average, men produce up to sixty times more testosterone than women.

Oxytocin is responsible for sexual arousal, feelings of bonding, as well as other social behaviors, including maternal behavior, trust, reducing fear and increasing generosity. Oxytocin is also what can addict us to one another, keeping us unable to spend long periods of time away from each other without aching.

Endorphins are responsible for many of the "highs" both men and women experience. Endorphins also help reduce pain and have a tremendous impact on both men and women's emotions. In my workshops, I often joke that these endorphins are what enable most men to enjoy having long conversations with their partner for hours upon hours.

Adrenaline in higher levels give couples a dramatic burst of energy and endurance. And, it is one of the leading causes of why couples are able to stay up so late into the night with reckless abandonment regarding any concerns about their schedules the next day.

Imagine all of these hormones "supersized" and this may explain the incredible charge we feel at the onset of a relationship, as this yearning stage of love begins. However, while these chemicals are vital in establishing "attraction," they were never meant to be sustained at such a high level, which is why they were never meant to be everlasting. Many believe these strong yearning feelings should last forever, but the reality is, they wane in two to three years. Have you ever noticed that many Hollywood marriages often end in just a few years? They never quite make it to the next stage, the earning stage of love.

These chemicals, whose strength lessens with time, should never be used to determine the integrity of a long-term relationship, nor should they be used to set the standard regarding what should be expected long-term. This is one reason why I smile anytime I hear couples invest a lot of time and energy talking about the "chemistry" they share for one another. Inevitably, all of this chemistry is going to be tested and some other source of love will have to take its place if the relationship is going to succeed.

One of the biggest illusions created in this stage is the idea that we learn to act for our partner because we have such strong feelings for him or her. In this yearning stage, we condition ourselves to do nice things for our partner because of these strong feelings. We serve our partner because we feel so much love for him or her. In fact, we serve our partner in ways that we have never served any other person in our lives, even to the shock and amazement of others who know us really well. This noble form of serving is powerful to us and makes us believe we are more committed and in love than ever before. However, I believe this is not the greatest sign of love. In fact, to me, the greatest sign of love comes when we are tested to see if we will offer our partner the exact same level of service when the feelings aren't as powerful. This test will come as we enter the next stage of love, Earning Love.

What we must also understand about yearning is that while intoxicated on these love chemicals, we are not our true self. In this stage, high on chemicals or endorphins, we often censor who we are for our partner, so our "human" side isn't shown too early. This is called self-censoring. Not only does it happen in our "love" relationships, but in other relationships as well, like with our friends, neighbors, and employers. Self-censoring happens in order to appear the way we hope other people might view us, or at least we present the image we feel will increase the likelihood of delivering the results we want. This is a very natural process in all types of human relationships. For instance, when Joe starts a new job, he usually doesn't tell his new boss or co-workers his worst habits, like being habitually late because he is not a morning person, or that he has a habit of "borrowing" company property, or that he sends and receives more than eighty personal e-mails a day. Similarly, in the early stages of love we self-censor to avoid showing our partner our worst characteristics, and put forward our best self instead.

For many of us, this first stage of love—often found in the dating and newlywed years—is obviously the most desirable because of all the wonderful chemicals that come with it, chemicals that deeply affect our memories, feelings, and understanding. Who wouldn't want to feel *this* good, *this* alive, and *this* in love all the time? In our society, Yearning Love is the type of love that is the most widely represented and sought after. Because these feelings are so pleasurable, it is the one most pleasantly remembered, which is why Hollywood depicts this love the most. Yearning Love is the theme behind most of the songs we hear on the radio. It is the theme in many of the television shows we become addicted to, and in the novels we absorb.

However, Yearning Love does have its downside. Because it appears to be so easy and there's not a lot a person has to do to earn it, this type of love creates an illusion and misconception for all future stages of love. In fact, most people actually believe Yearning Love is Enduring Love. They are under the illusion that Yearning Love is what love is really all about. Many of the people I coach have been together for three or more years, with most of them expressing their frustration that this Yearning Love has vanished. Like the old song, "The Thrill Is Gone," they tell me they want to have this love back, but do not know how to obtain it. They want so badly to go back to this stage. They want the "fog" back, where everything seemed okay. They want the "buzz" back that made their partner so irresistible. Simply put, they want love to be a lot easier than it really is. The sad truth about Enduring Love is that it will *never* be as free and easy as it first was in this initial stage.

The good news about all this is that the initial, superficial stage of love is what launches all of the deeper, enduring stages of love. Think of it like a space shuttle launch; every shuttle must be rocketed into space by massive amounts of intense chemicals in order to get 4.5 million pounds of spacecraft and cargo into the air. The rocket boosters are then shed as the transition into the long journey begins. This journey then leads to the discovery of countless wonderful and unexplored places that generate even greater knowledge. Just as these rockets must be shed for the deeper, long journey ahead, so must the chemical stage give way to the next, deeper stage of love, Earning Love.

Earning Love

The next stage of love is completely different. I like to refer to it as the earning stage of love, where each partner must *earn* the love he or she desires. Just as we have to work to earn a paycheck, we now must work to earn the love we both want to share. There are no more freebies; the relationship is not as easy, nor does it float as high in the clouds, as it once did. Most couples know when this stage hits because they often declare, "The honeymoon is over!" It is interesting to note that the majority of couples spend most of their long-term relationships in this stage of love.

EARNING

LOW CHEMICALS

HIGH CLARITY

COMMITMENT IN QUESTION

Lower chemicals and higher clarity signify this earning stage. This doesn't mean chemicals are no longer involved in the relationship, but it does mean these chemicals don't come along as easily as they once did. Instead, they have to be pushed and infused more. This change comes because the chemicals found in the yearning stage have now taken a backseat to clarity; now our feelings for each other are based on the "real" evidence of our day-to-day interactions, and not on the chemical highs that our "love" used to afford. The self-censoring that once filled the yearning stage of love has slowed down, and the true colors in the relationship begin to emerge.

The first reality check comes when the shift from the yearning stage to the earning stage feels anti-climactic. I hear clients say all the time, "But love shouldn't feel this way." Couples wonder, "Is this all there is?" People go through a serious withdrawal after the yearning stage. They say, "What's up with having to earn it? This makes no sense at all! Why do I have to earn this when it came so naturally before?"

I can't tell you how many times I've heard earning stage comments like, "If he loved me, he would just do it." Or, "I shouldn't have to tell her what I need, she should just know." And finally my personal favorite, "I love you, I'm just not *in* love with you!"

At this point, it is important to recognize that just as earning a paycheck is worthwhile and is the means for attaining many of the things you want most, so also is Earning Love worthwhile. For it is by earning this level of deeper love within your relationship that you will achieve the greatest amount of happiness and contentment.

One does not fall "in" or "out" of love. One grows in love.
—Leo Buscaglia

In the earning stage, couples sometimes feel overwhelmed with the new task of handling their relationship without all the chemistry. This is because while in the fog of yearning, both were bound together, excited, and committed to making their incredible journey. Do you remember in your own relationship how excited you both were while yearning to get the journey going? Do you remember talking with each other all day and late into the night about all of the possibilities your partnership could bring? Do you remember when the "honeymoon" officially ended and you began to see your partner with complete clarity as the chemistry began to wear off? Maybe it was the day those dirty clothes on the floor didn't seem so cute anymore, or the day you thought, "What have I gotten myself into here?"

When the chemistry dissipates and the clarity takes root, a couple's commitment truly begins to be tested in ways it has never been tested before. No longer can they rely on free chemistry. Now they must start making the chemistry or earning the love they so desperately desire.

This reminds me of my son, Jake, and the fifty-mile hike he took with his scout troop a few years ago. Before the hike, all of the boys were giddy with excitement, chemically charged for the weeklong hike. The fog my son was in about the entire hike was demonstrated by his comment, which sounded something like this: "Dad, this hike is going to be so awesome! What could be better than being with my friends for an entire week? We get to sleep in tents, carry everything on our backs, and we don't even have to shower if we don't want to. . . . It's going to be so much fun!"

I thought to myself, "This poor, poor boy has no clue what he is about to go through." For me, just like many parents of newlywed couples or couples who are about to have a child, I learned it is better to give support than to try to educate someone who is under the influence of misconceptions.

Guess how many miles down the trail my son was before the yearning wore off? About two-and-a-half miles! Then all the boys began asking,

"Are we there yet?"

"How much longer?"

"This bites! Can we go back?"

Notice how the excitement wore off and the reality set in. The feelings of fun and excitement no longer propelled my son's legs forward. And now the feelings were gone, the new lesson of earning had to be learned.

In the earning stages of life and love, feelings don't always precede actions like they once did in the yearning stage. It just can't be that easy. Instead, in the earning stage, the opposite is true. Actions precede feelings. If you want to have good feelings, you must first act. Actions actually are the drivers and creators of our feelings.

To illustrate this point, let's go back to my son's hiking trip. Once the chemicals wore off, my son no longer had any positive feelings for the fifty-mile journey he had committed to make. Devoid of these feelings, it could have become very easy for him to either abandon the journey altogether; find another troop with better, more alluring toys to make the journey seem easier; or look for another, more interesting journey that would be packed with more chemistry and opportunity. I believe my son made the best choice he could have made when he decided to continue with his original commitment and just keep climbing with his troop, even if he didn't feel like it. And every step he took, every action he made, set him closer to his original goal. By the end of day one, if he stuck through the many times his brain told him to quit, he would end the day eight miles into his goal, with only forty-two miles left. When the boys unpacked that night, tired and worn out, my son would feel bolstered by his newfound character and troop teamwork. He would begin to feel a flood of new feelings, like accomplishment, character, growth, and love for himself and those around him.

This is what the feeling of Earning Love is all about. These are the feelings love generates once we've acted on our commitments. Just as the journey of a thousand steps begins with only one, the first steps of my son's journey now needed to be earned one step at a time through character, giving, serving, and working for one another.

The same is just as true in our relationships. When the Yearning Love leaves us and the chemistry fades, this is when we have got to decide what path we're going to take. Are we going to leave our partner and return to the safety of our base camp? Are we going to look for another, greener pasture elsewhere that offers more excitement and fun for us along the road? Or, are we going to stick to our earlier commitment and find a way to create better feelings by working harder and smarter with our partner until we earn a more Enduring Love?

No man can climb beyond the limitations of his own character.
—John Morley

Altitude can be gained only by trusting one another, committing more and more to each other, and working together to finish the journey. This is because the more we go through together, the greater the potential we have of giving even more to each other.

This phenomenon is not new. The experience of highly charged chemicals and excitement that quickly fades has been around since the world first began and exists in many areas of our lives: attending school for the first time, the first day at a new job, or participating in a new adventure. Each of these experiences comes with an over activity of chemicals upfront, only to have them ebb after a period of time. Do you remember starting a brand-new school year? Do you remember the excitement and anticipation you felt and the extra attention you paid to what you were going to wear? You probably woke up extra early for those first few days to get ready in your new clothes and to gather your new school supplies. How long was it before that excitement wore off? Maybe a few days or a few weeks? Then the realization set in that school required work!

At some point or another, we will all pass through this second stage of love and have to deal with the reality that the feelings of lasting love must be earned. As I discussed earlier, most researchers feel Yearning Love usually only lasts two to three years. So how long will the earning stage of love last? It will last as long as you need it to! How long will it take my son to "earn" the fifty-mile hike? This entirely depends on him and how hard he is willing to work to earn it. But the wisdom, the growth, and the confidence he experiences along the way will bring a joy that lasts forever. This is when the climb can really get interesting. The same is true in relationships, as you will see in the final stage of love, Enduring Love.

Enduring Love

The final, transcendent stage of love is Enduring Love, the love where you are content with each other and committed to the end, where chemicals are no longer the source of your love, your clarity is crystal clear, commitment is enduring, and you *choose* to be with each other. For me, this really is the goal of the entire book: helping all who seek it reach a healthy and Enduring Love.

ENDURING

CHEMICALS IRRELEVANT
CLARITY CRYSTAL CLEAR
COMMITMENT ENDURING

Once you reach this enduring stage of love, it isn't realistic to expect everything to be perfect. There are still problems in the relationship. Money may still not be there, she may still burn the rolls, he may still leave his dirty socks on the floor, but you will feel gratitude for the person you have chosen to spend your life with. You will know that this is the person you want and this is the love you want to keep earning every day and every night. Here, you will know you are trusted and appreciated and, more importantly, you will trust and appreciate your partner. For all of us, this is possible. You just have to know how to earn it, to reach this Enduring Love.

Your friend is the man who knows all about you, and still likes you.
—Elbert Hubbard

Possibly Buddha was referring to long-term relationships when he said, "Endurance is one of the most difficult disciplines, but it is to the one who endures that the final victory comes."

A great example to me of Enduring Love was my wife's grandparents. My wife's grandfather, Bill, was an incredible man. He was a great example of decency and love throughout the many years I had the privilege of observing him.

Bill and his wife, Margaret, were married for sixty-four years. For about the first sixty years of marriage, they lived the typical married life of that time where Bill went to work, made money, worked hard, played golf, came home for dinner, and did what was expected of him. Bill was kind, supportive, and honest. Margaret was an incredible wife, who served him and performed all the typical tasks of a housewife. She fixed his dinners, took care of the kids, ironed his clothes, and kept him on track.

Bill was a "comfortable" husband. He was never mean or overly difficult, and like most men, he probably was more concerned with his own life than he was with spending long hours talking to Margaret about her life.

For the first sixty years of his marriage, Bill "loved" Margaret as much as he knew how. He loved her through all three stages of love—through the charged stage of Yearning Love, to the somewhat more difficult stage of Earning Love, and eventually to the most lasting stage of Enduring Love.

Margaret's investment in Bill was returned when, just a few years before Margaret passed away, she was diagnosed with Alzheimer's disease. Eventually robbing her of all her faculties and abilities to relate fully with others, Margaret's health deteriorated and her mind regressed. Her memory continued to leave her and her ability to care for herself decreased. Margaret then became totally dependent on the husband she had faithfully served every day for sixty years. With each passing day, Bill served his wife more and more. The last year or two, he fed her every bite of her food, fluffed up her henna-colored hair with his large hands, and served and cared for her in every way imaginable. For the last year of her life, he was her "constant companion." He held her hand while they walked, he pushed her in her wheelchair, and he drove her to her appointments. Bill provided Margaret's safety and allowed her to trust in him, day in and day out. He showed her appreciation, respect, validation, encouragement, and also complete dedication.

Following Margaret's passing, after the graveside service came to a close, Bill stood from his seat and instinctively reached his hand back—just as he had so many countless times before, to grab the hand of his Enduring Love, Margaret. Only this time, Margaret was not there. Instead, my sweet wife, Mardi, was the one who received the extended hand of Bill. Even after Margaret's death, Bill's acts of Enduring Love were clearly evident because Bill had chosen to go through all of the steps necessary to discover Enduring Love.

A few months later, at a family reunion, Bill talked about what happened to him through this process. He talked to the whole extended family about the love that grew for his wife during those last few years of their marriage. One of the most powerful lessons he taught us was that he learned to love Margaret more in the last couple of years he served her than during the first sixty years they were married.

Then he taught all of us an even more important lesson. Bill said, "I had always loved Margaret with all of my heart all of my life, but I never fully loved her as much as I did the last few years of her life, when I fully gave myself to her." He then added, "Do not wait until the end of your partner's life to begin serving them completely. Serve them fully *now*, give your love fully *now*, so you can have that Enduring Love *now*, so you can enjoy it while you're still together." To me, this was pure and true Enduring Love.

I believe the ultimate goal of each of us is to create a healthy and enduring relationship just as Bill and Margaret had. Each of us wants to know we are safe with our partner, that we can trust him or her, that we are appreciated, respected, validated, and encouraged. Each of us wants to know our partner is completely dedicated to us and our relationship. This is the final transcendent stage of love and what Enduring Love is all about.

For true love is inexhaustible; the more you give, the more you have.
—Antoine De Saint-Exupery

In order to obtain this kind of love, we must learn to overcome the obstacles we will experience in life, as will be discussed in the next few chapters, and then we must follow the solutions that are discussed at the end of the book. I want you to know that your goal of becoming a healthy and enduring couple is entirely possible. I have seen it in the lives of many people, including my own. Now let's work our way through these obstacles.

Chapter Review:

- Yearning Love is a stage of high chemicals, low clarity, and untested commitment. It lasts for two to three years.
- Earning Love is signaled by lower chemicals, higher clarity, and questioned commitment. Couples spend most, it not all, of their long-term relationship in this stage.
- With Enduring Love the chemicals are irrelevant, clarity is crystal clear, and commitment is enduring. This stage is marked by a choice to be dedicated to one another despite complete clarity of faults, idiosyncrasies, and difficult times.
- Enduring Love is earned through selfless service.
- Love you have earned is more valuable than all the chemistry in the world.

My Feeding Plan

In order to create a healthy diet that feeds your relationship, you need to have a plan. Use the "My Feeding Plan" activity to come up with some specific ideas from the last chapter that you can use to improve the health of your relationship.

Commitment to Keep Learning

What is the most important thing you learned in this chapter that, if lived consistently, would positively impact your relationship?

Dont wait to serve my wife completely. do it now.

Commitment to Keep Changing

Based on what you have learned, what will you commit to change in your life?

Work through the process of earning love stage.

Specifically, how will you do it?

I will make the decision that I want to earn her love and that she is the one that I want that with.

Specifically, when will you do it?

immediately, thats why I went to relationship coaching and am reading this book. So I can be better at loving her.

The Challenge:

The STARVED Stuff

Chapter 2

Focusing on the Smoke
Not the Fire

In the yearning stage of love, there tends to be a naive hope or belief that life is going to be all fun and games, and that we are going to live happily ever after. It doesn't take long for us to wake up from our dream, in the earning stage of love, and realize that life and love are not so easy. Problems arise and continue to arise, filling our once clean and clear view of life with a hazy, smoky, and choking environment. I believe smoke is a great metaphor for the many irritating and choking issues that block a couple's particular lovefest.

The smoke in our relationships symbolizes any and all of the issues about which we and our partners tend to disagree. These arguments can be numerous and as varied as each individual couple. Most couples feel these smoky, irritating issues on and off throughout their relationship. At times, these smoky issues can even seem to be suffocating their relationship to death. The important principle here is that conflict is smoke, and smoke can kill. In most relationships, when couples begin talking about their problems, the problems tend to spread like smoke in a fire. Here's an example:

A couple came into my office fighting about what they called "money issues." (Watch how the smoke spreads and see if this ever happens in your relationship.) The husband was so tired of how his wife spent their money—without any thought or care, and the wife was tired of being told she had a problem.

Mike began the discussion in my office with what he thought was a simple statement. "She just purchased a $400 handbag and I think that is ridiculous! Who needs a $400 purse? Does a $100 purse not hold your stuff well enough? Nobody needs a $400 bag! It's just selfish!"

"You just don't understand!" Carla snapped. "You say *I'm* selfish? How much was your golf bag? How much did you spend on that huge bag with rolling wheels, huh?"

Mike's face grew redder. "What does my golf bag have to do with this? We were talking about your purse. Besides my bag wasn't $400!"

"How much was it?" Carla asked again.

"Three something! I can't remember," he argued.

Carla crossed her arms in front of her. "Three what?"

Veins began to protrude from Mike's neck. "Three-seventy-ish something. But that's not the point."

"That sounds like $400 to me," said Carla. "I thought you said nobody needed a $400 bag and you just went out and bought one, didn't you? You're such a hypocrite!"

"That's different! I have to have a nice bag to put all my clubs in! It's an investment!"

Carla laughed. "Oh really, then how much of an investment were all your clubs?"

Mike sat back. "I don't know, but not as much as *your* junk!"

"How much?" Carla demanded.

"$1,800 to $2,000 dollars."

"What?" Carla exclaimed. "You spent $2,000 on golf clubs and you're complaining about my bag? Talk about ridiculous!"

Mike shook his head. "I didn't buy them all at once."

"You always did love golf more than me!" said Carla. "You'll do anything to get away from me on the weekends."

Mike's eyebrows rose. "You got that right!"

"I guess if that's the excuse you're going to use," said Carla, "then I need a $400 bag to put my $15,000 worth of credit cards in."

"The credit card is up to $15,000?" Mike exclaimed. "You said last month it was $12,000!"

Carla rolled her eyes. "Yes, well I've had to buy a few things since then to catch up with you."

"Of course you did," said Mike. "You're out of control. You're a shopaholic! You always did love shopping more than me!"

"Whatever!" said Carla.

"Whatever!!" exclaimed Mike.

Notice in the discussion between Mike and Carla how the "smoky" issues kept spreading and moving. The fight went from an expensive handbag to golf bags to golf clubs to debt to the love of shopping to golfing, and on and on! What was this fight really about anyway?

Think about the last time you sat around a campfire where there was a lot of smoke. What did you do with the smoke? Did you fan it away or walk away? The smoke kept following or coming back to you, right? This is just like the issues that come up in relationships.

One of the obstacles to creating a healthy and enduring relationship, during the earning stage, is to figure out how to keep the smoke from coming back. Sometimes there is so much smoke that eventually it chokes out the relationship.

It is difficulties that show what men are.
—Epictetus

Research shows that all couples eventually have issues in their relationship that create smoke. The key is not whether smoke is in the relationship, but what a couple does with the smoke and what each partner thinks the smoke means. In fact, one of the most paralyzing factors in a relationship is that most couples end up focusing on the smoke and not on the real issue—the fire. We all know that where there's smoke, there's fire. Just as the number one cause of death in a house fire is the smoke and not the fire itself, the same is true in relationships. The number one killer of healthy relationships is when couples spend all day fighting about the smoke and not getting down to the fire or, again, the real issues.

Throughout the rest of the book, we will learn how to cut through all of the smoke and get down to the fire, or the 7 Basic Needs of all Healthy Relationships. First, let's look at what researchers tell us are some of the most common "smoky issues" or "smoke signals" that couples struggle with in their relationships. See if any of these have made their way into your relationship:

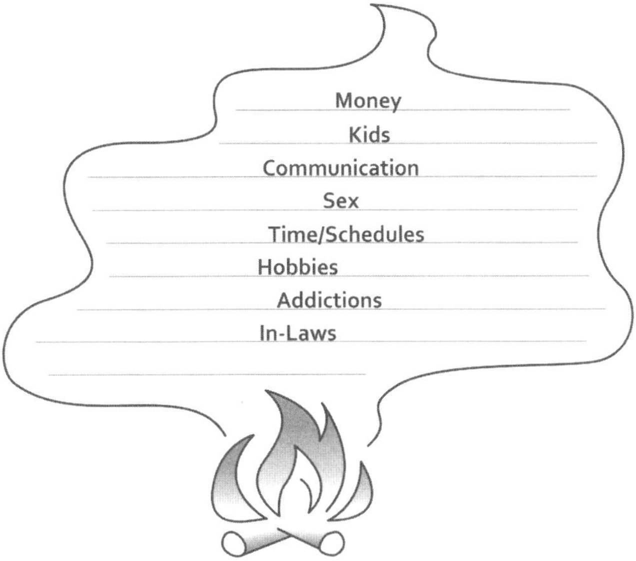

Money

Studies have shown that money is the number one issue couples fight about. Do you have so much money that you're constantly fighting about how to spend it? Wouldn't that be a great problem to have? Unfortunately, the problem with money is that we don't usually have enough to make ends meet. Money conflicts tend to spread into differences about how to spend and save the money, as was the case with the smoky argument between Mike and Carla. In your relationship, is one of you a spender while the other is a saver? It's not uncommon for couples to argue over how the money "manager" in the relationship manages the money. Whatever the facts might be, in any relationship, money is one big deal!

Kids

Another big issue couples fight about is kids. Children often create conflicts in a relationship because of the couple's differences in disciplining and parenting techniques. Like a domino effect, children can create a huge list of other issues such as money, communication, sex, time, and a myriad of other things. Some studies have even suggested that for every child you have, you decrease your marital satisfaction by up to twenty percent per child. As the father of six children, I'm hoping this isn't the case or I am in a world of hurt! On the other hand, there is no doubt that kids do impact relationships.

Some couples have even experienced the death of a relationship through the birth of a baby. Why is this? This can't be something that happens on purpose. When was the last time you heard new parents say, "Wow! We can't wait for this baby to ruin our relationship!" The conflict usually happens because with kids who are so cute and innocent at first, "the family" becomes the primary focus in the relationship instead of "the relationship." Countless studies show that only those things that are focused on have a real chance to grow and improve. Therefore, as the children become the benefactor of this growth and improvement, the relationship quite naturally takes its place on the back burner. This is one of the biggest ways that children impact a relationship.

Having children tends to take our eyes off our relationship and places our focus firmly onto the children. Then, by the time the last child is out of the house, too many couples look at one another and wonder, "Who is this person sitting across the table from me?" In this "empty nest" stage, divorce rates soar, most likely because two people learned to live completely independent lives.

Communication

Along with money and children, one of the top complaints I hear from couples coming into my office is in regards to communication. One or both partners will say, "We just don't talk anymore," or "She just doesn't get me," or "He's so busy watching television that he never hears what I have to say." Most of us do not understand how to communicate very well. Instead, we tend to chase each other or run away from each other and our problems.

True communication means that we are willing to hear the needs of our partner, strive to understand their needs, communicate our needs, and manage the typical and inevitable conflicts that may come into our lives.

Did you know that, nationwide, women file 70 percent of all divorces? My experience is that most of the husbands of these unhappy women had no clue divorce was coming their way. For a brief time in my career, I worked as a divorce mediator. I cannot tell you how many times men came into my office shocked, in complete disbelief that they were suddenly in this situation. "Is it really *that* bad?" the husband would ask. And the wife would quickly reply, "Oh brother! I've been telling you this for years!"

When I speak to large groups, I often ask people to raise their hands if they have taken courses in couples' communication or classes in conflict resolution. Sadly, very few have and yet we're surprised when couples have a hard time communicating. Isn't it interesting that we are required by law to spend more time learning how to drive a car than we are in learning how to communicate effectively with each other? Of course we need to take driver's education to learn to be safe on the roads, but I believe we also need to be instructed more on how to communicate better in our relationships.

Sex

Sex, or intimacy, can be another major issue in relationships—or the lack thereof. Many times, the man tends to be branded as the sexually charged one while the woman plays the contrary role as the one with the "headache." However, in my coaching, I have found this to not always be the case. More and more often, I see women complaining about their husband's lack of interest in the bedroom. Obviously there are many contributing factors, namely, time with each other, kids running in and out, work schedules, expectations about intimate roles, sexual drives, and partner communication.

How do couples get so far apart on this issue? Do you remember back in the yearning stages of the relationship when you couldn't keep your hands off each other? Where did those yearning chemicals go? What happens to sex in the long run and how do couples keep the thrill from going away?

Time/Schedules

How about work, time, and scheduling issues? This is a very common problem for many couples. How does your partner's work impact your relationship? Is he or she spending too much time away or not enough time? Does this impact other things like money or getting help around the house? Do you hear complaints like, "We never do anything together anymore," or "When is it my time to go out and play?" Was your last date together attending one of your children's soccer games or a quick bite to eat after your child's parent-teacher conference? If so, you've got a pretty common obstacle that will eventually turn into some major smoke.

Hobbies

What about hobbies? How can something as innocent and fulfilling as a hobby bring conflict into a relationship? Well, if your spouse is an avid golfer or hunter, or training for a marathon, you will have no problem answering this question. Often, a hobby can be a healthy outlet in which to exercise or expand one's talents, as well as a relief from the pressures of everyday life. However, in some cases, couples experience what is referred to as an "emotional divorce." In this case, one partner emotionally detaches from the other partner, seeking other outlets such as hobbies or friends to fill his or her emotional needs. These hobbies might be endlessly playing video games or constantly surfing the Web on social networking sites like Facebook or Twitter. It has been said that a problem isn't a problem unless it complicates your life. If a hobby is complicating your life and/or your relationship, it might be a sign that a problem exists that must be addressed before serious damage to the relationship occurs.

Addictions

Another issue that causes great pain in a relationship is that of addiction. Whether a person in the relationship is addicted to work, hobbies, pornography, gambling, alcohol, drugs, or even shopping, addictions create an intense amount of smoke in a relationship. If that smoke is not addressed, it can destroy the relationship. As the old saying goes, "An adulterer is a liar first," and most addictions are preceded by a trail of untruths. As the addiction grows, so do the lies. Desires are targeted more towards the addiction than to the partner as the addict becomes more loyal and dedicated to his or her addiction. This obviously has a huge impact on the innocent spouse, as well as on the one who is addicted. In this case, "What they don't know *will* hurt them." The degree of any addiction carries great risks for both partners. Because the addiction typically ends up coming first, the innocent partner is no longer married to the person, but to the person's addiction.

In-Laws (or Out-Laws)

Are your in-laws outlawed? Are you an outlawed in-law? When a relationship is no longer run by chemicals and a couple enters the earning stage of love, one or both partners can sometimes feel more and more irritated by external forces, including extended family members or intrusive in-laws who are sometimes too involved in the relationship. Issues with in-laws are commonplace and can create undue strain on a relationship. Every couple needs a fair chance to create their own relationship traditions and rituals, unhindered by extended family and friends. The most important role for extended family is to be a structure that can strengthen and support a relationship, not weaken it.

Obviously, we have not named every problem a relationship might have, as there are just too many to talk about, but these are the biggest ones I continue to see day after day and year after year, based on the thousands of couples I have coached. Some other issues we could talk about would be the negative impact of friends, social networking sites, cell phones, how time is spent, jobs, and religious differences.

When it comes to personal relationships, I have yet to see much deviation from these general themes in all of my work with couples, which tells me we are all much more alike than we are different. Carl Jung once said, "That which is most personal is most universal." Many couples believe their relationship is the only one suffering with certain problems, but the reality is nearly every couple seems to go through similar troubles. So although you may feel your problems are unique only to you, it is important that you realize most of the problems you face are universal to all people.

So, as a couple you can continue to argue and fight all you want about "stuff"—money, kids, time, communication, sex, schedules, etc., but I can promise, you are focusing on the wrong things. These issues are the smoke in the relationship. They are the noxious fumes that fill the air between couples and quickly destroy all the oxygen that keeps love alive. They sap away the very air needed to sustain the life of a relationship.

Activity: In the smoke below, take a moment to identify all of the issues that make it hard to breathe in your relationship. What is choking your relationship and sapping your energy and your desire to keep forging ahead?

Just as more people die from smoke inhalation than the actual fire, so too do many relationships die from chasing the "smoke" of these issues rather than getting down to the real fire behind the issues. In the earning stage of love, the smoke can become so thick and deadly that it makes it harder for us to look into each other's eyes and see each other clearly. Oftentimes these issues seem to appear out of nowhere. Like spontaneous combustion, smoke clouds suddenly fill the room, irritate us, then dissipate, only to reappear later and irritate us all over again.

One of the most tragic by-products of too much smoke in a relationship is the fact that one partner or both partners will eventually become uncomfortable in their own home. If we aren't comfortable in our own home, we are going to make our home elsewhere. This is when countless people stop earning the love of their partner and turn somewhere else. Sometimes it is the workplace or the golf course, and too many times it is in the arms of another person.

In order for a relationship to be healthy, couples need to realize that it is not the differences (the smoke) that creates the problems, but the inability to look beyond the smoke and into the fire. The fire represents the 7 Basic Needs of all healthy and enduring relationships. Instead of focusing on the "smoky" problems, we need to focus on the 7 Basic Needs. These needs will be discussed in further detail in the next chapter.

Through all my years as a relationship coach, the 7 Basic Needs are the ones mentioned most often as the reasons couples feel unfulfilled within their relationship; this is regardless of economic, social, emotional, and/or intellectual status.

Chapter Review:

- Conflict issues are the smoke in the relationship. These issues dissipate and then resurface throughout the relationship.
- All couples have smoke.
- Success in the relationship is determined by how the smoke is handled and how well conflict is managed.
- The number one killer of healthy relationships is fighting about smoke rather than trying to understand the fire, or the 7 Basic Needs of healthy relationships.
- Common smoke includes money, kids, communication, sex, time/schedules, hobbies, addictions, and in-laws.

My Feeding Plan

In order to create a healthy diet that feeds your relationship, you need to have a plan. Use the "My Feeding Plan" activity to come up with some specific ideas from the last chapter that you can use to improve the health of your relationship.

Commitment to Keep Learning

What is the most important thing you learned in this chapter that, if lived consistently, would positively impact your relationship?

To learn to look into the fire beyond the smoke.

Commitment to Keep Changing

Based on what you have learned, what will you commit to change in your life?

learning skills to help see beyond
the snake and to identify those things.

Specifically, how will you do it?

Study daily and use what I learn
in interactions with my wife.

Specifically, when will you do it?

Chapter 3

Feeding the 7 Basic Needs of Healthy Relationships

In order to get rid of the "smoke" that sometimes chokes a relationship, remember one simple truth: Where there's smoke, there's fire. As mentioned before, the smoky issues we fight about are always caused by the fire or, in other words, one or more of the 7 Basic Needs that are not being met.

Couples who successfully create healthy and enduring relationships, like Bill and Margaret, have learned how to meet these 7 Basic Needs of all relationships:

Safety

Trust

Appreciation

Respect

Validation

Encouragement

Dedication

Couples who know how to fulfill these needs for each other have learned how to make one another feel *safe*, *trusted*, *appreciated*, *respected*, *validated*, *encouraged*, and both partners are completely *dedicated* to the success of their relationship. Notice that the first letters of these 7 Basic Needs spell out the word STARVED. When these seven needs are not being met, a person begins to feel STARVED, which is exactly the opposite of what being in a healthy relationship means. Being STARVED is what stokes the fire and creates more and more noxious fumes in the relationship. However, when these seven needs are being met, we feel loved and the smoky issues of the relationship dissipate. After all of the yearning is gone, creating Enduring Love is simply recognizing and meeting the 7 Basic Needs of healthy relationships.

I cannot begin to count the number of couples who have come into my office STARVED for these most basic needs in their relationship. I have also learned, through each of these coaching sessions, there is no shortcut when it comes to learning how to feed each of these needs. The steps can be hard to achieve and, at times, take a lot of time and energy, but the fruits of feeding the STARVED relationship will pay off in great dividends through the stage of Enduring Love.

There is more good news: Even if your relationship is STARVED, you *can* turn it around! In my experience, working with even the most extreme cases, **85 percent of all starving relationships can be saved!** It's true. Even though your relationship may be starved now, you can choose to put out the fire and get rid of the smoke that's getting in the way of finding true love.

Remember the days when you were dating or first committed to one another? Most likely you were both excellent "feeders," and this is what originally attracted you to one another. You probably bought each other presents, wrote each other notes, rubbed each other's backs, and talked for hour and hours, right? Now, in this earning stage of love, things have likely changed quite drastically. Your days might now be filled with children, mortgages, and busy schedules—therefore feeding each other is not as easy as it used to be. Do not give up hope, though, if you are in a starving relationship! Everyone can learn to be good "feeders" again.

The 7 Basic Needs

In your own life, consider each of these basic needs and what each one means to you. How do you feel when one of these needs is not being met? How would you rate yourself when it comes to providing each of these needs for your partner? Let's take a closer look at each of these STARVED needs and see if we can figure out how to begin to put out the fire:

Safety

In your relationship, do you feel safe with your partner? Does your partner feel safe with you? When we think of safety, we usually think about physical safety, which is very important to having healthy relationships. In this case, I'm also talking about being financially safe, emotionally safe, socially safe, intellectually safe, and spiritually safe. Feeling safe in each of these areas means we feel secure and stable, not worried about any kind of potential harm. For me, this is the most basic need of all healthy and enduring relationships. As we take a closer look at the components of safety, evaluate how you and your partner are doing.

- **Physical safety** comes when you feel physically safe and protected, and knowing you will not be abused or physically hurt by your partner.
- **Financial safety** comes when you have shared financial goals and plans to meet those goals. It also means you both equally understand and work toward your shared financial goals.
- **Emotional safety** comes when you feel free to share your most personal ideas, feelings, and fears with your partner. This is one of the most important levels of safety because this need cuts to the core of who you really are and exposes your deepest feelings. When a person feels emotionally safe with another person, this creates a space where they can be vulnerable and can openly share their thoughts and feelings. Being able to risk emotionally together and in a safe space is what creates real intimacy and closeness, and eventually brings some of the strongest connections between two people.
- **Social safety** comes when you feel safety together in

connecting with friends and in building new, appropriate relationships with others. It also means you feel supported and encouraged to grow socially and your partner doesn't feel threatened by this. Feeling safe socially also means you never embarrass your partner and that you are never made to feel embarrassed by your partner.

- **Intellectual safety** comes when you feel safety in knowing your thoughts and ideas are valued and celebrated by your partner and won't be demeaned. It also means that you are seen as an intellectual contributor to the relationship, and your talents, intellect, and ideas are relevant and sought out in the relationship—that your ideas and input matter!
- **Spiritual safety** is not talked about very often. However, a large number of clients come into my office describing this as a major source of insecurity and a major factor in their starvation. Spiritual safety happens when we either share the same religious and spiritual belief system as our partner or we have an understanding and appreciation of our partner's individual religion and personal belief system. Spiritual safety also happens when we have confidence in each other's values, character, and life goals and we know that our value systems are aligned. The lack of spiritual safety usually leads to arguments about church attendance, specific moral issues, and/or values in the home.

Abraham Maslow, commonly known as "the father of humanistic psychology," taught that one of the most basic of all human needs is safety. The opposite of feeling safe is to feel in danger, in jeopardy, or threatened. Remember the example of Mike and Carla and her $400 purse and how it turned into a major fight about every other issue in their marriage? Odds are that the real, deeper issue was more about their financial safety than it was about the purse, golf bag or debt. Just as it did with Mike and Carla, safety issues can appear in a myriad of ways in relationships.

Trust

Every long-term, healthy relationship is founded in trust. It only takes a few bad moves, however, to destroy or erode trust. Trust breaks down because of someone's actions or inactions. Trust is usually broken when one or both partners behave in a way that is contrary to their mutually agreed upon standards or values. For example, one spouse may discover on the computer that his or her partner has been looking at pornography. This type of action is commonly referred to as betrayal.

From my experience, rebuilding trust is one of the most difficult things to do. Trust governs all effectiveness in human relationships. It is the glue that holds everything together. When this glue is weakened or affected, relationship bonds tend to loosen as well, which is usually when most relationships tend to start falling apart. Trust affects everything in a relationship, but most importantly, trust affects how we both see and hear our partner. For example, how do you communicate with someone you don't trust? What do you say to someone you don't trust? How do you listen to someone you don't trust?

Low trust cultures pay a high tax.
—Unknown

This means that in a society where trust is nonexistent, members of the community usually end up paying higher prices and higher taxes for the items they want and need. In addition, because our society is filled with so much mistrust, we must pay for insurance, locks for our front doors, streetlights, police services, fences, alarm services, and so on. In relationships, the price for having low trust is that couples pull back from sharing their true feelings, partners have to work harder to be believed, and everything takes more time and energy just to get simple points across. When this happens, emotional disconnect can result, as well as a tendency to "check out" of the relationship.

Appreciation

Long-term relationships require a sense of feeling appreciated. Appreciation means the relationship increases in value, or appreciates, rather than depreciates in value. In relationships, we desire to feel appreciated by our partner and not taken for granted. Most humans also need to feel loved, needed, and supported. Regardless of gender, age, or circumstance, each of us needs to know our efforts are noticed, remembered, and valued.

The deepest principle of human nature is the craving to be appreciated.
—William James

The ways to express appreciation are many. The key is in knowing what means the most to your partner and what makes you feel most appreciated as well. Does your partner feel most appreciated when you give gifts to him or her? Do you feel most appreciated when your partner serves you, or spends time with you? My wife, Mardi, feels most appreciated and loved when I help around the house, doing dishes or just spending time actively engaged with the family. I, on the other hand, prefer more touch and positive talk to feel most appreciated.

What is it that makes your partner feel most loved? Perhaps it is a simple "thank-you," a hug, a loving note, a bill paid on time, vacuuming the house, or some other sincere act of kindness.

Respect

Respect is key in any healthy, long-term relationship and can actually work as a barometer to rate the level at which a relationship functions. Respect means treating your partner not as an object, but as a person of endless worth. To respect means you have a higher vision of what your partner is all about. Your partner is not just a body, or a label, or a bunch of traits or characteristics, but instead he is a human being—changeable, influenceable, and honorable. To respect your partner means you don't make unilateral decisions in your relationship. Instead, you confer with one another and collaborate on all solutions, making sure both of you are onboard before moving ahead with decisions. It also means you defer regularly to your partner's positions and views, always recognizing that his opinions, thoughts, and ideas are just as valuable as yours.

When couples engage in serious disagreements about in-laws or power in relationships, the STARVED issue of "respect" usually creeps into the conversation. When one feels the other partner listens more to his or her parents than to them, respect is usually the real issue. They want to know that the other person, who means more to them than any other person in the world, has a high regard for them, reveres them, and actually wants to be with them.

Validation

Validation happens when one partner or both feel that his or her individual thoughts and feelings are real, sound, justified, well-founded, and valid in the eyes of the other partner—that who they are, including how they think, feel, and act, is of value. Have you ever expressed your thoughts or opinions about something only to have them shot down or ignored? This is the opposite of validation. To validate other human beings doesn't mean you have to agree with them or their position. Validation simply means you recognize that another person's viewpoints have merit and have an equal place in the discussion. Validation is a very basic and profound human need. Everyone has the need to be viewed as a valid and legitimate person, to feel that others want to hear her voice and even yearn to hear her opinions, thoughts, feelings, and desires. Validation shows support, caring, and acceptance. Sadly enough, I've found in my coaching practice that validation is one of the least understood skills of human relating.

I'll never forget an instance when I felt immediately invalidated. One muggy summer day in Mississippi when I was out consulting with a company, I walked out of a wonderfully air-conditioned building into the hot, wet warmth of the Gulf Coast. As a desert boy who was raised with very little humidity in my town, the wall of heat overwhelmed my senses and I moaned out loud, "Oh, this place is so muggy!" One of the men I was walking with, apparently offended by my negative remark, quickly replied with disgust, "This is nothing! Try Vietnam!"

What is someone supposed to say to that? Isn't it possible that a desert boy can feel like a hot summer day in Mississippi is pretty muggy? And isn't it also possible that a Mississippi boy can think Vietnam is ten times muggier than even his hometown? Can't these two ideas exist at the same time without competing? Validating another person means instead of taking my reality and discounting it to make your reality work, we both try to understand one another's reality.

In the above exchange, all this man needed to do was "get into me" for a minute and find out why I was so affected by the heat. If he had invested time in me, then he would have earned more favorable feelings from me and I would have loved to have heard about how Vietnam's humidity affected him. Validating another person helps that person want to validate you.

Encouragement

Encouragement is a powerful tool in any relationship. Each of us can think of people in our past that went out of their way to encourage us to reach our potential. Encouragement comes when you can support and empower the dreams of your partner and his desire to grow.

Hidden in the word *encouragement* is the word *courage. Courage* comes from the Old French word for heart (*coeur*). The French word *coeur* means "the center of your feelings," like knowing in your heart that someone loves you. Encouragement is getting to the center of your partner's feelings to see what is really in his heart—his interests and deepest dreams—and then being supportive, and even promoting those interests.

In order to feel encouraged, we need to know that someone else is behind us, supporting us in what matters most to us. Sometimes encouraging someone else who doesn't encourage us is one of the toughest tests of a relationship. So ask yourself some tough questions about your own heart and identify what keeps you from being your partner's biggest cheerleader.

This is the unpardonable sin—to talk discouragingly to
human souls, hungering for hope.
—Ella Wheeler Wilcox

Dedication

Dedication is about commitment and devotion to each other. For many couples, their vows of commitment are sacred. Yet for others, their wedding vows are nothing more than words that mean, "Until my partner messes up so much that I can't tolerate it anymore." Dedicated couples spend more time worrying about why they love being with their partner (also known as "deal makers"), than they do thinking about what or who they would leave their partner for (also known as "deal breakers").

Dedication is apparent when you know your partner is more committed to you than to any other thing, being, or activity. Dedication means you put your partner first in your life, and that you each receive a sufficient amount of time, energy, resources, and emotions. Dedicated couples are secure in the knowledge that they each would choose one another first over anything else in life. Now this doesn't mean things like education, work, or childrearing don't sometimes get in the way and take precedence over the relationship, but, in the grand scheme of things, the truth is well-established as to who really comes first in each other's lives.

Couples who are dedicated show deference to their partner over all others including even their own parents, family, friends, co-workers, or boss. Dedication comes when you and your partner are truly committed to each other *no matter what.*

From the Smoke to the Fire

I had a couple I'll call the Telfords come into my office one day. After many years of marriage they were seriously considering a divorce. We sat down to discuss "the problem" and I asked the wife to tell me the source of her excruciating pain, a pain that was so awful she was considering ending her marriage.

She quickly replied, "My husband is so lazy! He never finishes *anything* he starts. In fact," she continued, "he started working on our bathroom door years ago, but never finished it. I haven't had a bathroom door for years. I'm just tired of it!"

At face value, this woman appeared to be ending her seventeen-year marriage because of an uninstalled bathroom door (a "smoky" issue). So, I asked her, "What if we found someone to hang that door? Would you then want to stay in your marriage?"

"No," she quickly replied, "it goes much deeper than that."

Notice that when she initially presented the issue, all she talked about was the bathroom door. Now we know that this was just the "smoke" and not the "fire." The actual fire, or the real issue, was what? What were her basic needs that were not being met? Was it that she didn't feel *safe*? Or that she couldn't *trust* her partner? Or that she didn't feel *appreciated* or *respected*? Was it about her not feeling *validated* or *encouraged*? Or was her anger about not feeling *dedication* to the marriage?

In the end, together we concluded she didn't feel appreciated, or her husband would have satisfied her needs by finishing the bathroom door years ago. Because of his behavior in this matter, she didn't feel respected because she had no privacy, and she never felt validated because she would complain and he never did anything about it. His lack of response made her feel discouraged. Her issue was never about the door, but about her STARVED needs.

When her husband considered the issue from the big picture of how the door fit into the seven steps of feeding a relationship, he finally felt moved enough, and understood her enough, to go home and fix the door. This couple had fought about that door for years, but in reality, the real issue was that his wife was STARVED to have her basic needs met.

As you can see, there is enormous power in the 7 Basic Needs. It's important to remember that these needs are universal to all long-term relationships. Everyone wants to feel safety, trust, appreciation, respect, validation, encouragement, and dedication. Any time these needs are not being met, this will alter our relationships. When we feel STARVED in our relationships, our natural tendency is to turn around and starve our partner right back! Then we have two starving people trapped in a downward spiral, a subject we will discuss in-depth in the next chapter.

The STARVED Standoff

Whenever I see clients starving each other to death, or caught in the STARVED Standoff, as I call it, I envision them both completely emaciated. Facing each other, with sunken faces and bloated bellies, they sit before some of the most delicious food in the entire world. Yet, in order to really enjoy this food, they must first learn to feed each other. But, because they are unwilling to do this, or unaware that the answer to their starvation could be found in simply feeding their partner, their clothes hang off their skeletal bodies while each one waits to be fed by the other. Focused only on themselves, they have no idea how emaciated their partner really is. They are now fully involved in a STARVED-induced delirium, each so blinded by their own selfishness that the condition of the other becomes irrelevant.

Remember when we were first in love, the assumption was that our partner would always be there to feed us. During the yearning stage, we assumed we would always be able and willing to meet one another's needs before our own, and vice versa. In fact, the greatest symbol of mutual feeding takes place at weddings when everyone gathers for the cutting of the wedding cake. The bride and groom cut their cake together and gently feed each other, demonstrating how they will feed each other and not starve one another in their life together. Sadly, many brides and grooms just don't get the concept of mutual feeding and instead turn this loving gesture upside down. Although done in fun, many times this feeding symbol turns into a food fight with both the bride and groom shoving cake into each other's faces. Sadly, for just under half of the couples getting married today, this foreshadows the tougher days of starvation that may lie ahead. For me, there is nothing less attractive than a bride in her expensive wedding gown and beautifully coiffed hair, now covered with cake, trying to blow frosting out her nose like a lumberjack in an Oregon forest.

Eventually, in most relationships, when we exit the yearning stage and enter the earning stage, we begin to tire of not being fed by our partner and begin to feed ourself. We feed ourself more and more, but then we discover that this is not as satisfying as being fed by our partner. Not knowing what to do or how to reach out, we end up finding ourselves firmly entrenched in a standoff with our partner. We both end up waiting and waiting for the other to begin feeding us while we continue to starve. Both feel justified in not feeding the other, yet both crave nothing more than to be fed and nourished by their partner. The result of this relationship formula is that both waste away.

When you are right, you have no need to be angry.
When you are wrong, you have no right to be angry.
—Mahatma Gandhi

So how do we stop this standoff, which happens to be one of the greatest obstacles getting in the way of creating a healthy and enduring relationship? First, we must learn how to recognize this cycle and become aware, as a couple, that we are slipping into the cycle. Most importantly, we must learn to cut through the smoke in our relationships and get down to the fire that really causes all of the pain: the STARVED Stuff. We need to figure out which of these needs are not being met. Interestingly, even though this sounds like a lot of work, it really isn't, and honestly, it only takes one person to really make a difference. Although two would be better, one person can start feeding and stop starving the relationship. Once they do, usually his partner will notice what is taking place and will begin to provide nourishment in return. As the saying goes, "Two heads are better than one, but one head is better than none."

As a relationship coach, I try to teach couples how to take every issue they face and show exactly where their particular issue falls within the 7 Basic Needs. This process is actually heartbreaking to see. None of these couples got involved in their deeply committed relationship with the plan to starve each other. This just became a habit that many couples fell into somewhere along the way as the result of a few destructive thought patterns, such as, "Because she won't serve me, I am not going to serve her." Or, "Because he won't feed me, I am not going to feed him."

In the STARVED Standoff, both partners wait for the other person to make the first move. Oftentimes each partner is unwilling to seek and meet his or her partner's needs first. Why? Maybe it's because of stubbornness or selfishness. Or perhaps because most of us *react* to one another instead of *acting* in the best interest of the relationship. For some, a fear exists, based on history and old habits, or each partner is afraid the other partner won't reciprocate. We all know that there are no guarantees that if you feed your partner, he will feed you back. But by taking the first step, by being the first one to feed your partner, you will greatly increase the likelihood that over time, something great will happen to you in return.

You cannot not communicate.
—Paul Watzlawick

The fact is that when we are treated with love and respect by another person, we want to treat that person the same way. This is human nature. When someone does nice things for you, doesn't it make you want to do nice things for him?

Starvation is the absence of love. Why would we starve another human being of love, let alone one to whom we have made a lifelong commitment? A basically good person—a person with a conscience and a good heart—wouldn't purposely choose to deprive or withhold love from another human being, right? Good people do not starve their partner because this is part of their value system. They starve their partner because *they* are personally hurting and in pain. They also may starve their partner in the hope that by starving them, they will kick-start their partner's desire to love them in return—an attempt I've rarely seen work long-term.

This reactivity is a part of every unhealthy relationship I have ever coached or observed. For some couples, they never question their "eye for an eye" mentality because it feels so justified or natural to hurt another when you are hurting. However, just because it feels natural doesn't mean this approach should ever become the avenue of choice for any relationship. Just because it might feel natural or satisfying to have a hamburger and fries every day for lunch doesn't mean we should do it. Eventually we're going to have to learn to lead our lives not solely by what feels most natural or comes easiest to us. If we want to be healthy, we're going to have to start making some different choices—choices that are based more on our highest values and principles and less on what feels good. These choices over time will change us to a point where healthy living and relating become our normal pattern rather than reactive living and relating.

How STARVED Is Your Relationship?

Take a few minutes and run through the following inventory to see how your relationship adds up on our STARVED scale. Then, share this quiz with your partner and have him or her answer both sets of questions. Then, exchange the list and see how you both feel when it comes to your individual levels of feeding or starving your relationship.

Most long-term relationships are STARVED to some degree at one time or another, so do not feel disheartened or ashamed if your score is low. You may not even be completely STARVED, but a relationship with the munchies is still painful and possibly dangerous because any STARVED relationship affects how we see things, meaning how we perceive our partner is meeting or not meeting our needs.

Assess the health of your relationship. Rate your marriage in each of the following categories by circling a number between 1 and 5:

5	Your marriage is full and healthy:	You are satisfied in this area.
4	Your marriage has the munchies:	You could use a little improvement in this area.
3	Your marriage is hungry:	You feel a little pain and need some improvement.
2	Your marriage is famished:	You hurt and absolutely must improve in this area.
1	Your marriage is STARVED:	You are in dire need of improvement NOW.

1. Do you feel safe with your partner?	1	2	3	4	5
2. Does your partner feel safe?	1	2	3	4	5
3. Do you feel trusted by your partner?	1	2	3	4	5
4. Does your partner feel trusted by you?	1	2	3	4	5
5. Do you feel appreciated by your partner?	1	2	3	4	5
6. Does your partner feel appreciated by you?	1	2	3	4	5
7. Do you feel respected by your partner?	1	2	3	4	5
8. Does your partner feel respected by you?	1	2	3	4	5
9. Do you feel validated by your partner?	1	2	3	4	5
10. Does your partner feel validated by you?	1	2	3	4	5
11. Do you feel encouraged by your partner?	1	2	3	4	5
12. Does your partner feel your encouragement?	1	2	3	4	5
13. Do you feel dedication from your partner?	1	2	3	4	5
14. Does your partner feel your dedication?	1	2	3	4	5

The STARVED Standoff in Action

Check your own experiences and see if the following scenario sounds familiar:

You arrive home after a long and difficult day at the office. Upon arriving home, you see the breakfast dishes still on the table while your children whine for dinner. Your partner arrives home shortly after you, also totally overwhelmed from the day. They walk in and immediately plant their behind firmly on the couch, with remote in hand.

How do you feel? Do you feel Appreciated? Respected? Validated? Encouraged? Probably not, but you are still experiencing feelings and, most likely, these feelings are negative ones. So what do you do with these feelings? Do you say something, knowing this will only lead to a fight and worse feelings? Do you get mad and take it out on your partner in other ways, as in the tit-for-tat scenarios mentioned earlier? Or do you just keep quiet?

Now fast-forward through the evening to bedtime. Your partner leans over and begins to cuddle with you, and you know very well, cuddling isn't all that is on her mind. All you can think of is how STARVED you felt earlier in the day when you were left with all of the family responsibilities. As a result, you are definitely *not* in the mood for cuddling, let alone anything else. So you roll over in the other direction, clearly communicating that it's "bedtime." Imagine your partner's reaction to your cold-shoulder treatment. Do you think your partner feels Appreciated? Respected? Validated? Encouraged? Dedicated? Do you even care if she feels any of these feelings right now? Probably not.

Based on this experience, you can predict how the following morning might play itself out. More silence, an early departure by your spouse, and you are left to clean up the breakfast mess and get the kids ready for school. Can you see how this mutual starvation can keep going and going and going? This STARVED Standoff sounds like a competition or event of some kind, doesn't it? But this is not an event anyone enjoys participating in!

Why Not Just Live the Golden Rule?

The solution to the great STARVED Standoff is so simple. From the beginning of recorded human behavior, people have been battling their natural desire to inflict painful penalties upon people they feel have wronged them. Every major faith and culture has created a "vaccination" to this human ailment of relational starvation in the form of a social or religious rule. In the Judeo-Christian ethic it's called the "Golden Rule" and goes something like this: "Do unto others as you would have them do unto you."

It is the ability to choose which makes us human.
—Madeleine L'Engle

In my workshops with STARVED couples, I ask how many of them believe in the "Golden Rule." Almost without exception, everyone in the room raises their hand in the affirmative. I then ask, "How many of you have ever been stuck in a STARVED Standoff and refuse to treat your partner the way you would like to be treated, but instead treat him or her the same way (or worse) than he or she was treating you?" All of them can see the contradiction.

In most cases, when it comes down to being STARVED, we just don't live what we say we value. We don't walk our talk. There is a definite disconnect between what we believe and how we act. This disconnect is the core problem when it comes to relationship starvation. Once we develop a STARVED perception, we have no choice but to contradict our own belief systems with some really great excuses like, "I've tried everything else already, so this is all that is left." Or, "What am I supposed to do, just sit around and take this?" Or, "He deserves exactly what he gets." I've also found that the minute we stop living our own value systems, the more guilt we end up feeling, and the more guilt we feel, the angrier we get. This anger should be directed at ourselves to get us to change, but in reality, the anger usually gets turned back on our partners, which only fuels the STARVED Standoff even further.

It Really Doesn't Matter Why We Starve Others

A common excuse I hear is, "I only starved my partner because she starved me." And while this may be a very real statement, what this statement actually says is, "I only inflict pain on my partner because she inflicted pain on me first." Notice how childish this statement is! Two adults are in pain and therefore two adults feel justified in continuing to inflict pain on one another. Locked in a cycle, they only know to perpetuate more pain, and because they feel their actions are justified, they don't seem to suffer the pain as badly. Sound familiar? This always reminds me of watching my young children fight over a toy and in the end both are crying, both end up alone in separate time-outs, and neither of them have the toy that caused all of the conflict.

A man who wants to do something will find a way;
a man who doesn't will find an excuse.
—Stephen Dolley, Jr.

I often use the following example with couples to show that justification for ineffective behavior doesn't matter:

I tell them to imagine I am standing on top of a ten-story building. I then ask, "If I'm on top of this tall building and I *jump* off, what is going to happen to me?"

Most answer, "Splat!"

"Right," I say, "I'm probably going to die. How about if I'm on top of the building and I *accidentally slip off*?"

"Splat again!" they say.

"How about if a gust of wind comes up and *blows me off* the building?"

"Splat!"

"What if my partner *pushes me off* the building?"

"Splat!"

"What if I jumped off the building because my mother was a building jumper and I wanted to be like my mother?"

"Splat!"

"How about if somebody *shoots me off*, then what?"

Usually they say, "Bang and then splat!"

You see, it doesn't really matter how or why I fell off the building, does it? The reality is that whether I accidentally slipped off, was blown off, pushed off, or shot off, or even if it was my mother's fault, I am "off" the building, and while I'm taking the short plunge to my death, it is not going to make me feel any better knowing why I fell off the building or having someone to blame for my fall. The results are the same—splat, splat, splat! In this same way, *why* your partner is starving you, or *why* you are starving your partner doesn't really matter because, in the end, the relationship will be "splat" no matter how the "splat" occurred.

There is only one very real consequence when a person feels justified in not living the basic promise of, "Loving one another, until death do us part." I always tell couples, "Good results are what create positive relationships, not good excuses."

The other problem created by looking at excuses is that it is a victim mindset. Blaming someone or something is always easier, right? We must stop looking for excuses—or even really good explanations—for why a relationship might be struggling and instead start doing what is needed to make the relationship work.

One of my favorite quotes (based on the fact that I have repeated this comment so many times to so many couples who want to cling to their excuses) is "Having someone to blame for the fall of your relationship doesn't soften the reality that your relationship is dead."

If you want to see more appreciation in your relationship, be more appreciative. If you want to feel greater safety, help your partner feel safe. If you want to be fed more, do more feeding. Do not wait for the other person to make the first move. Make the choice to be the one who takes action.

As a disclaimer, I'm not talking here about abusive relationships. If you are in an abusive relationship, you need to get out and find help now. An abusive relationship is on a much more destructive path than what we are talking about here, and a person must seek the help he or she needs in order to remain safe.

The relationships I work with appear to represent the vast majority of relationships out there, and these relationships involve people who have developed patterns of interaction that have become so unhealthy that really great people are no longer interested in being the kind of partner they would really like to be. Again, when it comes right down to it, excuses don't strengthen relationships; they only explain why the relationship isn't working. I can honestly say that what I have seen in all of my work through years of coaching is that the key to strengthening relationships, long-term, is for couples to learn to get positive results together. Inevitably, if a couple wants to create a healthy and enduring relationship, both partners need to get in the game and start feeding one another.

A few promises to yourself and to your partner must be made as you rearrange your thoughts:

- Promise you won't fall back into any more excuses for why you're not doing your part in the relationship. The "whys" don't matter because excuses do not make others feel loved.
- Promise you will live your deepest principles and values more

explicitly, which means you'll begin to live the "Golden Rule" and other principles that you already believe in, such as love, respect, honesty, service, sacrifice, and commitment.

One reason I am confident your life will improve if you keep these promises is that, regardless of what happens in your relationship, you will always end up with yourself. So, if you do not live up to your own values or belief system first—in thought and in action—who and what are you ultimately walking away with?

Without fail, the best place to start working on your relationship is to begin to find the power within your own character to be who you know you truly are and want to be. Living your values will help you replace "could have," "should have," and "ought to" with the knowledge that you, at the very least, always tried to do the right thing.

The following is inscribed on the tomb of an Anglican Bishop in Westminster Abbey (1100 A.D.):

> *When I was young and free and my imagination had no limits, I dreamed of changing the world. As I grew older and wiser, I discovered the world would not change, so I shortened my sights somewhat and decided to change only my country. But it, too, seemed immovable. As I grew into my twilight years, in one last desperate attempt, I settled for changing only my family, those closest to me, but alas, they would have none of it. And now, as I lie on my deathbed, I suddenly realize: If I had only changed myself first, then by example I would have changed my family. From their inspiration and encouragement, I would then have been able to better my country, and who knows, I may have even changed the world.*

There is no other more effective way to go about changing

your relationships, your marriage, your family, and even your world than by changing yourself first. And, if you are going to change yourself, there is no better place to begin than to work on how you see your situation, your relationships, and your life. It is your thinking that most impacts your ability to relate to others, including your partner.

As discussed in the next chapter, the first step to turning your relationship around is in comprehending the impact your misunderstandings have on your relationship and how these misunderstandings are perpetuated, all based on your perceptions.

Chapter Review:

- There are 7 Basic Needs in every relationship. When these needs are not being met, couples begin to feel STARVED.
- The 7 Basic Needs are Safety, Trust, Appreciation, Respect, Validation, Encouragement, and Dedication.
- A STARVED person generally starves others and perpetuates the STARVED Standoff where both partners wait for the other person to feed them first.
- The solution to the STARVED Standoff is to treat your partner as they would like to be treated.
- It doesn't matter why the relationship is STARVED, it only matters that both partners take responsibility to start feeding each other.
- Having a healthy relationship means at times feeding because it is right, not because you are being fed.

My Feeding Plan

In order to create a healthy diet that feeds your relationship, you need to have a plan. Use the "My Feeding Plan" activity to come up with some specific ideas from the last chapter that you can use to improve the health of your relationship.

Commitment to Keep Learning

What is the most important thing you learned in this chapter that, if lived consistently, would positively impact your relationship?

Be the catalyst for change, don't wait for your partner. Don't live in a starved standoff.

Commitment to Keep Changing

Based on what you have learned, what will you commit to change in your life?

live my Values and build my character by acting first to feed my partner

Specifically, how will you do it?

I will not ignore the starved moments.

Specifically, when will you do it?

Chapter 4

The STARVED Spiral

When we begin to feel STARVED, we start to operate out of a new way of seeing the world around us, as if changing rose-colored glasses to smoke-filled ones. Because of this, we begin to operate with more and more negatively charged feelings. This negative mindset drastically changes the entire basis of our interactions from an opportunity for growth to an opportunity for pain. We tend to feel more fear, anxiety, selfishness, vengeance, anger, and frustration. The opposite of loved is STARVED, so when we are STARVED, we feel everything but love in our lives. Yet it is when we feel love in our relationships that we have the power to overcome anything.

One of the most powerful, negative feelings that swell in the hearts of STARVED people is fear. In her book, *A Return to Love*, Marianne Williamson claims, "Fear is the absence of love and the best way to remove fear from your relationships is to learn to love others more fully."

In the STARVED mindset, fear impacts every part of our relationships from how we act, to what we say, to what we don't say. From my observation, the following reactions occur when fear overtakes love in our interpersonal relationships:

When we fear looking weak	then we talk or act tough.
When we fear feeling guilty	then we blame others.
When we fear being judged	then we criticize.
When we fear the truth	then we don't ask tough questions.
When we fear our insecurities	then we pretend we can't be hurt.
When we fear people who are different	then we judge & label them.
When we fear being hurt	then we ignore those who hurt us.
When we fear words aren't working	then we get louder or forceful.
When we fear feeling inferior	then we put others down.
When we fear we don't know the answer	then we act as if we do.
When we fear being wrong	we turn everything into debates.
When we fear admitting we're human	then we act as if we're not.

When we feel STARVED within our relationships, we naturally begin to lose the confidence of when we feel loved. Love creates confidence and feeling STARVED creates fear. Feelings of starvation tend to perpetuate more starvation, which moves the relationship further and further away from healthy and sends it spinning into a downward spiral.

The STARVED Spiral

When we experience the starving process long enough, we see no hope in sight. It is then that we begin to shut down in a variety of ways. The relationship lacks trust, communication breaks down, and time is spent on everything but each other. Individual activities take precedence over couple activities, and loving traditions or rituals that we once shared are discarded. With each shutdown, the relationship becomes less and less likely to survive. This dangerous shutdown is what I call the STARVED Spiral. The downward spiral is as real to a relationship as starvation is to a person in need of life-sustaining food.

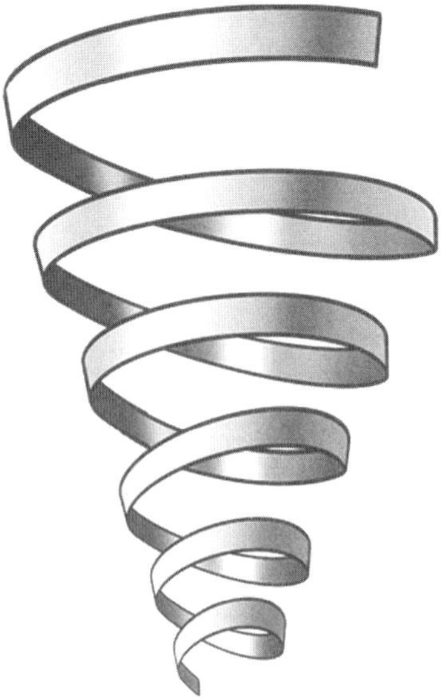

The STARVED Spiral is an enormous obstacle that must be dealt with if couples ever want to get the love flowing back in their relationship. The STARVED Spiral passes through six different levels, with each level inevitably starving your partner more and more as the process wears on.

The STARVED Spiral is different than the STARVED Standoff because in the Standoff both partners are staying in the same position, just waiting for the other partner to change and neither is really going anywhere. In the STARVED Spiral, however, partners begin to take the relationship into a destructive downward direction that usually ends up leading to complete abandonment. I first noticed the STARVED Spiral while working with couples who were on the verge of divorce and found that couple after couple demonstrated the same STARVED-induced pattern of ending their relationship. While teaching my "Feeding the STARVED Relationship" workshop, I also noticed that with a few quick adjustments and a lot of character, the STARVED Spiral could be permanently reversed.

Character is not made in a crisis—it is only exhibited.
—Robert Freeman

I have worked with hundreds of couples in the very depths of the STARVED Spiral and witnessed their ability to turn the situation around. If you find that you are suffering, as they were, I am confident you will be able to turn your relationship around by learning some new skills and simply infusing your true character back into the relationship. The first change you can make is to begin to operate out of love instead of fear.

To explain the Spiral further, take this quick True/False quiz and see how many of the *Top 10 Signs* apply to you or your relationship:

The Top 10 Signs You and Your Partner are in a STARVED Spiral

Circle the appropriate answer:

1. Little things in your relationship turn into big things. **True/False**
2. You and your partner often seem to be angry and take it out on others. **True/False**
3. You feel more and more cynicism in your conversations. **True/False**
4. You question everything your partner says and avoid eye contact. **True/False**
5. Your relationship feels stale, boring, and stuck in the same routine. **True/False**
6. You feel taken advantage of by your partner and share your frustrations with others. **True/False**
7. You have a hard time finding any positive memories from your time together. **True/False**
8. You find ways to not be together and when you are together, you rarely have "real" conversations. **True/False**
9. Everything about your partner seems to bother you and you put each other down in front of others. **True/False**
10. You're confident that the grass is greener somewhere else and think about being with someone else. **True/False**

How did you do? If you answered "True" to more than three of these questions, you're probably already in a STARVED Spiral. However, keep in mind that it doesn't matter whether or not you are in a STARVED Spiral, it only matters which way you are headed: upward or downward. If you are in a downward spiral, this book is going to help you change that direction. If you are starting to climb out of the STARVED Spiral, this book will give you plenty of tools and ideas to keep you heading in the right direction. The key to pulling yourself out of a STARVED Spiral is to learn to create new and better conditions in which your relationship can grow and thrive.

The 6 Conditions of the STARVED Spiral

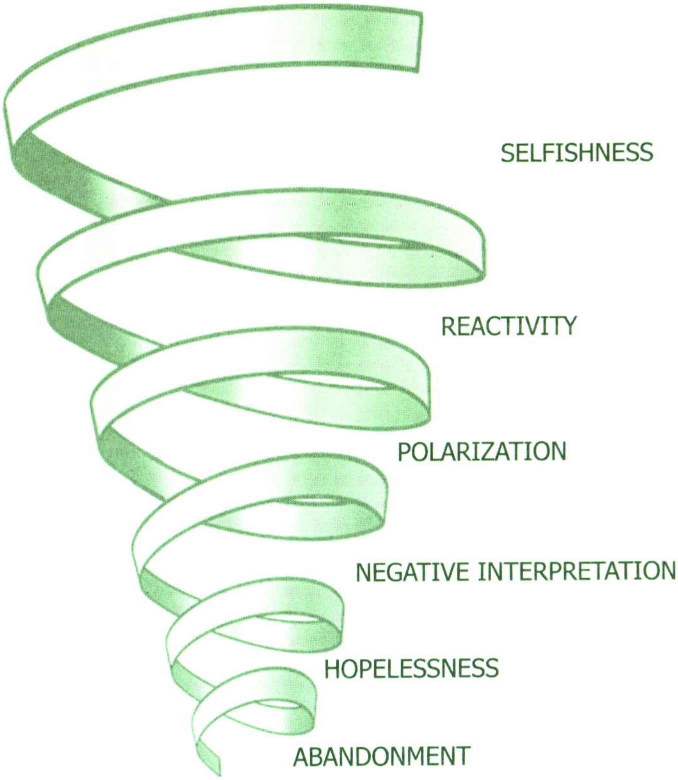

Selfishness

Entrance into the STARVED Spiral happens when selfishness takes over and you begin to demonstrate a spirit of being self-absorbed and self-focused. If you really think about it, this makes a lot of sense. Think of someone who is starving to death, who doesn't have enough food to keep herself alive and well. Wouldn't it make sense for this person to become selfish and no longer worry so much about what everyone else is eating, but instead simply focus on herself? Just as "looking out for number one" is the governing paradigm of physiological starvation, it is also true for those who suffer from relational starvation. Selfishness is truly one of the greatest acids to every healthy and enduring relationship.

Habits change into character.
—Ovid

The more you feel your needs aren't being met, the more you focus on yourself and your unmet needs. This is where the little things become big things. Little oversights and miscommunications become big issues. Once this happens, your agenda, your needs, and your feelings become more important than your partner's. This isn't because you are an innately selfish person, but because you don't know how to stop what's happening.

So you read books, talk to friends, and seek counseling to reassure your "rights," to have your needs met, and not just met, but met *your way*. In this selfish frame of mind, having what you want takes precedence over being together. Your goals are no longer about being *interdependent*, but instead are about being *independent*.

Now, do not mistake what I am saying. I'm not against getting what you need out of your relationship. What I am saying is that once you have been STARVED, or have felt STARVED long enough, having your needs met becomes paramount in your life. Some people become obsessed with this and feel their needs are the only ones that matter anymore. These people begin to throw out ultimatums and threats, simultaneously justifying their actions based on the fact that they've already met their partner's needs for ten years, "and now it's *my* turn."

This condition of selfishness is very understandable. It makes total sense and almost everyone has felt this way, to some degree or another, at one time. But no matter how well we understand this feeling, it doesn't change the reality that selfishness will never improve our life or our relationship.

A popular Internet story tells the tale of an old man on his deathbed who laboriously makes his way downstairs looking for one final cookie to remember his loving wife by before he dies. After reaching for the cookie with his withered hand, his wife, self-absorbed with all that has to be done before the funeral, smacks his hand with her spatula and yells, "Leave those alone, those are for your funeral!" Perhaps the woman baking the cookies was so overwhelmed by the stress of her husband's impending death that she could only focus on her list of "to dos" rather than think about her life without him. However, in her focus to get her list done, she overlooked the very relationship she was preparing to mourn.

There are times when we all hold tightly onto our own lists, our own needs, our own expectations, and our own dreams, all at the expense of our relationships.

Feeding Rule – Change Your Focus
Instead of focusing on getting "my" needs met, focus on how "we" can work together to get all of "our" needs met.

Feeding Homework – Plan a date
Plan a date with your spouse for this week. Spend time doing something you both enjoy. Better yet, plan the date together. Keep it simple and stay away from "issues" right now. While you are together, use "we" language rather than "you" or "I." Just enjoy each other and what you're doing together.

Reactivity

Reactivity is the most common fuel for the STARVED Spiral. Reactivity happens when we make decisions based upon our moods, circumstances, or events, not on what is most important. Reactivity also happens when we act out of being STARVED and not out of what we want most in the future with our partner.

Take the example of a young, newly married couple who experienced reactivity in a very big way. Both partners had a child from a previous marriage, but genuinely wanted children together. They had been married only a few months when the husband brought up the subject of trying to get pregnant soon. To this the wife answered that because the couple had experienced a very short courtship and engagement, she wanted to wait longer before having a baby. The young husband immediately took her comments personally and a negative emotional reaction was the result. The situation escalated out of control as he felt her comments indicated a lack of trust in him and their relationship, although she didn't mean to have her comments taken this way. Their argument turned to talk of splitting up and ending the marriage right then and there. No amount of trying to explain what she meant seemed to help. It was not until they took a break from each other, and with the help of a close family member, that they were able to talk through the issue and come to an understanding. They are now expecting their first child together with all of the excitement and anticipation for which they had hoped. This couple learned two valuable lessons from their experience: she learned to choose her words more carefully and he learned to stop and think before reacting.

The problem with reactivity in relationships is that the big issues are repeated and perpetuated. Luckily, the couple in the story above learned from their mistake; they are working hard to make sure this never happens again. Reactivity is what greases the spiral, making it so slippery that some people are unable to pull themselves out of it.

Reactivity is most often the inability to choose to do something better or different—it's basically a dog chasing its tail. A dog does not chase its tail because this is in the dog's best interest. The dog chases its tail because this is all the dog knows; when the tail wags, the chase begins. Many couples are in a similar pattern. "Because she won't serve me, I'm not serving her." "Because he won't feed me, I'm not feeding him." Reactivity is a self-perpetuating pattern that only ensures more STARVED issues will follow. It is also why "self-fulfilling" prophecy takes place, because if people say something bad is going to happen, a lot of times they react in a way that makes it happen.

The key to stopping the spiral is to begin making choices based on long-term goals, not short-term factors like mood or circumstance. When people stop reacting to their STARVED needs and start proactively choosing to love, the direction of the spiral begins to change.

Feeding Rule – Clearly identify and live by your values
When you clearly identify and live by your values, your relationship decisions become we-centered and not me-centered. They are based on long-term needs and not circumstantial situations and events. In this case, values might include integrity, honesty, family, home, community, and humor.

Feeding Homework – Make a list of your values
Make a list of all the things you value most. Once you've made your list, prioritize your values. How do your values impact your relationships? If you were really living your values, how would your relationships change for the better?

Polarization

Polarization is the natural result of a relationship that is reactive. Polarization happens when couples reactively take opposite stands on positions and ideas. If he goes right, she reacts and goes left.

When she wants black, he argues for white. When he wants it colder, she wants it warmer. When I talk about polarization in relationships, I'm not talking about the natural differences in preference that are common to all couples. Instead, polarization is the ineffective pattern many couples share, a pattern that leads to creating unhealthy communication habits that inevitably begin to tear every conversation apart. Polarization makes couples feel like they're complete opposites in everything, eventually becoming polarized on many of the smoky issues discussed in chapter one, like child rearing, sex, money, home chores, religion, and so on.

Accept me as I am—only then will we discover each other.
—Federico Fellini

In the self-assessment that follows, score yourself from 1 to 10 for each potential polarization area. Once you've done this, score where you believe your partner would fall. Use an X to mark the male's answers and an O to mark the female's answers.

Saver **Spender**
1 2 3 4 5 6 7 8 9 10

In-laws **Out-laws**
1 2 3 4 5 6 7 8 9 10

Saint **Sinner**
1 2 3 4 5 6 7 8 9 10

Sexually Charged **Headache**
1 2 3 4 5 6 7 8 9 10

Over-achiever **Under-achiever**
1 2 3 4 5 6 7 8 9 10

Social **Anti-social**
1 2 3 4 5 6 7 8 9 10

Together-focused **Self-focused**
1 2 3 4 5 6 7 8 9 10

Spontaneous									**Structured**
1	2	3	4	5	6	7	8	9	10
Neat									**Sloppy**
1	2	3	4	5	6	7	8	9	10
Strict Parent									**Relaxed Parent**
1	2	3	4	5	6	7	8	9	10
Morning Person									**Night Person**
1	2	3	4	5	6	7	8	9	10

Ideally, each partner should fall somewhere in the middle, but if a relationship is experiencing polarization, the scores will most likely be on opposite ends of the scale.

People's reactive tendencies tend to lead them to compete with each other, and it is this competition that leads to the polarization of ideas and positions. Competition is a marvelous tool to spur creativity and performance when we have the same goals and purpose. However, without balance, competition in conversations can become the by-product of a more individualistic mindset—one that reinforces selfish tendencies and fears, and one that is not conducive to an intimate, long-term relationship.

The opposite of *competitive* communication is *cooperative* communication. This concept is far better adapted to those relationships that generate a more interdependent reality and a greater sense of companionship. Cooperative communication is exactly what a relationship requires in order to get down to the real STARVED needs, which then results in more unifying conversations and decreased polarization.

When the conditions of the STARVED Spiral take over, the spiral begins to pick up momentum, hurling a couple towards the demise of their relationship. Every passing day without change only encourages a couple to become more and more comfortable with selfishness, reactivity, and more polarization.

Now imagine a relationship that is so far down the spiral that both partners are STARVED enough that they don't want to be hurt anymore. In this case, they are not acting with integrity to their values. Instead, they become self-focused, highly reactive, and highly competitive in the relationship. What hope does this relationship have? When couples are at this point and a new problem arises, there becomes only one way to handle the problem, and that is simply to take the exact opposite position from the other partner, even if their position isn't what they really think or believe.

In my coaching experience, most couples do not start out their relationship strongly polarized, but when they become STARVED, they tend to become polarized and stay polarized because, in a very weird way, this keeps them balanced and stable because this behavior is so predictable. When couples are first married, they create predictability because they are both so overcome with yearning that they serve each other incessantly. This constant service and attention creates predictability in the relationship. To some extent, predictability creates trust.

However, as the yearning fades, the predictability of the relationship lessens through decreased service towards one another. The relationship seems less safe, less predictable, and less stable. Thus, in order to create some form of predictability, many couples subconsciously follow one of the most ineffective relational patterns that exists: the pattern of polarization. One partner wants the thermostat set lower; the other wants it higher. One partner wants more sex; the other wants less. One partner wants to go to a movie; the other partner wants to eat at a restaurant. All of the things that tend to drive each other crazy about one another begin to appear. Ironically, this pattern of behavior actually forces people to create emotion around the relationship again.

Feeding Rule – Look for opportunities to cooperate, not compete
Competition belongs in the sports arena, not in intimate relationships. Competitive Communication begins when couples find themselves polarizing on issues. For the sake of the relationship, this cycle must be stopped immediately, and cooperation must begin.

Feeding Homework – Choose one area of improvement
Refer to the polarization assessment contained in this chapter and choose one area to work on this week. Set up a time with your partner to openly and cooperatively communicate about your feelings on this issue without judging, criticizing, or arguing about who is right. Set up guidelines and rules, if necessary, and see if you can come closer to the middle together. You don't have to totally agree. Just see if you can understand, accept, and honor your partner's opinions, and see if the two of you can somehow find a way to come to a more common ground.

Negative Interpretation

Negativity is another common sign of the STARVED Spiral. It is the inability to see that there is anything positive left in your relationship. Negative thinking begets negative interpretations.

Every interaction you have with your partner is interpreted and given a meaning. When you interact with anyone, you interpret what the other person does and you choose to see the interaction or conversation as positive, negative, or neutral. In your relationship, once you have slid into negativity, you begin to see everything your partner does as negative. These negative interpretations doom the relationship, because even if your partner is actually changing and trying harder than ever, honestly delivering results, a negative interpreter is not able to see these changes and instead chooses to see things as more of the same or "too little, too late."

Whatever we focus on is bound to expand.
Where we see the negative, we call forth more negative.
And where we see the positive, we call forth more positive.
—Marianne Williamson

Another problem with negative interpretations is that they lead to negative feelings about your partner and the relationship. These feelings lead to negative actions, which only starve your partner more. Seeing your relationship in such a negative way is dangerous because you not only see your present state as negative, but you usually begin to rewrite your entire past together as negative.

I hear this from couples with phrases like, "I should have known this relationship was never going to work because on our honeymoon he . . ." or "I'm not sure I really ever loved her at all. I think we were just young and stupid." As you rewrite your stories with a negative bent, you can't help but begin to feel more negatively about each other. Some couples take these negative rewrites and project them into their future as well, ensuring that "It's never going to work," or, "Our future is only going to be more of the same."

Anne and Armond were a middle-aged couple who both had been married before. Armond had experienced a particularly difficult first marriage, separation, and divorce. When Anne and Armond met and were getting to know each other, Armond's descriptions of his first marriage included little to no happy or positive times together, not even when he talked about his past with his children. Anne questioned him on this and related her experience with her first marriage. It was no picnic, but she was able to recall many happy times they had had together as a couple and as a family. She told Armond she could hardly believe that nothing positive happened in the eleven years of his previous marriage. When he stopped and thought about it, Armond knew he was rewriting some of his life. The negativity experienced in the last part of his marriage and the ensuing separation and divorce had influenced his memory of many happy times in the early days. Now that's not to say that Armond should have stuck it out with his first wife, but recognizing that there had been good times helped him in his healing process.

The biggest problem with becoming a negative interpreter in your relationship is that no matter what your partner does, his or her actions will be turned into a negative. If your partner buys you a dozen red roses, you'll be mad that they aren't pink. If your partner does everything to make you feel happy on a fun weekend together, you'll still bemoan the fact out loud that this will probably not last.

Negative interpretation is the death knell of a relationship because, when it hits, it means the end of the relationship is near. This is because both partners begin to project this negative self-fulfilling prophecy. Negative interpretation is the natural follow up to selfishness, reactivity, and polarization. This type of interpretation is what ensures the downward direction of the spiral because today's interpretations beget tomorrow's interpretations or perceptions, and the negative spiraling continues. It is this negativity that actually maintains the direction of the spiral and drives us into the next condition of the STARVED Spiral.

Feeding Rule – Take the High Road

When you take the High Road, you choose to go the better way—the higher way. You choose to avoid negativity and all that comes with it.

Feeding Homework – Make a choice

The next time negativity creeps into your relationship, stop, take a deep breath, and choose otherwise. Make a conscious choice to avoid negativity at all costs and find a way to see your partner in a healthier, more realistic mindset. Write these new interpretations down, and then refer back to them when you need to.

Hopelessness

The fifth condition of the STARVED Spiral is a great sense of hopelessness. If selfishness, reactivity, polarization, and negative interpretation are the roots of the STARVED Spiral, then hopelessness is the fruit. Hopelessness comes because of the expectation that nothing will ever change. Almost universally all couples who struggle in the STARVED Spiral combat intense moments of hopelessness. An interesting example of this hopelessness is how completely alone you can feel in your bed even though your partner is just one foot away. In the STARVED Spiral, hopelessness is a reflection of every other level that has already been discussed:

1. ***Selfishness***: A partner feels hopeless when he becomes convinced that his needs are never going to be met, therefore he shifts into a self-focus and becomes selfish.
2. ***Reactivity***: A partner becomes hopeless when she perceives the other partner does not possess the character, or the apparent desire, to live according to her values and is instead reacting to the emotional pain that surfaces through the differences expressed or other environmental factors, like mood or circumstance.
3. ***Polarization***: A partner feels hopeless as she sees that communication patterns are so ineffective that even the simplest issues turn into disagreements. Not only do polarizing couples argue, but even more damaging is the fact that they end up pulling away from each other and taking positions on opposite ends of their issues.
4. ***Negativity***: A partner feels hopeless because he no longer sees anything positive in his partner, their future, or their relationship.

Hopelessness is the absence of three very basic components in a relationship: (1) a shared positive vision, (2) a focused plan for that vision, and (3) consistent action on the couple's shared plan. Partners become hopeless because they no longer have the "eyes" to see the relationship as it could be—healthy and productive. Without this long-term perspective, couples begin to struggle with daily decisions and wander aimlessly, no longer sure what their relationship is about.

This hopelessness is what I call the "Groundhog Day" syndrome. If you've ever seen the movie *Groundhog Day*, Phil Connors (Bill Murray) is stuck in an endless loop of reliving the same day over and over and over again. What a torturous cycle to watch! At first, hopelessness sets in on Phil as he lacks the vision to get out of this predicament. Like Phil, couples can also experience this hopeless feeling, believing no power exists to change the dreary life we sometimes find ourselves in.

There is no such thing as darkness; only a failure to see.
—Malcolm Muggeridge

The thing that finally pulled Phil out of his hopeless state was when he devised his own plan. Phil took it upon *himself* to change his circumstances rather than wait for someone else to do it for him. He began learning from others, discovered what made people tick, and began to progress. He started seeing life more positively as he quit reacting and started regaining hope.

Do not rush this process and soon you'll experience amazing results. Most importantly, promise yourself to do anything you can this week to improve your situation.

Feeding Rule - DO SOMETHING
Nothing is more hopeless than not having a vision, not having a plan, and not doing anything to improve your situation.

Feeding Homework - Make a plan
If one of the biggest reasons people tend to lose hope in their relationship is because they see their life filled with major challenges and do not have a plan to deal with these challenges, then it is time to do something about it. Plans help us stay focused so we know what to do. People without plans have nothing to do. With nothing to do to improve their life, hopelessness settles in. Grab a journal and get started on a plan for how you will begin to change the five conditions of your STARVED Spiral we have talked about so far, namely selfishness, reactivity, polarization, negative interpretation and hopelessness. Take each condition one small step at a time. Some things can be done individually. Other items will need both partners. Do not rush this process and soon amazing results will be experienced. Most importantly, promise yourself to do anything you can this week to improve your situation.

Abandonment

The final stage of the STARVED Spiral is the state of abandonment. Abandonment of the relationship, of a partner, and of one's responsibility to the relationship is a tragic ending to an even more tragic story. Abandonment is where one partner walks away from the relationship, either literally or emotionally.

Most couples abandon the relationship before they ever really understand what happened and it almost ensures that they will repeat their problems again. There is a reason 60 percent of second marriages fail, and 70 to 80 percent of third marriages fail. I believe these statistics are because people often abandon their partner, assuming the partner was the problem, and they never really know exactly what happened or how they themselves contributed to the end of the relationship.

Mistakes are a fact of life. It is the response to the error that counts.
—Nikki Giovanni

Again, let me state that I'm not saying you should always stay in a relationship. There are good reasons and appropriate times to end a relationship. What I am saying is that abandoning a relationship without understanding what went wrong, and how to prevent it from happening again, is a dangerous move for future relationships. Without learning some new ways of relating, the odds are that in time you'll see the STARVED Standoff and Spiral rear its ugly head in your next relationship.

The six conditions of the STARVED Spiral are universal conditions that we all face any time we're dealing with people. If you feel like you can no longer stand being in the STARVED Spiral, don't give up quite yet. You still need to learn how to stop the spiral, whether you choose to stay with your partner or not. This book is about learning to work through these conditions, to stop the downward spiral, and begin to move upward to new heights. Remember the real antidote to the STARVED Spiral and STARVED relationships in general is to begin loving one another again.

Chapter Review:

- Being STARVED brings a negative mindset that changes a person's thought process during personal interactions from a positive outlook to a negative one.
- Over time, being STARVED creates a STARVED Spiral. The Spiral creates a shutdown of the relationship and if not reversed will result in its end.
- Selfishness is the beginning of the STARVED Spiral and happens when personal needs aren't being met and the focus turns on self rather than on others.
- Reactivity, or acting based on moods, circumstances, or events rather than what is most important, leads to polarization where couples continually oppose each other.
- Negative interpretation is the inability to see that there is anything positive left in the relationship and leads to hopelessness and then to abandonment.

My Feeding Plan

In order to create a healthy diet that feeds your relationship, you need to have a plan. Use the "My Feeding Plan" activity to come up with some specific ideas from the last chapter that you can use to improve the health of your relationship.

Commitment to Keep Learning

What is the most important thing you learned in this chapter that, if lived consistently, would positively impact your relationship?

That we are definitely in a downward spiral. I feel almost all of those conditions and I would assume she does as well.

Commitment to Keep Changing

Based on what you have learned, what will you commit to change in your life?

Specifically, how will you do it?

Specifically, when will you do it?

The Solution:

Four Courses to Feed the Healthy Relationship

Chapter 5

Let the Feeding Begin

Now that a solid foundation for a relationship has been laid, the rest of the tools needed to feed our relationships will be introduced. To review, the stage has been set as to what the primary **Goal** is about. It is to create healthy and enduring relationships. We've also discussed the major **Challenges**, which can be broken down into three categories: focusing on the smoke and not the fire, feeding the 7 Basic Needs of healthy relationships—the STARVED Stuff, and getting caught in the STARVED Spiral. Now it is time to introduce the largest section of this book, the part you've all been waiting for: **Solutions** to feeding a healthy and enduring relationship.

There is hope in our relationships, no matter what **Challenges** we have faced or will face. No matter how deeply or quickly we find ourselves circling the drain of the STARVED Spiral, the situation can be improved. We shouldn't give up on ourself or our relationship until we have learned and internalized the **Solutions** that I am about to present. I have seen these principles, when incorporated into a couple's way of life, revitalize even in the most dysfunctional, broken relationships. In fact, with the couples with whom I work, I'm so confident about the effectiveness of these principles that I "guarantee" they will begin to create change in the lives of those who use them or I will give them their money back. In my many years of this guarantee, I've never had one couple who has gone through the program and then asked for their money back. The Four Courses you're going to learn about have worked for thousands of my clients, and I'll guarantee they'll work for you. The only real question is, will you put these principles to work or will you keep using the ineffective habits that have STARVED your relationship, or at least left you with the munchies?

A critical principle I teach about all relationships is that they are going to change. Remember, change is inevitable. You and your partner are going to change. The question is what will your relationship change into? Will your love grow stronger and stronger, more complete, deeper and enduring? Or will it keep changing as it goes deeper and deeper into the abyss of the STARVED Spiral? If change is constant and inevitable (and we've already asked the question of what are we going to change into), the only other question is—who is going to start loving whom first?

The smallest good deed is better than the grandest good intention.
—Duguet

Surprisingly, I've found that it doesn't always take two people to begin to improve a relationship. It only takes one. I can't tell you how many of my clients have started the program alone and then single handedly created conditions in which their partner became more and more influenced to come and learn the program themselves. There is truly power in one!

Think about it—if it only takes one selfish partner to starve the other or to be reactive, polarizing, negative and hopeless, then wouldn't it also just take one person to begin being selfless, proactive, unifying and positive? A well-used saying in my office is: "Two heads are better than one, but one is better than none."

Try this. Think of a relationship or situation you're struggling with right now. Now think of one negative thing you could do to make it even worse. Pretty easy, huh? So if it's that easy to come up with something negative that could change a situation, then doesn't it make sense that it could be that easy to make positive changes, too? Even small changes are worth the effort!

Just as you created a downward spiral by starving, you can also create an upward spiral by effectively relating and becoming the partner you need to become. The **Solutions** section of this book is all about where and how you begin to lift the relationship out of the STARVED Spiral and into the Loving Spiral. It's about how you reverse the spiral, stop the starving, and begin feeding the 7 Basic Needs of all healthy relationships.

Reversing the STARVED Spiral

Someone once said that the definition of insanity is to keep making the same mistakes over and over again and expecting a different outcome. When we are in the STARVED Spiral and repeating the same mistakes over and over again, we might be a little insane. So, how do we stop the insanity, reverse this STARVED Spiral and begin creating more love?

The reversal of the STARVED Spiral is really about creating more love in a relationship. Remember, the opposite of STARVED is loved. Love, once out of the yearning stage, is really about meeting the 7 Basic Needs: Safety, Trust, Appreciation, Respect, Validation, Encouragement, and Dedication.

In my experience, the STARVED Stuff is fed, and therefore reversed, most effectively through four very basic courses or meals. Just like in a meal, each course adds a different flavor and experience. Whereas individually each course may stand alone, collectively they come together to create a meal that is completely satisfying. For me, the four courses that feed the healthy relationship are sequential; each builds upon the earlier course and is dependent upon the other.

Four Courses to Feeding the STARVED Relationship

As I've tried to help couples learn to solve their problems together, I've experimented with every possible relational solution, skill, or technique I've ever come across. I've altered the sequencing of the skills, the focus, scope, and intensity of the activities all with the hope of unlocking the door to healthier relationships. Through all of this experimentation, I've found four powerful principles that I believe are at the root of all healthy relationships. These four principles with their accompanying skills and tools, I call the Four Courses to feeding the STARVED relationship. The principles are Character, Communication, Companionship, and Commitment. These four principles, when operating alone, are incredibly powerful tools. However, when operating together I've seen the synergy between these principles truly transform the relationships of people. Together they meet the concise description of being both profoundly simple and simply profound.

I have tried serving my clients the Four Courses in every order possible. I've tried to teach the course on Communication or Companionship before the course on Character, only to find out that many people lacked the character necessary to truly communicate or be good companions. I've served Commitment first, thinking that this was where it all started, only to find that every commitment was limited by one's ability to be both a companion and communicator. After a lot of testing and practice, I have found that teaching Character first, followed by Communication, then Companionship, and then Commitment creates powerful results in the lives of couples.

You will notice that each course has a governing principle and resulting benefit if the principle is exercised. It is the synergy between the lived principle and its inherent benefit that begins to change the relationship. So, let's now dig in deeper and explore the power of the Four Courses:

#1- The Course on Character results in Mutual Trust.
#2- The Course on Communication results in Mutual Understanding.
#3- The Course on Companionship results in Mutual Benefit.
#4- The Course on Commitment results in Mutual Growth.

Each of these courses helps create a more healthy and productive relationship while simultaneously reversing the STARVED Spiral. These Four Courses nourish our relationships. They give us strength and ability to not just put up with each other in our relationship, but more importantly, to begin to thrive together. Here is a brief look at the Four Courses:

The Course on Character: The Choice to Create Mutual Trust

The first course for feeding the STARVED relationship is Character. In this course, the goal is to teach you how to keep your head in the game, which will prove critical for all of the other courses you will study and put into practice. Character is the governing principle of this course, with the result being the benefit of creating Mutual Trust. My experiences in both life and my profession have taught me that each relationship is nothing more than a composite of the choices we make in that relationship. In this section, we will talk a lot about our choices and the Choice Points, or moments of choice that we need to focus on that will change the entire direction of the relationship.

We define *Character* as having the ability to make decisions based on our values and principles, not based on our moods, circumstances or events, or, in other words, the STARVED Stuff. In this course, we will begin to see the strength of our own character and the impact our character has on our relationships. We will also learn how our head gets in the way of effective relationships by hijacking our emotions and turning on our fight or flight responses. We will learn valuable skills that will help us regain control of our head and will suspend our need to react to our partner. We will learn how to "take the High Road." As a result, our own confidence will grow as we begin to turn around the old, ineffective habits of the past. Finally, we will learn about recognizing the ruts in relationships in order to make better choices that ensure we don't keep living the same old problems over and over again.

The Course on Communication: The Choice to Create Mutual Understanding

The second course for feeding the STARVED relationship is the course on Communication. Communication is the governing principle with the end result being to create Mutual Understanding. You will notice that the course on Communication follows the course on Character because how do you communicate with someone who doesn't have character? Character determines the quality of communication.

Conversation means being able to disagree and
still continue the discussion.
—Dwight MacDonald

We will learn the skills and tools we need in order to truly understand our partner and to be able to *show* our partner that we do understand. We will begin to learn the process of "Getting REAL" by accepting our partner where he or she is, exploring the issues and energy, and taking the conversation out of the "senseless smoke" and down into the real fire—the STARVED Stuff. We will learn how to use communication to actually reverse the negative "Vital Signs" and bring new life back into a conversation.

We will also learn how to stop the dangerous STARVED Spiral condition of polarization by turning old fight or flight patterns into more healthy and productive conversations. Finally, we will learn about the four directions we can take any conversation and about how to lift our conversations upward. We will then see that all of these skills can be practiced effectively, even if only one party knows how to do them.

The Course on Companionship: The Choice to Create Mutual Benefit

Once we have partaken of the courses on Character and Communication, the third course on Companionship seems to fit right in as the next course in line because we have the character to try to feed our partner their way and the communication skills to understand what their way looks like.

In this section, we will discuss how to both give and receive love to those who matter most. Companionship is the principle of this section and the result created is Mutual Benefit. Every long-term relationship requires Mutual Benefit. For instance, how long would you stay at a job where you were not benefiting? Or, how long would you shop at a store where you began to see that the quality of their product was so poor that it fell apart and you had to replace it often? The same is true in our relationships. If we don't have great companionship with our partner, where we are both benefiting, we will probably lack the drive to communicate or show character with one another.

Course on Commitment: The Choice to Create Mutual Growth

The fourth course for feeding the 7 Basic Needs of healthy relationships is the course on Commitment. Now that the courses on Character, Communication, and Companionship are in place, this final course can be taught. This is really the course that ensures all three previous courses will continue to be strengthened and delivered.

My belief is not that we should be committed to having the perfect relationship or to be the perfect partner, but instead we should remain committed to learning and improving ourselves in the other three courses of Character, Communication, and Companionship.

In this section, we will explore the keys to creating long-term hope in the relationship. The governing principle of commitment results in the benefit of Mutual Growth. Through my work with couples, I have found that when two people are truly committed to continually learn and change for each other, there is nothing they can't accomplish. I have found that having a true commitment to our partner, and a willingness to act every day on that commitment, will lift our relationship higher. However, what kills the hope is having all of the tools we've learned throughout this book, but realizing our partner is unwilling to act on this knowledge.

A high degree of empathy in a relationship is possibly the most potent factor in bringing about change and learning.
—Carl Rogers

In this course on Commitment, I will focus on three key steps to create movement and hope in the relationship. First is to create a combined vision of where both of the partners want to be, or what we call the Best Possible Marriage (BPM). Second, I'll teach how to put together solutions around any problems we encounter, solutions that will help us eventually overcome the issues and create movement toward our long-term goals as a couple. Finally, and perhaps most importantly, the key to creating hope is action. Nothing creates more hope than focused action around mutually agreed upon solutions.

We will begin to see the importance of taking the understanding we have acquired and using this information to create better solutions together. With this new plan, we can then create a focused action on the plan, which will inevitably begin to create hope.

Whether you know it consciously or not, these are the principles that get results, and always have, for you and your partner. Now it's time to sit back and enjoy your four-course meal. Take in what you can, commit to finish what's on your plate, and let the feeding begin!

The understanding and practice that will come with each of these courses will create even greater strength to create the changes that need to be created. Inevitably, by utilizing the tools of the Four Courses, we will inherently begin feeding the 7 Basic Needs of healthy relationships and simultaneously reverse the STARVED Spiral by filling the voids of starvation with the benefits of the Loving Spiral. The outcome will naturally be selflessness, proactivity, cooperation, positive interpretation, hope, and togetherness.

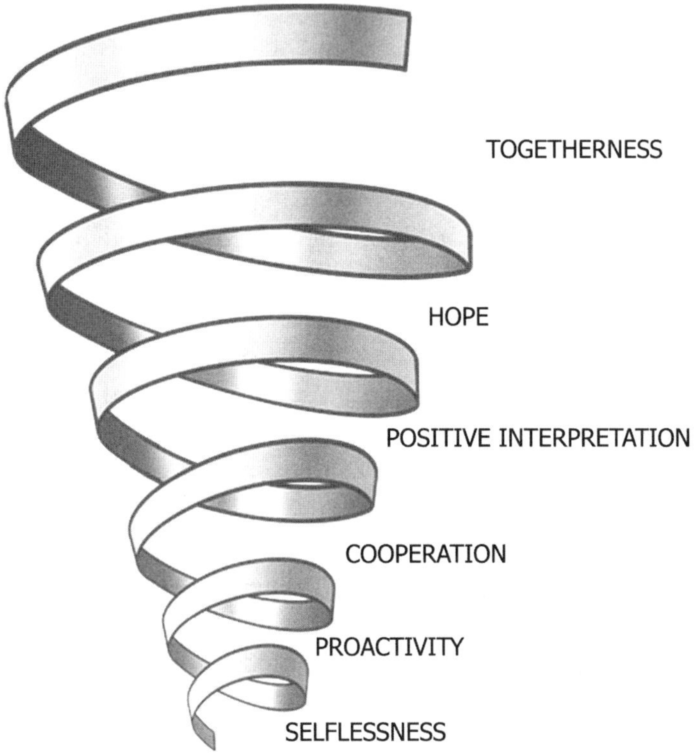

So here begins the journey. I know it may seem overwhelming for some and exciting for others. Much of this depends on whether our relationship is STARVED and emaciated or whether it just has the munchies. I want you to know that there is hope for your relationship. You can make it better. This doesn't mean these principles are always going to improve everything about our partner, but we can definitely improve how we view our partner and interact with them. The key to all of this is to go through the solutions of the book seriously, learn what we can, and take something we learn today and begin to use it. As we do all of the exercises, we will see that the more we act on these principles, the more each of us will understand how to be and do more in our relationships. Phillip Venier describes this process of change best when he said:

> *Do not wait for great strength before starting out, or immobility will weaken you further:*
> *Do not wait to see very clearly before beginning, for one must walk toward the light.*
> *Have you the strength to take this first step?*
> *The courage to perform this one small act, the necessity of which is obvious to you?*
> *Take this step!*
> *Perform this act!*
> *And you will find that the effort thus spent, rather than exhausting your strength, has doubled it and you will see clearly what to do next.*
>
> *—Phillip Venier (translated from French)*

Take the steps you need to take, perform the acts you need to perform, and you will see the energy and hope in your relationship begin to soar. Let the feeding frenzy begin!

Chapter Review:

- No matter how far down the STARVED Spiral a relationship has gone, there is always hope for the relationship. It takes only one person to make significant change and progress in the relationship.
- The Loving Spiral is facilitated by learning to effectively relate, and it begins with selflessness and moves through proactivity, cooperation, positive interpretation, hope, and ends in togetherness.
- The opposite of STARVED is loved, and love is really just meeting the 7 Basic Needs of Safety, Trust, Appreciation, Respect, Validation, Encouragement, and Dedication.
- The STARVED Stuff is fed, and thus reversed, through Four Courses: Character, Communication, Companionship, and Commitment
- The result of Character is Mutual Trust and is defined as the ability to make choices based on integrity and knowledge, not based on emotions and circumstances.
- The result of Communication is Mutual Understanding and is the ability to truly understand another and show that understanding.

- The result of Companionship is Mutual Benefit and is the ability to both give and receive love.
- The result of Commitment is Mutual Growth and is the ability to continue learning and changing together.

My Feeding Plan

In order to create a healthy diet that feeds your relationship, you need to have a plan. Use the "My Feeding Plan" activity to come up with some specific ideas from the last chapter that you can use to improve the health of your relationship.

Commitment to Keep Learning

What is the most important thing you learned in this chapter that, if lived consistently, would positively impact your relationship?

Commitment to Keep Changing

Based on what you have learned, what will you commit to change in your life?

____

____

____

____

Specifically, how will you do it?

____

____

____

Specifically, when will you do it?

____

____

____

The Course on Character

Building Mutual Trust

Chapter 6

Defining Character

By definition, *Character* means "moral excellence or firmness." It is the ability to live our values and the commitments we make. Character is the root to building trust and creating long-term growth and connection with other human beings. Character is what allows us to put other's needs before our own. It is what leads us to act in the best interest of our partner and the relationship. A lack of character, by one or both partners, is the leading cause of the STARVED Spiral we talked about in chapter four. Lack of character causes the demise of most of our closest relationships and is the root cause of reactivity. In my coaching practice, I have seen hundreds of breakdowns in character that have lead to the starvation of both partners.

The force of character is cumulative.
—Ralph Waldo Emerson

Almost universally when couples come to me for help in their relationships and they hear I am a communication expert, they immediately begin peppering me with questions about how they can improve their communication, assuming that if only they could talk better, this would mean they would immediately relate better. I have found that the answer lies not in immediately addressing their communication problems, but in first teaching them the importance of character in a relationship. Our character is the primary driver in both our ability to communicate and to cooperate with our partner.

I have already discussed some definitions of character; however, there are two more that I feel are critical to creating healthy and enduring relationships:

- Character is the ability to stick to a decision long after the emotion of the decision has passed.
- Character is the ability to make a decision based upon values and principles, and not upon mood, circumstances, or STARVED Stuff.

As we can see by these definitions, no principle is more important to feeding the 7 Basic Needs of healthy relationships than the principle of character. A great example of character is a story about Mahatma Gandhi.

> *During the 1930's, a young boy had become obsessed with eating sugar. His mother was very upset with this. But no matter how much she scolded him and tried to break his habit, he continued to satisfy his sweet tooth. Totally frustrated, she decided to take her son to see his idol—Mahatma Gandhi; perhaps her son would listen to him.*
>
> *She walked miles, for hours under scorching sun to finally reach Gandhi's ashram. There, she shared with Gandhi her predicament. "Bapu, my son eats too much sugar. It is not good for his health. Would you please advise him to stop eating it?"*
>
> *Gandhi listened to the woman carefully, thought for a while and replied, "Please come back after two weeks. I will talk to your son."*
>
> *The woman looked perplexed and wondered why had he not asked the boy to stop eating sugar right away. She took the boy by the hand and went home.*
>
> *Two weeks later they revisited Gandhi. Gandhi looked directly at the boy and said, "Boy, you should stop eating sugar. It is not good for your health."*
>
> *The boy nodded and promised he would not continue this habit any longer. The boy's mother was puzzled. She turned to Gandhi and asked, "Bapu, Why didn't you tell him that two weeks ago when I brought him here to see you?"*
>
> *Gandhi smiled, "Mother, two weeks ago I was eating a lot of sugar myself."*
>
> *—(www.avani-mehta.com)*

I honestly believe that if you can master only one of these Four Courses, it should be character. People with character will eventually find the way to healthier communication, companionship, and commitment. So dig deep into the course on character and watch the positive impact on your relationships. Especially pay attention to how character enables six key benefits that will feed even the hungriest relationships.

Character:

1. Builds trust.
2. Helps us act on what matters most.
3. Enables us to overcome our weaknesses.
4. Facilitates forgiveness.
5. Empowers us to be the "Wizard" in our own life.
6. Helps us manage Choice Points.

Character Builds Trust

Axel and Celeste came into my office complaining about the lack of trust they felt in their marriage. Neither trusted the other. Celeste complained that the collapse of their marriage started when her husband spent the entire 10 years of their marriage falsely accusing her of having multiple affairs. Instead of loving nicknames, Axel called her derogatory names like tramp, slut, flirt, and player—all of which were intended to belittle her. Axel also spent a lot of time talking with his buddies about how "crazy" Celeste was in the bedroom. He shared private details about their intimacy and often made suggestive comments about her when they were out with other couples and friends. He chose to accuse, blame, and degrade, with no evidence to back up his beliefs about Celeste.

Telling the strained story of her past, Celeste's eyes welled with tears as she explained, "For ten years I was completely faithful to Axel and he still treated me this way." In the eleventh year of the marriage, Celeste's will broke and she had a year-long affair that she felt destroyed her family. And guess who she had the affair with? Axel's best friend—the person to whom he had told all their marital secrets.

When Axel found out Celeste had the affair, he angrily turned to her. Pointing his finger right in her face, he yelled, "I *knew* I couldn't trust you. You always were a slut and you always will be."

Ironic isn't it? Because he perceived he couldn't trust her, he chose to treat her in ways that showed so much distrust that his perceptions actually influenced her into living "down" to his derogatory remarks.

Trust is a very powerful factor in any relationship and is clearly a two-way street, meaning that building trust is the responsibility of *both* partners. Each partner should live in a trustworthy way, and each should also be willing to see his partner as trustworthy. It's a continual path back and forth—giving trust and being trustworthy. When we are governed by fear (or mistrust), we usually get that which we fear (or mistrust) the most.

The difficulty with marriage is that we fall in love with a personality, but must live with a character.
—Peter De Vries

In Axel and Celeste's situation, character was lacking in both partners. This fact disabled any true ability to build trust in the relationship. Obviously, Celeste's affair was a breakdown of her character; she made choices that did not align with her values. However, Celeste's character was not the only breakdown in the relationship. Axel's constant questioning of Celeste's morals and character also contributed. Whether we like to accept this fact or not, the reality is that our actions do impact our partner's psyche and vice versa. It is inevitable that your character flaws (and we all have them) will eventually make their way into your relationship with your partner. As Peter De Vries, the American editor and novelist, alludes to, sometimes we end up being married to a character that lacks character.

One of the keys to creating more trust in our relationships is to watch carefully what we reflect back onto our partner. If our reflections of our partner are respectful, full of dignity and validation, then over time our partner will be influenced. He will eventually begin to see himself in a more respectful light. Sometimes this is referred to as self-fulfilling prophecy. If we tell someone long enough that they're fabulous, talented, and amazing, they start to believe this. The reverse is also true—just like Celeste, who was told over and over again that she was having an affair. Over time, she began to fulfill this prophecy. We need to be strong enough to project our partner's great worth and potential. Our partner doesn't need or want us to dwell on what is most obvious about how he is not performing up to our expectations.

Let's break this down even further:

Long-term relationships demand Mutual Trust and high character, and then both parties in the relationship will be much more likely to stick it out to the Enduring years when the fruits and harvest appear.

About ten years ago I was in Indianapolis, Indiana, teaching this concept. I asked the class, "What does having character in a relationship guarantee? Does it guarantee everything will go perfectly in your life? Does it guarantee you'll never have problems or that your marriage will always be perfect?"

Obviously the answer to the last two questions was a resounding, "No!"

To further clarify this point for me, near the back of the room, a man raised his hand and taught me a very profound lesson. I never got his name, but he was a retired military officer who had worked for years as a recruiter for the U.S. Army. On April 19, 1995, he was working in the Alfred P. Murrah Federal building in Oklahoma City, Oklahoma, when Timothy McVeigh blew the building up with a bomb that killed 168 people, the deadliest domestic terrorist attack in the history of the United States, until September 11, 2001. The army recruiter and his team were on the upper floors of that building when the bomb went off.

This man described how he had always tried to live his life with character and discipline. He then said, "No matter how much character I had that day, it didn't protect me from a bomb that exploded and killed half of the people in my charge. Life happens, and character can't protect us from everything."

But then he continued, "Although my character couldn't protect those who lost their lives that day, the habits of character I had demonstrated so many times with my team, before that explosion, created a trust that enabled the remaining survivors to follow me out of that dangerous building, through the darkness of all the smoke, rubble, and fire. My history of character with them allowed them to trust me enough that they would follow me down the dark stairs, even when their world had just been shattered."

Character will determine if others will follow us. Our character can act as a light for others—especially our partner—exuding confidence and direction. Our character won't guarantee we won't be hurt or that times won't be tough. Character won't guarantee that we won't be disappointed in our relationship or have disagreements with each other, but our character will guarantee that we will have the Mutual Trust and power to make it through almost anything life throws at us.

Character Helps Us Act on What Matters Most

International Business Consultant James Skinner shared this story with me many years ago when we were working together on a project. This example perfectly describes how character enables your ability to focus on what matters most.

Yoko was a young girl born mentally handicapped and suffered from severe learning disabilities. Her mother died at Yoko's birth and her physically incapacitated father was unable to give her the extensive care she needed.

Yoko was placed in an institution. She was treated well and the doctors did everything they could to help Yoko prepare to live an independent life. While many things would always remain beyond her capacity, the doctors felt it was especially important that Yoko learn to handle money if she was to ever live outside the institution. They carefully taught her to distinguish amongst various coins and bills. At last the day arrived to test Yoko's ability to live outside the institution walls. Her caretakers and doctors sat with her and laid out various denominations of money: 10 yen coins, 100 yen coins, 1,000 yen notes, and 10,000 yen notes. The doctors questioned, "All right Yoko, which of these is of most value?"

Yoko smiled and without question pointed to the 10 yen coin. The doctors couldn't believe it! They were devastated. After all of their work, it seemed maybe Yoko would never make it on her own. Holding out hope, they rearranged the money on the table and decided to try again.

"Okay, one more time. Yoko, which of these is the most valuable?"

Again, without hesitation she pointed to the 10 yen coin.

The doctors were downhearted and discouraged. In a last-ditch effort they asked, "Why do you say that? You know these coins are not the ones of most value!"

Yoko looked down and frowned. She started to cry and replied,

"You don't understand. When I put the 10 yen coin in the phone, I can hear the loving voice of my father."

When asked which was most valuable, Yoko chose not the monetary aspects of the coin, but the emotional value of what that coin meant to her character—the loving voice of her father. Imagine how this impacted Yoko's father.

Each of us needs to learn what is most important in our relationships. And this can be accomplished only through character, through knowing first what is important. There are times when putting our partner's needs or wants above our own is what is most important in the relationship—even if it's when you are feeling most vulnerable and under attack. Altruistic, but true.

Character Enables Us to Overcome Our Weaknesses

I was never very good at math. It's no wonder that all of my degrees are in the arts and not the sciences. It doesn't matter though that I'm not good at math, because "I'm a Townsend!"

Let me explain. When I was a freshman in high school, I had an algebra teacher named Mrs. Larson. She was a well-experienced teacher who taught every one of my older sisters and, to be quite honest, none of us were her best math students.

One day, while I was home and suffering through my math homework, my mom came over to check out what I was doing.

"I hate math!" I told her. "I'm not good at it. It's not important anyway. Nobody ever uses algebra in real life."

Following this, my well-intentioned mom said the most beautiful words I had ever heard. To this day, I can still hear her say, "Well, to tell you the truth, honey, no Townsend has ever been good at algebra. We don't do math. Townsends aren't math people. Most of your grandparents weren't math people, your dad wasn't good at math, I'm not good at math, and your sisters aren't good at math. We just aren't good at math."

When she was finished talking, I had this overwhelming peace, as the expectation of having to learn something nearly impossible began to leave me. "Excellent!" I thought to myself. "I can't do algebra, because 'I'm a Townsend!'"

How simple was this? I couldn't do math because of my genes! I began to treat my last name as if it was a clinical diagnosis like Alzheimer's or Parkinson's. In fact, just for the record, when I got married I made sure to give my children a fighting chance by marrying someone who did do math and didn't carry the bad algebra gene!

From that moment on, I quit worrying about my inadequacy. I quit trying to learn something I was never going to "get." Instead of preparing to do a math retest on Monday, I spent time hanging out with my friends and having fun. I just knew Mrs. Larson would understand my "genetic" condition and make all kinds of allowances for me. I was confident all would be well with the world.

So, I went to school the next Monday and didn't turn in my math assignment. My conscientious algebra teacher called me up to her desk and expressed her frustration with me, "Matt, where is your homework? Are you ready to be retested?"

"Well," I answered, "I've got something important to tell you about why I'm struggling so much in this class. You see, Mrs. Larson, I talked to my mom about it and we discovered that I can't do algebra, because 'I'm a Townsend.' You see, Townsends just don't *do* algebra. My grandparents couldn't do it, my parents can't do it, and my sisters can't do it. We're all 'Townsends' and we're all afflicted."

There was silence as Mrs. Larson peered over her glasses into my face. She looked stunned, obviously overwhelmed by the tragic news of my condition. She then began laughing and shaking her head. She said, "You've sure got that right! Townsends don't do algebra. After having all of your sisters, I couldn't agree with you more!" Then, with a serious look on her face, she added, "However, *this* Townsend," she pointed to me, "is going to do algebra. I won't take any excuses; you're going to learn it!"

It is our choices that show what we truly are, far more than our abilities.
—J. K. Rowling

This was one of the first moments of my life when I realized I was learning an important lesson about character. Building character and, in turn, building trust happens when we choose to not go for excuses or the easy way out. Character is choosing to overcome our genetics, our conditioning, our environment, our habits, and ourself, and instead doing everything we can to make our life better. It means that we don't rely on excuses.

Character is choosing to overcome those things that "others" say determine who we are. Character means that, even though we have every excuse in the book to let something remain in a less healthy state, we choose a more healthy state and do our best to improve our condition.

I won't kid you, I never really did turn my math skills around and master higher math like trigonometry and calculus. I did, however, pass Mrs. Larson's algebra class and went on to take college algebra as well as many other advanced statistics classes. I'm not a mathematician, but I didn't let "my genes" stop me from being willing to learn and, in so doing, this helped my character become tougher and stronger.

Having character in our relationship is the same. We each get to make choices, regardless of what history, genes, or examples have gone before us. Axel made choices about how he treated Celeste, and Celeste made choices about whether or not she would listen to and believe Axel's critiques or not. And we already know where this got them.

Researchers tell us there are certain conditions that increase the likelihood of divorce, such as having parents who divorced and having different religious and socio-economic backgrounds. Blended families can also have a harder go of it, and differences in education might also come into play.

But none of these factors compare to the power character plays in the lives of the couples with whom I work. Conditions don't determine our relationship results—character does. At some point, our character determines the choices we make and our choices determine our results.

Character Facilitates Forgiveness

Sometimes when we have been hurt or offended, it is hard to forgive or let go of the pain and sadness. We carry the problem with us, being burdened by the load and the feeling of its impact in every step we take in life.

Nelson Mandela had a great understanding of what character and forgiveness are really about. After being imprisoned for over 27 years, Mandela was freed, and soon after he became the first elected black leader of South Africa. As a sign of his character and a symbol for the future of an integrated South Africa, he invited the jailors to his inauguration—those men who for 27 years had held him captive. He even reserved front row seats for them and treated them as honored guests. At that same inauguration, Nelson Mandela read a quote from Marianne Williamson that I believe beautifully captures the difference between what character does for humanity and what fear does:

> *Our deepest fear is not that we are inadequate.*
> *Our deepest fear is that we are powerful beyond measure.*
> *It is our light, not our darkness that most frightens us.*
> *We ask ourselves, who am I to be brilliant, gorgeous, talented and fabulous?*

Actually, who are you "not" to be?
You are a child of God.
Your playing small doesn't serve the world.
There is nothing enlightened about shrinking so that other people won't feel insecure around you.
We were born to make manifest the glory of God that is within us.
It's not just in some of us, it's in everyone.
And as we let our own light shine,
We unconsciously give other people permission to do the same.
As we are liberated from our own fear our presence automatically liberates others.

It was the power of Mandela's character that allowed him to forgive his captors. This also impacted the level of trust his countrymen and the world had for him. If Nelson Mandela can forgive 27 years of oppression and mistreatment to millions of his people, then certainly we can forgive our partner for accidentally shutting the electric garage door down on our new car. Our character allows us to forgive our partner, not only for his sake, but maybe, more importantly, for our sake.

A powerful example of character and forgiveness was demonstrated by one of my clients after she found out her husband had an emotional affair with a co-worker. Rosa was devastated by the news that her husband, Carlos, had been unfaithful. For months she came into my office and, at times, cried about the pain she felt. She didn't know quite how to move on and let go of the pain, anger, and frustration.

Rosa's husband was seriously apologetic for his mistake and fully realized that regaining her trust was going to be a difficult and long road. He was also frustrated with himself for having the affair and, at times, was even frustrated with his wife for her inability to let the affair go after some period of time.

On the spur of the moment, they had a chance to leave their children and fly to Hawaii for a vacation. While on the vacation, Rosa decided it was time for her to take charge of some of the feelings she had about Carlos and let them go. She recognized that if she continued to make him suffer by not forgiving, she would create conditions that would inevitably starve their relationship more and bring about its demise.

While sitting on the beach, she calmly stood and without saying a word walked away from her partner. She walked over to the water and picked up some rocks. With each rock she thought about the pain she felt and then replaced the painful thought with a healthier thought about her future with Carlos and her family. She accepted his desires to be closer to her and she accepted how she had STARVED Carlos, just as Carlos had STARVED her. She identified how they could rebuild and, with each of these thoughts, she intentionally made the choice to let her negative feelings go and replace them with love and forgiveness. She then tossed the rock into the ocean. Rock by rock, she felt more and more love for Carlos. With tears streaming down her cheeks, her heart opened wider than it had been for years. It was then that she realized forgiveness was a choice and a gift she had to give. Trust in marriage was something that had to be worked for on his part, and given on her part—the two-way street we talked about earlier.

Forgiveness is a gift of high value. Yet its cost is nothing.
—Betty Smith

Notice that the title of this section is *Character Facilitates Forgiveness*. By definition, the word *facilitates* means to make something easier. Character makes easier the ability to forgive another. Nothing will make it completely pain free; however, our character is something that at least puts us on a healthier path.

Character Empowers Us to be the "Wizard" in Our Own Life

Remember the man behind the curtain in the classic film *The Wizard of Oz*? The wizard was the one controlling all of the events of Emerald City. He was the one Dorothy and her friends went to because they believed he controlled their fate. Remember the revealing scene near the end of the movie when the lion, the scarecrow, the tin man, and Dorothy finally had the chance to be presented to the wizard, and Dorothy's dog, Toto, opened the curtain and exposed the real "brain" behind the wizard of Oz?

Just as Dorothy and her friends didn't know who was behind the curtain "pulling all the strings," most of us are not aware of who is actually pulling the strings behind our own curtain or the curtain in our own relationship. Just as in the movie, we tend to take advice from the little voice in our head that says, "Pay no attention to the man behind the curtain."

Yet there really is a lot of progress made in the movie when the secret is revealed. If you remember, Dorothy could not go home until the wizard's secrets were exposed and his power or powerlessness was dealt with, and in turn, each one of the characters in the film discovered that what each person so desperately sought after could not be given to them by the wizard. Instead, each of those gifts was already beautifully contained within each character. Remember, the scarecrow wanted a brain, the tin man desired a heart, and the lion wanted courage. This then became an empowering motive for good within each of them.

Having and expressing character empowers us with the truth of who we are, and then helps us recognize how we interact with others.

Once Dorothy realized she didn't need the man behind the curtain to grant her wish to go home, she realized she had all the power she needed to stand on her own two feet. In our relationship, we must find the power within us and be willing to trust this power. Character allows us to balance the paradox that we truly are an incredible person who can make amazing changes for the better and yet, at the same time, realize that we're still very human and prone to weakness and ineptitude. Just as Dorothy found out that you've got to believe in yourself, we too will be able to just be ourself and know who we really are with all of our hopes, dreams, visions, wishes, intelligence and great wisdom.

Character Helps Us Manage Choice Points

Relationships don't just appear—they are created. Every relationship is created through our interactions with each other. These interactions are like the bricks that, one by one and side by side, slowly join together to either create a strong, beautiful building or a thick impenetrable wall. Depending on how they are created, every interaction a couple engages in will either generate positive, hopeful experiences or potentially negative, painful experiences. Over time, the accumulation of these experiences creates the couple's view of what constitutes their relationship. Not one interaction is created without our influence and guidance.

One of the most critical moments of any relationship, and one of the greatest moments where character is demonstrated, is during what I call the Choice Point. The Choice Point occurs during any critical moments of interaction that could affect our present and our future relationships. It is the moment where the direction and the health of the interaction, and eventually the direction and the health of the relationship, are determined. We have hundreds, if not thousands, of Choice Points per day and each of these Choice Points make up the quality of the bricks used to build our relationships. In these moments, our relationships are molded and future stability is decided. It is in these Choice Points that the soundness of the relationship is determined.

Choice Points are really nothing more than a moment where a choice is going to take place. This choice could be either a healthy decision that strengthens the relationship or a less healthy decision that actually weakens the relationship. A non-relational example of Choice Points could be of the person who is trying to lose 20 pounds before her big summer vacation. The Choice Point would take place when someone at the office brings in a box of doughnuts for everyone to enjoy. What would the dieting person do at this Choice Point? Would she stick with her goal and exercise character during this temptation, or would she give in to the momentary satisfaction of a rich, moist doughnut with fresh glaze? Notice what a powerful moment this Choice Point is. So much is riding on this moment, and yet the dieting person may not stop to think about the importance of this moment of choice.

Whatever decision we make at the Choice Point will have far-reaching effects. Perhaps this Choice Point might even impact our mood, our self-esteem, our self-worth, the ability for others to trust us, as well as our future goals, such as our ability to fit into that swimsuit. The same is true in all of our relationships as well. Our goal of having healthy relationships can be just as big of a test as sticking to our "doughnut-free" health regimen. In the end, our health, both physical and relational, is directly affected by how we handle the Choice Points of our relationships.

There is a great quote from Eleanor Roosevelt that describes our role in the moment of the Choice Point:

> *One's philosophy is not best expressed in words; it's expressed in the choices one makes. In the long run, we shape our lives and we shape ourselves. The process never ends until we die. And the choices we make are ultimately our responsibility.*

This statement suggests that our focus should be directed in the Choice Point. Instead of looking for others to be the one who should change in the Choice Point, we must change our self. This is not a quick, fleeting, short-term change, but a long-term permanent change in who we are and how we see our partner—a change that isn't conditional, but a real change of character in which we agree to love our partner first and unconditionally.

When we both begin to realize how much *our own* choices in the Moment of Choice have caused so much of the STARVED Stuff in our relationship, then we can truly begin to change how we interact with one another. Doing this enables us to move away from the hard feelings we hold toward our partner. Living in the present, in the Choice Point, fully accepting responsibility for our feelings and choices, we become the change we seek in our relationship.

Over the years I have found that there tends to be three empowering principles that enhance our strength at the Choice Point:

1. **The Choice to Keep Our Head in the Game** and not react to our partner or the situation we're facing.
2. **The Choice to be an Empowered Communicator** who takes responsibility for interpretations instead of transferring all power to the speaker.
3. **The Choice to Take the High Road** with others as we interpret their actions and words.

At the foundation of each of these points are principles of character. These principles constitute a large part of the course on Character we will be reviewing in the next few chapters. When we exercise character with these rules, in the Choice Points of our lives, we begin to gain ground in our relationships because these rules enhance our ability to be trusted by our partner. These are the battles we must win, the tiny little battles in the Choice Points that will determine if we can change the future of our relationships.

So, get your character ready and let's dive in deeper to each of these rules and learn how to choose to bring power and trust back into your relationships.

Chapter Review:

- Character is the ability to live one's values and commitments and leads one to act in the best interest of his or her partner and the relationship.
- A lack of character is the leading cause of the STARVED Spiral and is the root cause of reactivity.
- Building trust is the responsibility of both people in the relationship. Trust is built when positive words and actions are reflected within the partnership.
- Character helps overcome weakness by rising above excuses and instead choosing to create a better self. In this same way, character also facilitates forgiveness.
- Relationships are created from interactions. Each interaction between partners generates either a positive or negative feeling in the relationship.
- The Choice Point is a critical moment during an interaction, when one or both partners can choose to either relate in a healthy and positive way or in a negative way that creates more STARVED Stuff.

My Feeding Plan

In order to create a healthy diet that feeds your relationship, you need to have a plan. Use the "My Feeding Plan" activity to come up with some specific ideas from the last chapter that you can use to improve the health of your relationship.

Commitment to Keep Learning

What is the most important thing you learned in this chapter that, if lived consistently, would positively impact your relationship?

Commitment to Keep Changing

Based on what you have learned, what will you commit to change in your life?

Specifically, how will you do it?

Specifically, when will you do it?

Chapter 7

The Choice to Keep Your Head in the Game

No matter how important a role character plays in a relationship and in life, there are times when struggles with overcoming reactive tendencies still happen and times when exercising true character seems nearly impossible. This is especially true in most personal relationships when we either feel threatened or we are afraid that we might be emotionally hurt or STARVED. So how do we overcome this struggle with character? Character is strengthened in the Choice Points as you make the choice to keep your head in the game, then the choice to be an Empowered Communicator and, finally, the choice to take the High Road. These three choices are actually skills for maintaining character and helping you on the way to a healthy and enduring relationship.

One of the fastest ways to bring character back into our life is to understand what it is that's getting in the way of staying focused on doing what is right. Believe it or not, the number one impediment to character, so many times, is our very own thought process. The principles found in the following pages will help us change our thought process and form a healthier one.

Just remember, character ensures that what we say can be trusted, what we learn will be acted upon, and how we say it will be in the best interest of our long-term goals. It is the first and most foundational course and, as mentioned before, if we choose to master only one of the courses, this is the one to master, because all other principles are built upon its foundation.

Character is the foundational building block of any relationship. Upon the foundation of character, trust and every other principle of effectiveness are built, resulting in more success in all of our relationships. Relationships come together for a variety of reasons, but most of them usually fall apart for the same reason—a lack of character. A healthy long-term relationship cannot be created unless both partners choose to manage the relationship from a foundation of character.

Keep Your Head in the Game

Have you ever experienced the following?

You're driving home after a long day at work, your commute goes well, you arrive at your destination safe and sound, and you don't remember any part of the trip? You don't remember merging onto the freeway. You don't remember exiting or driving through any of the stoplights.

Almost universally this, or some version of this absentmindedness, is experienced by everyone. Is this not unbelievable or frightening? Sometimes we are so out of it that we don't bother to be engaged, even while doing one of the most dangerous things we can do, like driving an automobile at 65 miles per hour. As humans, we sometimes have an extremely hard time keeping focused on what is most important in our life. There are just too many distractions that vie for our attention. So is it any wonder that relationships suffer? If we can't even pay attention while driving 3,500 pounds of machinery along a highway at 65 mph, what makes us think we can pay attention to each other's needs all of the time?

How many of us have gone weeks and maybe even months without ever really paying attention to our partner's needs, dreams, and/or desires? How many times have we had conversations, interactions, discussions, maybe even fights, and our head wasn't in the game at all? How much do you think you miss by living your relationship this way? By being distracted about other matters, how many "innocent bystanders" in your relationship have you run over or how many conversations could you classify as a "hit and run"?

If you don't know where you are going, any road will get you there.
—Lewis Carroll

As learned earlier in this book, once we leave the yearning stage of love and enter into the earning stage of love, losing our head in the relationship is much more likely to occur, and this can be just as deadly as losing our head during our commute home. This is where character and discipline at the Choice Point come into play.

After years of my research and coaching thousands of couples, this experience has proven to me, over and over again, that the divorce epidemic is largely a result of an inability to keep one's head in the game. As mentioned before, women file 70 percent of divorces across the United States. Half the time the husbands are shocked to hear such news. "What? It's not that bad! If it was that bad, why didn't you say anything?" Rolling their eyes, these women shake their heads in disbelief and wonder aloud where he's been for the last five years.

The Reactive Brain

Brain scientists could spend years teaching us exactly how the brain works, but simply put, there are two parts of the brain that greatly affect our relationships. One part of the brain builds character and relationships. The other part of the brain reinforces reactivity, usually for the preservation of humankind. For our purposes, I will refer to them as the "Relating Brain" and the "Reactive Brain." Let's talk about the Reactive Brain first.

Have you ever driven down the freeway, going a little too fast, and all of a sudden you see a car that looks like a State Trooper parked on the side of the road? What do you immediately feel? You pull your foot off the accelerator while your heart pumps like crazy. This is the great "Reactive Brain" at your service.

Imagine now that you're walking through the mall and you see somebody you would prefer not to see. Maybe it's an old boyfriend or a girlfriend who hurt your feelings, perhaps a boss who fired you. Your heart starts beating out of your chest, you get flushed, warm, and you feel all the blood leave your brain and go to your extremities and you think, "I've got to get out of here!" Nervously, you cruise through the mall wondering if they saw you. Again, your Reactive Brain is at work. Let's find out what causes this.

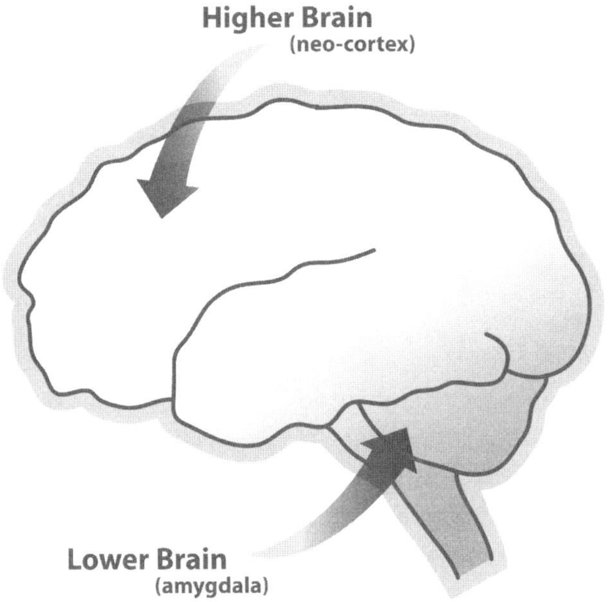

The Reactive Brain is made of two, almond-shaped fragments fixed at the base of the brain near the spinal column—the amygdalae. The amygdalae's primary function is to ensure our physical survival by quickly initiating the fight or flight reaction whenever our life is threatened. In other words, these two reactions are designed to save our hide. The problem with the amygdalae is that it's not designed to produce long-term relationships. The amygdala is what I call the "Reactive Brain"; however, others call it the reptilian brain, the fight or flight brain, or the lower brain. Its greatest strength is its ability to ensure the survival of the species. It is the most primitive part of the brain and is the same part of the brain we share with the animal kingdom.

The amygdalae or reactive brain is concerned with three basic needs: threat management, food, and reproduction. This very "primitive" brain asks three very basic questions at its Choice Points in order to filter the millions of pieces of data it must sort through on a daily basis:

1. Can it hurt me?
2. Can I eat it?
3. Can I mate with it?

Every time I list these three needs in a workshop, inevitably some woman yells from the back of the room, "That sounds like my husband!" to which contagious laughter always breaks out. At times, this is true. Men may function from the amygdalae more often than women do; however, both genders fall prey to the Reactive Brain.

The hardest victory is the victory over self.
—Aristotle

Can you see how the Reactive Brain creates a very narrow and shallow potential for beneficial and workable relationships? Staying in the Reactive Brain tends to create very selfish and self-serving relationships. The Reactive Brain works only to ensure that "I" will minimize the amount of pain in my life, that "I" will be well fed, and that "I" will get plenty of loving.

Now for some people this may sound like the perfect relationship, but for many others, women in general, they seek to have much more in their relationship. Most likely, you decided to get into your relationship because you wanted more than to have just these three very basic needs and instincts met.

Besides selfishness, the Reactive Brain—although it may save our lives at times and ensure survival of our species—creates other problems that are hard on relationships. The Reactive Brain fosters a spirit of competition rather than cooperation, depletes rather than builds trust, and tends to quickly polarize couples. It ensures key issues rarely get resolved and, inevitably, this increases the likelihood of divorce.

By contrast, the Relating Brain is the higher brain. This part of the brain refrains from reactivity and selfishness. Character is fostered in the Relating Brain and decisions made in the Choice Points are in the best interest of the relationship. The Relating Brain moves us from thinking about our own needs to, instead, paying attention to the needs of our partner. In the Relating Brain, we think about what is best for our partner and what is best for the relationship, and we act accordingly. We keep our head in the game by staying in the Relating Brain.

Getting Hijacked by the Reactive Brain

When we feel threatened, immediately our Reactive Brain kicks in. As we just learned, the Reactive Brain is meant to take over and cause instant action on our part. This is great if a tiger walks in the room, but not so great if we just interpreted our spouse's words or actions as hurtful. In relationships, we spend far too much time interacting out of the Reactive Brain. Once we've worked out of the Reactive Brain, we have six seconds to shut it down or the amygdalae will start pumping adrenaline and endorphins throughout our body, priming the fight or flight response. Once our body is primed chemically, we are hijacked. And it is this hijacking that starves most relationships.

In a heated argument we are apt to lose sight of the truth.
—Publilius Syrus

When we are hijacked, we feel no motivation to improve our relationship. Instead, we are chemically driven to react by becoming either a fighter or a flighter, a pursuer or a withdrawer. Safety then goes out the window and trust follows closely behind. I doubt if any of us feel appreciated or respected when our partner "goes off" on us. Validating words are not reactive words. It is impossible to consistently validate or encourage another human being while in the Reactive Brain. Dedication may be shaken when the other six basic needs are plummeting. Doctors have found that traces of the hijacking chemicals of adrenaline can be found in a person's system 24 hours after a stressful event. You may have experienced this in one of your late night "discussions" that went bad and you were unable to sleep for hours. It is at this point that our primal emotions hijack any real meaning we wanted to create. We cannot lift our relationship or increase understanding or show love when we are hijacked.

Take a second and think about your relationship. When we feel our partner is starving us and we feel threatened, what is our most typical response? Do we become more of a fighter who aggressively pursues or chases after our partner in search for answers that we hope will feed us? Or do we typically turn into a flighter who aggressively withdraws from the conflict in search of peace? It doesn't matter which method we tend to employ when our lower brain starts to fire, the mere fact that we are in the Reactive Brain will severely limit our ability to produce stronger relationships.

The Two Ruts of the Reactive Brain

The fight or flight reaction wired into our systems creates two ruts when we don't keep our head in the game. The fight or flight reaction is the battle between the physiological wiring of our bodies for self-preservation and protection, and the relational realities of our complex interpersonal interactions. Where the amygdalae was once vital in helping our early ancestors outrun a predatory animal, it is of little use to us today, because rarely are we ever threatened by such physical realities. Instead, we battle with our amygdalae the minute our partner brings up a difficult issue or wants to give us feedback about our poor relational performances. These fight or flight ruts are called many different names and are discussed abundantly by scholars in the field of marriage and family research. Here's just a sampling of terms describing the amygdalae responses. See if you use any of these terms to describe how you and your partner interact in your relationship.

Fight	Flight
Demander	Distancer
Engager	Avoider
Violent	Silent
Pursuer	Withdrawer
Talker	Walker
Escalator	Evader

In my practice, I prefer to use the terms "Pursuer" and "Withdrawer" and "Talker" and "Walker" to capture the essence of what is going on in most reactive communication patterns. Pursuer and Withdrawer are the two biggest ruts of the Reactive Brain. I follow the definitions posted by two expert researchers in the field of Marriage and Family Conflict, Clifford Notarious and Howard Markman:

Pursuers—These people "often feel an urgency to express anger and deal with upsetting events sooner rather than later. Are you unable to leave a problem unsettled for even an hour, even if your partner is not interested in talking?"

Withdrawers—"On the other hand, are you a partner who wishes to maintain peace and harmony above all else? Is it your tendency to see everything as a really small problem, so small that you feel it does not merit discussion?" (Notarius & Markman, p. 45, 1993).

In order to learn to get out of our reactive ruts, we must first acknowledge that we are in a rut. Then from this point, we can choose healthier patterns and tools to improve our relationships. Remember that conflict in relationship is normal, but how we deal with the conflict is what inevitably matters most.

Every person responds differently to conflict. Pursuers approach issues head on that potentially threaten their relationship, and they discuss things outright. Withdrawers believe any conflict in the relationship may be too hazardous to the relationship and opt to avoid the conflict or issues in order to ensure more peace and safety.

Pursuers tend to push the discussion because they seek answers and closure. They feel that a discussion around their concerns or complaints, if reciprocated and mutual, will bring the answers they need to not only solve the problem at hand, but, maybe more importantly, to reaffirm that their partner is engaged in the relationship and that they are safe to be together. For many pursuers, the issue of safety seems to be paramount and many times they push the conversation in an effort to eliminate their fears. Their fears create a stimulus that must be answered through conversation.

Withdrawers have a completely different goal when it comes to conflict. They tend to see conflict not as an opportunity to create safety and closure, but as a threat to the relationship, and in their own altruistic way, they've learned that avoiding conflict is the healthiest way to ensure peace. So, as the pursuers pursue to get answers, the withdrawers withdraw to get peace. Yet, in the end, this is a battle in which one person's need for answers robs another's need for peace, and the other person's need for peace robs their partner's need for answers. Both partners are desperately seeking safety using two diametrically opposed methods to obtain it. Counter-productivity like this only ensures the failure of not only their partner's goals, but inevitably their own.

The pursuers' drive for answers is so real that you can see an aggressive look in their eyes that shows they truly feel their "safety depends" on having this conversation! If the pursuers approach their partner with either intense fire or fear in their eyes because of the newly received tax bill (feeling financially unsafe) that they knew nothing about, there is some potential for problems. This aggressive presentation prompts the withdrawers to feel unsafe, which easily explains why withdrawers are so quick to start running. When the pursuers come out with fire in their eyes and the withdrawers immediately start moving away, then the chase is on. The pursuers are chasing only because the withdrawers are running, and the withdrawers are running only because the pursuers are chasing.

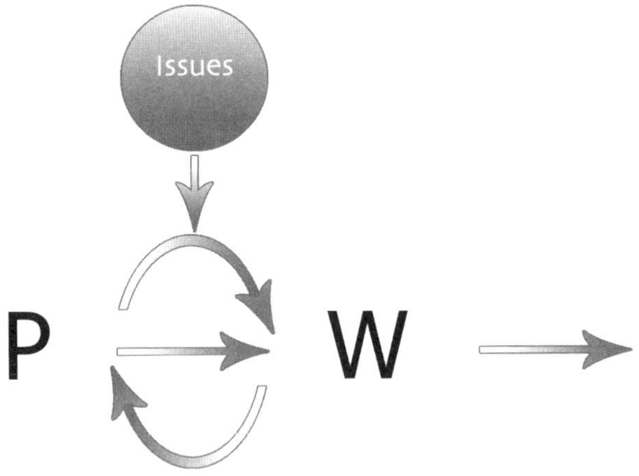

A similar pattern is demonstrated in the example of a dog chasing its tail. The faster the tail moves, the faster the dog chases it; and the faster the dog chases it, the faster the tail moves. Yet, in the end, the dog-chasing-the-tail routine will simply have one of two outcomes: either the dog will get its tail and there will be pain (which the withdrawers hope to avoid) or the pursuers will never catch the tail and will give up exhausted (which is what the pursuers hope to avoid). Either way, the pattern ensures pain or exhaustion, which is not the ideal goal of any relationship.

Another important point here is that dogs that chase their tails don't do so because they're brilliant, and they don't chase their tails because they're stupid. In fact, they do it because of an "instinctive drive" called the prey drive. They're just reacting to this natural, instinctive drive, even though this instinct is not bringing them any immediate benefit. Just as dogs instinctively chase, so do humans. This drive comes when we act out of our Reactive Brain to meet our STARVED needs instead of making a choice out of our higher or Relating Brain.

Escalation

In the pursuer and withdrawer cycle, once the difficult issues have surfaced and the reactive fight or flight pattern has already taken hold of us, we begin to play out our patterns and escalate them to a higher level. Pursuers pursue harder, louder, faster, and more aggressively, while withdrawers become stealthier, avoidant, and illusive. For most couples in the throes of a very difficult conversation, even the slightest escalation from their partner fosters their own slight escalation, fueling the chaos even more. Both parties escalate as they react to each other, not because they feel this method is working. They escalate out of their deepest fears and concerns and not out of their highest values and goals of creating the healthiest and strongest relationships.

Escalation ensures that we'll just keep getting "more of the same," only at a faster pace and with a more exaggerated result. For example, pursuers feel the need to heighten their pattern by getting louder, angrier, and more belligerent and offensive. The withdrawers then feel forced to withdraw in more complete and permanent ways, by either leaving the house, putting on headsets, going to bed, or

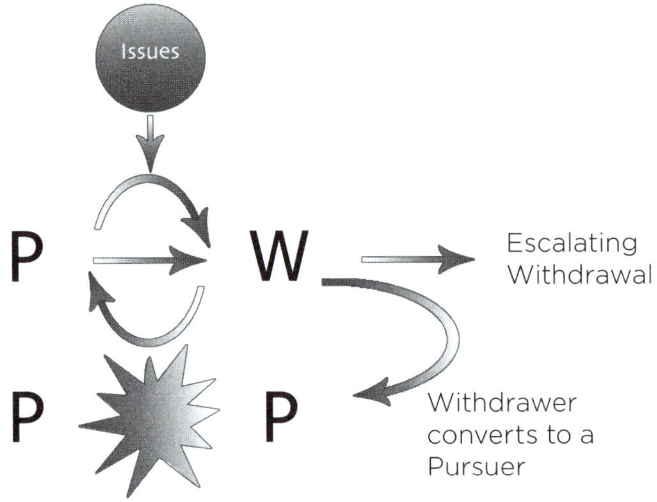

ignoring their spouse. All of these are a sign to their partner that they are never going to talk about the issue.

The best way to escape from a problem is to solve it.
—Brendan Francis

Sometimes, in the middle of this commotion, a quick reversal of roles appears. When a withdrawer is pushed to the edge, or just wants to end the discussion more quickly, the withdrawer turns into a pursuer and comes back to take on the pursuer head to head. This will create an explosion, some smoke, and a great diversion that allows the withdrawer to disappear and usually starts with an, "Oh yeah, well what about…?" This change by the withdrawer is inevitably seen by the pursuer as reinforcement to keep pushing. Now you have two pursuers facing each other with fire in their eyes and the real fireworks are about to start. In my experience working with couples, it is in this explosive state of interaction that we end up saying and doing things we might regret, things that are hard to fix later. In a worst case scenario, the police might get called in and people don't come home for a few days.

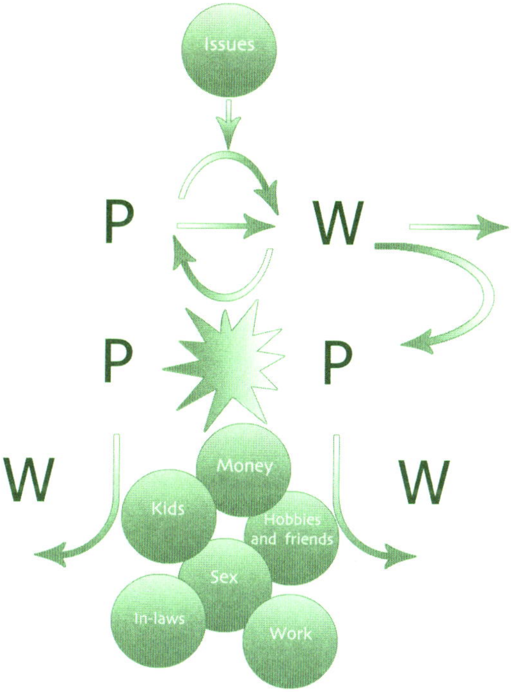

The collision of two pursuers creates such intense frustration and gridlock that both pursuers eventually end up withdrawing from each other in opposite directions and the issue goes unresolved, along with every other issue they haven't been able to solve because of their ineffective ruts. Once the escalation, drama, negativity, and distractions have taken place, both members are now hurt and exhausted and decide that it is best to just stay away from one another and avoid the subject all together. As a matter of fact, they avoid it so well that it never gets solved.

This is why the pursuer/withdrawer pattern is seen as polarizing. In the model, you can see how far apart the reactive pattern of pursuer/withdrawer has driven the couple. They now stand in different worlds, and all they see is a pile of issues between them that can't be dealt with, and both feel the pain from the carnage of all their failed conversations.

This pattern is consistent with many couples and begins with reactivity, then turns into polarization or fight and flight, and then negativity, hopelessness and abandonment. The pursuer/withdrawer pattern is a seriously treacherous rut that is suffered by many couples in relationships. A large sign is posted at the entrance to the Alaskan Wildlife Reserves, an expansive holding of untouched nature up in Alaska, and it reads, "Choose your rut carefully . . . you'll be in it for hundreds of miles." This saying also rings true for couples I work with every day. Choose your ruts in your relationship carefully because you'll be in them for a very long time. The rut of the pursuer/withdrawer is one trap that has immense costs associated with it and one that, until we learn to turn it around, will only leave us feeling hurt and exhausted.

Using Choice Points in the Ruts

Understanding about the negative ruts found in the Reactive Brain helps us begin to notice our patterns better and to see that in the middle of the rut is an enormous Choice Point. This is truly a moment that can be improved only by engaging our character to stop one of us from pursuing and the other from withdrawing. This is where we have the choice to move from the Reactive Brain into the Relating Brain.

So how do we get into the Relating Brain? You probably already know how to do this, whether you realize it or not. In fact, you probably do this all the time in your other relationships or you wouldn't have any. When you are at work, whatever success you enjoy in your relationships is most likely the result of managing your Choice Points and keeping your head in the Relating Brain rather than the Reactive Brain.

Here are a few quick solutions to managing your Choice Points and moving out of the Reactive Brain and into the Relating Brain with your most important relationships:

Stop and pause

Take a second and let the initial wave of emotion roll over you, just as you would while trying to walk out into pounding surf; just turn, stay in your place, and let the wave of negative energy roll by you.

Count to 10

This doesn't usually work for me because I'm still reacting while I'm counting to 10. In order to get into the Relating Brain, you're probably going to have to do higher math, so instead of counting to 10, count backwards from 10 million by 9's.

Take a deep breath

Sometimes just taking in a few calming deep breaths can help clear your head. One of the best things about any breathing technique is that it forces you to focus, which takes time and attention, and distracts you away from reacting to your partner.

Ask for a time-out

Sometimes you may feel like you are being run over by your Reactive Brain. You may become hijacked by thoughts that you don't want to have. If this is the case, you should just call a time-out on the subject and agree to come back to it when you and your partner have calmed down.

Understand the other's position

Instead of reacting to your partner's ideas, spend your energy trying to understand his or her position by listening. Then clarify your understanding by stating your interpretation of what your partner is saying.

Ask yourself a question

One of the best things to do in order not to be taken over by the Reactive Brain is to ask some higher brain questions like, "What part of the problem am I? What is my partner really trying to say? How can we work this out together?" These questions help you immediately get into the Relating Brain and think beyond yourself to what you want most from your relationship.

Anticipate and build rules together

During difficult times, in order to keep your head in the game, try to anticipate that problems are going to happen. Make rules together for how you both will handle being taken over by the Reactive Brain. Talk to your partner about what you should both do the minute you see you are reacting in your amygdalae. What should you say to each other? What should you do in the moment? How should you work together to get into the Relating Brain?

There are many other solutions that also help. We will discuss those later as we discuss the other three courses.

Chapter Review:

- The choice to keep your head in the game means to pay attention to your partner's needs.
- The Reactive Brain hijacks understanding and healthy interactions and leads to the biggest communication rut, the pursuer/withdrawer pattern.
- The pursuer/withdrawer pattern polarizes couples and results in issues being unresolved.
- Using Choice Points can help overcome the ruts of the Reactive Brain.

My Feeding Plan

In order to create a healthy diet that feeds your relationship, you need to have a plan. Use the "My Feeding Plan" activity to come up with some specific ideas from the last chapter that you can use to improve the health of your relationship.

Commitment to Keep Learning

What is the most important thing you learned in this chapter that, if lived consistently, would positively impact your relationship?

Commitment to Keep Changing

Based on what you have learned, what will you commit to change in your life?

Specifically, how will you do it?

Specifically, when will you do it?

Chapter 8

The Choice to be an Empowered Communicator

As we just discussed in the last chapter, nothing is more foundational in a relationship than learning to keep our head in the game and not reacting to our partner. Now, let's review what to do with all of this newfound energy we'll have when we're not always pursuing and withdrawing. The goal is to start exercising our character and choose to be an empowered communicator.

We live in a day and age when our communication patterns are changing like crazy. As a kid, I used to go out and play with my friends right after school until about 6:00 p.m., when my mom would come home from work. She never knew where I was and I hardly ever talked to her during the day. Nowadays, my oldest children all have cell phones and we can track them through calls and text messages regularly. I have the ability to reach my older children any time, any place, and anywhere. Whether this is good or bad is not the topic of this chapter. What is the topic, however, is the fact that change brings about new ways of seeing and thinking about our relationships and this is what I'm hoping you will see here.

Just as we need to change some of our thinking with the newer times, we also need to remove from our heads some of the older myths that we might have about communication and how it works. For many, communication is something another person does to you, as the communication model below demonstrates.

As shown in this model, most people view communication as having a sender and a receiver. The sender creates the message, then encodes the message into a language of symbols either verbal or nonverbal, and then sends the message through the channel to the receiver. The receiver then decodes the message exactly as it was sent, and, voila, communication takes place. This model is called the transmission model because it symbolizes that communication is nothing more than a transmission of verbal or nonverbal messages from one person to another.

What do you think about this? Is it really this simple to communicate with your partner when you think about the complex interactions that you have with each other? Think about body language, misinterpretation, and mixed messages, just to name a few communication complexities. Maybe it's time we begin to exercise more character in our communication and develop a new view of how communication is actually supposed to work. I believe that communication should be an empowering process. Empowered Communication is the premise that every person is *response-able* or, in other words, *able* to choose his or her *response* to any situation. This means that we are all participants in communication, not just victims of its meaning. Dispelling some common myths might help us see communication with a different perspective.

The Myth: Communication Is One Way

Many people believe communication is something we just do to one another, like talk or listen. However, communication is not one way, but definitely two way. As you talk to me and I listen, simultaneously I communicate back to you how I feel about what you are saying. The old transmission model seems to demonstrate that a speaker packages his or her message and then sends it out without being influenced by the listener.

Although this may be possible, I have found the speaker to be greatly influenced by the listener and how the listener receives the message as the message is being given. How many times have you altered what you were saying because you sensed the person you were talking to wasn't listening or understanding you? If you've ever had a teenager roll their eyes or shake their head in disgust as you were talking to them, then you know communication is a two-way street and not a one-way street. A speaker is usually encouraged to make eye contact with the listener. Why? To see how the listener is reacting as the speaker speaks. Sometimes the listener leans towards the speaker, showing the speaker he or she is open and listening. This is how, together, both the speaker and the listener create healthier and more helpful conversations.

The Myth: The Communication Channel Is Always Open

Many people tell their partner that they are always open to communication, but nothing could be further from the truth! We all have a ton of history, baggage, past experiences, STARVED Stuff, expectations, gender differences, and current interference (including ringing cell phones) that dramatically impact our ability to receive another person's message, let alone understand it.

The problem with communication . . . is the illusion
that it has been accomplished.
—George Bernard Shaw

In communication theory, all of these distractions are called "noise" or "static" and they interfere with the clarity of the messages we are trying to receive. With all of these distractions, it is a wonder we are able to get anything through the channel at all. Think about all of the noise you have in your relationship. Does this impact how you communicate with each other?

The Myth: You and Your Partner Speak the Same Language

Another possible myth you may have bought into is that your partner will receive the same message you fully and completely delivered. Again, in my experience, very few, if any of the messages I have communicated have ever been received exactly as they were sent or intended. The problem is that if we were so in tune with one another's way of thinking, then why would we have to do any talking at all? Couldn't we just have a conversation with ourselves and be equally satisfied? The reality is, each of us encodes and decodes our messages differently. In every communication, we see things a little differently because we all have varying experiences, backgrounds, gender differences, filters, and expectations. These variations ensure that every person sends and receives messages differently.

The Myth: The Speaker Has All the Power

The final communication myth that must be debunked if we want to take back some of the power in our relationships is the myth that what people say is what really matters most. In fact, the old myth says that in most communication the power is found in the speaker, since he or she is the one who created the message, encoded it into a language and sent it to the listener, in essence because he or she did all of the work. However, I don't believe this is true. Is the speaker really the most powerful person in conversations? Is it what people say that really determines the meaning of the message, or is it what people hear? Or think they heard? Or wanted to hear?

Think about this revolutionary idea: when it comes to the meaning of a message, the receiver holds as much, if not more, communication power than the sender. As the receiver, we decide how to accept each message we hear. We also get to interpret the sender's intent, timing, and the context in which he or she is speaking. In reality, the receiver is in the driver's seat, so to speak. This is called Empowered Communication, in which the receiver is empowered to decide how to accept the message of the sender.

In the Empowered Communication approach, communication is seen not as something that we do *to* one another, but instead as a process we create together as we build healthier and more meaningful communication. Our goal is to speak, with the hope that understanding will take place. Our goal is to communicate and together create new meanings. This approach has huge rewards because communication is not a perfect science, so, more often than not, the message intended was not received the way it was meant to be. The new method changes the conversation to a deeper focus on understanding what is meant (or intended) behind each word spoken.

Now think about this for a minute. You are in the middle of a conversation when the person you are speaking with says things that are hurtful or offensive to you. You are now at a Choice Point. As the listener, you get to decide how you will interpret this message. You get to decide if you will take this person's words literally or not, whether or not you believe what he or she is saying, and how you will respond to what was just said. You also get to decide if you think the other person is being hurtful because he or she is in the Reactive Brain or because of STARVED Stuff or if he or she is just plain out of his mind. The power to determine how you're going to interpret this interaction is entirely in your hands; and again, how you choose to deal with this Choice Point will determine the health of not only this interaction, but undoubtedly even the future health of your long-term relationship as well. The biggest difference between the Empowered Communication approach and other forms of communication is in the power both you and your partner now possess to interpret in healthier ways each other's communication.

This is why character plays such an important role in the Choice Point, because you have the opportunity to take the role as the leader in your relationship. With Empowered Communication, you have the power to use your character to influence that part of the communication you have control over as the receiver of the message or, as I call it, the interpreter. As the interpreter, you get to decide what the speaker means, and whatever you decide his or her message means will inevitably influence the entire future of this conversation and your relationship in general. Using character, you can lead the relationship into the healthiest interactions possible, instead of just simply reacting to what you thought your partner said and meant. How many times in your relationships, in a moment of weakness or because you were tired, frustrated, or hijacked, have you said something that was rude or offensive to your partner? Did they believe your offensive remark? Did they forgive you? Did they run right over you? Or did they give you the benefit of the doubt, seeing through all of your smoke, and understanding your pain? We each have the choice to interpret anything we want, any way we want to. In the long run, if we believe the words spoken are really what hurt us, then we are in for a very long road. Instead, we should take the advice of every kindergartner who has ever quoted these empowering lines, "Sticks and stones may break my bones, but names will never hurt me."

Now, even though all of us have, most likely, used this phrase in the earliest arguments of our life, apparently many of us still believe names *will* hurt us. Have you ever considered that possibly you could choose *not* to allow "names," or whatever people might say to you, to hurt you? In your relationship, what would happen if you chose *not* to receive negative messages, but instead reinterpreted these messages into more healthy meanings that would be less reactive and more focused on things that would heal your relationship and make it stronger? With Empowered Communication any person can truly change the entire meaning and direction of any conversation by changing its context or by reframing the conversation in a healthier or more positive light.

Men are disturbed not by things that happen,
but by their opinions of the things that happen.
—Epictetus

For example, let's say after a long day of work, you walk into your home forty-five minutes later than you told your partner you would be home. Because of this, she yells out in a loud, angry, and sarcastic voice, "Where have you been? Thanks for coming home and spending time with us!"

Now, according to the myths of communication, your partner has all the power in the world because she is the speaker, right? You have no power to reinterpret her insensitive remark because your partner doesn't care to know why you're really late. She doesn't care how hard you've been working or how tired you now are, so you just reactively shout back some typical, sarcastic remark. You're trapped and feel forced to act like a jerk because your partner's acting like a jerk. The problem with this old way of thinking is that it just keeps setting up the same old broken-down fights couples have always had. Just because she judges you with a negative, angry tone—that uses sarcasm and a flippant remark to put you down—doesn't mean you understand what's going on with your partner or that she understands what's going on with you.

You may have very good reasons for being late and, as you can imagine, based on your partner's mood, none of them really matter right now, do they? You might think your partner is trying to condemn or attack you. If so, these thoughts immediately lead you into the Reactive Brain, causing you to begin the fight or flight process. For some couples, especially those who are constantly hijacked by their Reactive Brains, negatively charged messages might be easier to accept. However, when it comes to communication, particularly misunderstandings, there are so many other factors to consider other than the literal transmission of the verbal or nonverbal message, factors such as missing data, emotions, timing, context, and STARVED issues that precipitated the miscommunication. Therefore, these things must be part of the communication equation.

To be upset over what you don't have is to waste what you do have.
—Ken Keyes

Stop your reactive feelings and see if she is trying to communicate painful feelings rather than just trying to be offensive. Most likely, your partner is trying to communicate deeper, inner feelings, probably a STARVED need that is wrapped up in a message that comes out as frustration at your lack of being punctual. Run through the STARVED Stuff and mentally check which one, or ones, might be causing your partner to react in such a highly emotional way. Does she have an issue with Safety, Trust, Appreciation, Respect, Validation, Encouragement or Dedication? Use your character to discover how your partner might be starving, then use this STARVED need to reframe the issue in a way that can help the relationship improve. This is the process of reinterpreting the message in a way that helps view the message not as an attack, but instead as an ineffective, outward expression of feeling let down because your partner was looking forward to spending time with you, or having a break from the kids, or maybe even just some time alone. See how the new interpretation helps you to not immediately react to this attack? Eleanor Roosevelt obviously understood this point when she said:

No one can make you feel inferior without your consent.

See how much change takes place with Empowered Communication when, instead of accepting the message as negative, you reinterpret the message into another context, perhaps one that includes giving your angry spouse the benefit of the doubt. Now, instead of just giving an angry person the power to make you angry as well, you have the power to interpret the message in a more positive way and to take your communication in a more productive and healthy direction.

If we choose positive interpretations, we get more positive feelings from those we interact with. More positive feelings get more positive actions. Remember there is no guarantee, but chances are we are much more likely to improve our relationships if we feel more positive.

It is important to understand that *we* have the power to make things better just simply by responding in healthier, more positive ways to what our partner is saying. Many relationships continue spinning in the STARVED Spiral because neither one of the parties will muster enough character to get out of their reactive brain's emotional response. If we are committed to our relationship, it is our responsibility to pay attention to where our head goes when we are at the Choice Point. It is within the heat of the battle that we must find new ways to see our partner if we truly want to change the direction of the STARVED Spiral.

Because of the critical roles that both the sender and receiver play in communication, a new way of thinking about communication is needed to deal with all the messy myths and confusing chaos of human relationships. Empowered Communication is all about healthy communication and learning to interpret positively based on what we want most in our relationship.

Chapter Review:

- Listeners have just as much power in conversations as speakers.
- Noise or static interferes with the clarity of the message between the speaker and listener.
- The message that is intended is not always the message that is received. Every person sends and receives messages differently.
- In Empowered Communication, the receiver decides the meaning of the message and how to accept it.
- The Choice Point in Empowered Communication comes when potentially negative messages are sent and reinterpreted as positive.

My Feeding Plan

In order to create a healthy diet that feeds your relationship, you need to have a plan. Use the "My Feeding Plan" activity to come up with some specific ideas from the last chapter that you can use to improve the health of your relationship.

Commitment to Keep Learning

What is the most important thing you learned in this chapter that, if lived consistently, would positively impact your relationship?

____

____

____

____

____

Commitment to Keep Changing

Based on what you have learned, what will you commit to change in your life?

Specifically, how will you do it?

Specifically, when will you do it?

Chapter 9

The Choice to Take the High Road

Now that we've successfully utilized character to keep our head in the game and to be an Empowered Communicator, it's now time to find a way to tackle what is one of the biggest and most productive Choice Points: Taking the High Road. In every conversation and interaction couples have, they come across moments when they are required to make some interpretations of what is being said and done. This Choice Point is where interpretations are created, and where conversations usually end up diverging in two different directions. One is called the High Road, or the road less traveled, and the other is referred to as the Low Road.

Two roads diverged in a wood, and I—
I took the one less traveled by,
And that has made all the difference.
—Robert Frost

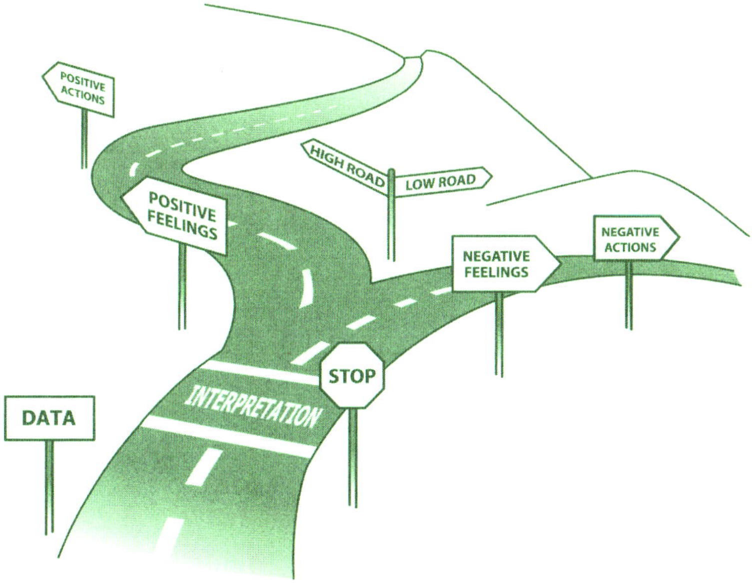

On the model of the High Road you can see how the High Road leads to more positive feelings and actions, while the Low Road leads to more negative feelings and reactions. As taught in the last chapter, what we choose to do at the Choice Point and the road we take with our partner is entirely up to us, a statement that should be very empowering. And remember that the direction taken in interpreting the data creates the direction the relationship will go. Also remember, it is the sum of all of our interactions, or the sum of all the High Roads and Low Roads we take, that overall determines the value of our relationship.

Everything we know and everything we have ever experienced has taken us down the Road to Relating. As we journey down this road, we meet up with certain interactions that create data. We interpret this data, eventually determining if we will create positive interpretations or negative interpretations. Whichever way we interpret this data determines both our feelings and our future. So I'll show how to begin to turn relationships around by turning our interpretations around.

Interactions

No interaction has inherent worth until we personally attach value to the event; all events reside as neutral and do not have any positive or negative value until we assign the meaning and results we want out of each of these events. In other words, as we have discussed extensively, because we are the one in the driver's seat, we decide which roads we will take with our partner, what meanings we will create, and what results we will get out of our relationship.

For example, here are a few interactions that command a positive or negative value. See how you feel as you read each statement:

- Your partner comes home from work late after working on a project.

- Your partner arrives home early from work with a dozen long-stemmed red roses.
- Your best friend calls at the last minute to cancel your lunch appointment.
- You receive a note on your car from a stranger who hit your car while backing up in a parking lot.

These interactions are neutral events, as they exist at their Choice Point, until we decide what each interaction means to us.

While we go through each interaction, we begin to accumulate certain data or facts about the situation. Here is an example of some data from an interaction between a husband and a wife:

- It's the day after your anniversary.
- Your husband has yet to mention anything about your anniversary.
- He's missed three other anniversaries over your 11-year marriage.
- Neither one of you mentioned anything about the anniversary yesterday.
- You spoke only 20 words with him last night.
- You left the house and went out to a movie by yourself without saying a word to him.
- He sat home watching a basketball championship game on television.

Each of these facts is relevant to the current status of your relationship, yet I will argue that none of them really mean anything quite yet. Now, for some people, this is a difficult thing to swallow. You may already be getting a little angry at this "uncaring and unfeeling" idiotic husband. If you are, then notice how you have already moved down to the Road to Relating and formulated a meaning based on the limited data you have before you. Also notice that these negative feelings should be the first clue that you are headed down the Low Road.

Never ascribe to malice that which is
adequately explained by incompetence.
—Napoleon

One important point to remember about the data surrounding the events we experience is that we never really have all of the data or facts, even when we feel confident we do. It's just not possible to obtain all of the data about each situation because things like motives, assumptions, biases, and intentions are all mostly hidden from view. My basic rule of thumb about understanding someone else is that we are usually going to find what we are looking for. If we want to prove our partner is an ignorant, selfish clod, we'll probably be able to pull out all of the applicable data to confirm this.

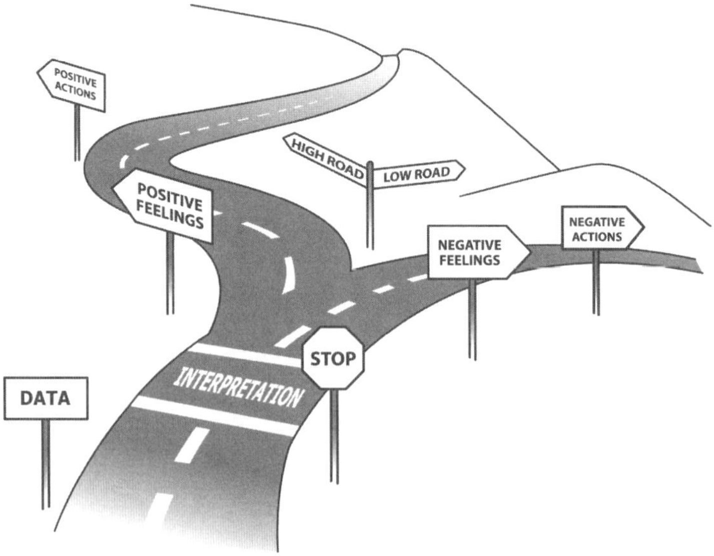

One of the greatest tools we all should learn, when it comes to receiving data along the Road to Relating, is to be careful to suspend our need to make quick, negatively slanted interpretations about it. Quick interpretations usually mean incomplete interpretations. Whenever we're in a conversation and find ourself beginning to react to the data being given, we should take a second and dig deeper. We should try to obtain even more data and facts about what is going on and then try to discover how this person might be STARVED or what expectations have been broken. In other words, we have to "assume our partner is innocent until proven guilty," instead of assuming he is "guilty until proven innocent."

This difficult step, which is governed by character, ensures we will make sure to obtain all of the data we can before moving further down the Road to Relating. For example, in regard to the example listed above about the husband, the wife and the anniversary, these responses might diffuse an otherwise tension-filled situation:

"Honey, we haven't talked much in the last 24 hours. What's up?"

"I noticed you came home last night and didn't mention anything about our anniversary. Are you okay?"

"I noticed you watched the basketball game all night last night and never said a word about the fact that I left for a couple of hours. What's going on?"

By communicating some of this data we've acquired, along with a soft, inviting question and not a cold attempt to lead the witness into a confession, we can open up some discussions that might give us some information about what is going on inside our partner's head.

Interpretation

Now we move to the point of interpreting all of this data. As in the case with the couple and the anniversary, the wife is now in an interaction with her husband. She has collected some data and is now at a Choice Point. This is the moment in which she must decide what all of this data means to her. This is where she will place a value on all of the facts she has uncovered and will decide which direction *she* is going to take this conversation.

What makes the Choice Point so difficult is that, by now, the brain exercises the simplistic path of trying to narrow down the choices. The brain does an incredible job of trying to make our life easier by turning all data into very simple answers of good or bad, positive or negative, black or white.

A great many people think they are thinking
when they are really rearranging prejudices.
—William James

Now, take a minute and think back to the facts regarding the husband who "forgot" his anniversary. What kind of interpretations did you find yourself naturally making about the guy? Were they positively or negatively slanted toward the husband? In your mind, was he a jerk or was he just forgetful? And what was your level of confidence about his position? Notice how quickly, and in fact seamlessly, you were able to jump to conclusions. When you heard the scenario about the forgetful husband, did you relate it to any experiences you have had with your partner? Did your history with that person influence your decision about how to interpret this situation? Of course it did. One of the key rules on the Road to Relating is, don't jump to conclusions!

Feeding Rule - Remember not to jump!
Look both ways and make a conscience choice for the betterment of your relationships.

Stop Sign

Look back at the diagram on the Road to Relating. The stop sign is posted in the diagram for a reason. It is there to bring us to a safe stop at the critical Choice Point. Years ago, the instructor in my driving class taught me that STOP does not mean a **S**light **T**ap **O**n **P**edal. STOP means coming to a complete stop for at least three seconds. Whenever I drive down a road, I become frustrated when drivers ignore a stop sign, because this action puts so many people's safety at risk. The same is true on the Road to Relating. Have you ever blown through a stop sign in any of your relationships? In your interactions, you need to make sure you are completely stopped at the stop sign before you interpret the data and choose which road to take. Notice how much better your journey will be and how much more safely you will be able to enjoy your journey when you don't blow through the stop sign.

Remember the decisions that need to be made at the Choice Point, and then remember what your options are. What are the consequences of each choice for the couple on their anniversary? Your ability to see so many options increases the likelihood of finding success during difficult conversations.

Negative	Neutral	Positive
My husband is a selfish pig who worries only about his needs and wants.	We've let our marriage celebration be too easily ignored.	He's not big on holidays or public displays of affection, but he is very good to me.
My marriage is over! My husband's obvious loves are his work and basketball.	This is a sign that we need to get some help.	My husband is simply overwhelmed with his life, work, and family.

We must remember that any interpretation ascribed to the facts listed above is nothing more than an educated guess.

When we are in a STARVED relationship, we tend to see things more negatively, which means our guesses tend to be more negative. This cycle creates a self-fulfilling prophecy. For example, have you ever noticed how when you're in a bad mood and seem to be looking for a fight, you usually find one? If our head is filled with negative details, interpretations and feelings, we usually respond more negatively to anything our partner does or says. So feeling confident about our negative interpretation about our partner doesn't actually make us any more accurate, just more energized and sometimes wrong. When we are at the Choice Point, hijacked by the Reactive Brain, STARVED and finding negative data, what do you think your natural tendency will be? I'll bet you are most likely going to turn your partner into the worst possible human being on the earth. Isn't it easier to fight with a jerk than to fight with a wonderful, charming, decent, God-fearing person? What we unfortunately do too often is dehumanize and make our partner an ill-intending villain.

We judge others by their behavior. We judge ourselves by our intentions.
—Ian Percy

Many times when I teach people this concept I have individuals in the audience who get really upset by the idea of positively interpreting somebody who has forgotten an anniversary. They will say something like, "There are no good reasons to forget such an important day of the year, and anyone who does forget their anniversary should be shot!" After checking where the exits are, I usually respond by saying something like, "I totally agree. Anniversaries are incredibly important and I can see by your energy (and your willingness to maim someone) that anniversaries are really important to you. Would you be willing to set aside your preexisting interpretations about anniversaries and try to understand how someone could possibly miss something as important as an anniversary?"

If they say yes, then I usually start with another question like, "Have you ever in your life forgotten to do something for someone else, whether intentionally or unintentionally, that was really important to them?"

Usually the response is "Well, sure!" And this is the beginning of change. Once a person understands that we are all human, change begins to take place.

If we can create just a little space to begin understanding another person's rationale, reasoning, and point of view, we can usually begin to relate and communicate better with that person. Truly understanding another person, from their perspective, can change a lot of things. It can change how we approach and interact with that person and can also create an awareness that this is someone who really is unable, unwilling, or uninterested when it comes to meeting our needs, and then we can deal with this better as well. This is what I call taking the High Road.

Feeding Rule –
Our feelings always follow our interpretations...and our actions or reactions always follow our feelings.

Based on the scenario stated above about the husband who missed his anniversary, let's test the above rule out and see how it works. If feelings follow interpretations, then they would look something like this:

	Negative	Neutral	Positive
Interpretations	My husband is a selfish pig who worries only about his needs and wants.	We've let our marriage celebration be too easily ignored.	He's not big on holidays or public displays of affection, but he is very good to me.
	My marriage is over! May husband's obvious love is his work and basketball.	This is a sign that we need to get some help.	My husband is simply overwhelmed with his life, work, and family.
Feelings	STARVED Angry Cheated Victimized Abandoned Hate-Filled Reactive	Disappointed Surprised Nervous STARVED Let Down Lonely Tolerant	Understanding Optimistic Committed Empathic Human Realistic STARVED
Actions	Leave him Major blow up Hurt him back Make him pay Ignore him Have an affair	Do something different Try to understand Call a counselor Go to classes Read a self-help book	Collaborate solutions that meet both needs Plan a couple's trip away from stress Learn Adapt Resolve

Don't get me wrong. I'm not saying that by taking the High Road we still won't feel hurt or have some negative feelings, but it is important to keep our eye fixed on the long-term goal of what we want most out of the relationship. The High Road begins with positive, healthier interpretations that will eventually lead us to have more positive and healthier feelings. Conversely, the Low Road begins with negative, less healthy interpretations that generate more negative, less healthy feelings. Our interpretation of events creates feelings that will either make us feel threatened—throwing us into the Reactive Brain, or they will help us feel positive, leading us back into the Relating Brain where we will find healthier answers and solutions to change the painful things in our relationship.

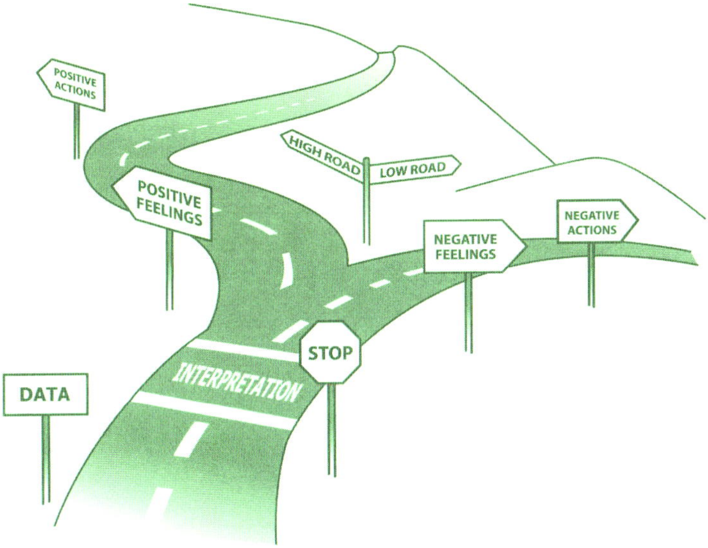

Actions or Reactions

As we continue down the Road to Relating, the only sign left to discuss on this road is the resulting Actions or Reactions that follow our feelings. It's natural to think actions follow feelings. For example, how do we act at a party if we're feeling sick, or how do we react to good news if we're feeling thoroughly exhausted? Just to be clear, character can override feelings any day of the week as we've been discussing through the entire course on Character. However, on the Road to Relating, interpretations generate feelings and then naturally, feelings lead us to take action or to react to what is going on. Because of this, the choice can be made to either handle the situation and improve it or to react and continue sliding downward into the STARVED Spiral.

I have always thought the actions of men the
best interpreters of their thoughts.
—John Locke

If we are on the High Road, our positive feelings will help us create positive actions and responses to the situations. If we are on the Low Road, our negative feelings will lead us to feeling threatened, and the starving will continue as we do more of the same old ineffective behaviors.

The Low Road tends to enable the debilitating downward spiral we've talked about because our reactions cause our partner's negative interpretations and our partner's negative interpretations cause our reactions. It is of critical importance that a partner responds positively if that partner wants to stop the downward STARVED Spiral and reverse its direction back toward the positive.

The following actions flow most naturally from the reactive, Low Road:

- Being focused on the Reacting Brain or Lower Brain
- Being problem-oriented
- Being misinformed and misunderstood
- Being filled with blaming, criticizing, and complaining

- Being filled with no character, no communication, no companionship, and no commitment
- Having a cold shoulder and/or an attitude of avoidance
- Playing an intense game of cat and mouse
- Being a pursuer or a withdrawer
- Focusing on abandonment and further starvation

Here are some of the positive actions that naturally flow from the High Road:

- Being focused on the Relating Brain or Higher Brain
- Being solution-oriented
- Being informed and filled with understanding
- Being filled with acceptance of mutual responsibility
- Being filled with character, communication, companionship, and commitment
- Reflecting positive language, understanding, expression of feelings and finding solutions in which both partners can plan ahead

More than likely, when we feel negative emotions, we react and do not take time to really think about what we want in the future. Simply speaking, taking the High Road means making a conscientious decision to interpret data positively at the Choice Point. While we may not always take the High Road with everyone, taking the High Road with our partner may be in our best interest because this is so good for our character and our personal sense of well-being. Whether the interpretation we're dealing with is about an event or a conversation, the decision to go to the positive always lifts a person and usually the relationship as well. It may not always fix the problem, but it does help.

Remember, our job is not to fix the problem, at least not at this point. More tools will be given in the remaining chapters of this book that will help with fixing the problem. The job at hand is to change the interpretation, to improve the feelings, and alter the course of action. If a disagreement arises, there is a better chance of actually solving the problem if at least one partner positively interprets the comments being said or the actions being taken. What other option is there? Carry the venom?

It's not the snake bite that kills you. It's chasing the snake that drives the venom to the heart.
—Stephen R. Covey

We can't change the negative consequences of life; all we can change is our interpretation. Good or bad, our interpretations are only guesses, because we don't know the intent of another person, even though we might think we do. So, if we're guessing anyway, why not guess in a positive direction?

If negative interpreting has become a habit, we will probably continue to take the Low Road, and we will most likely feel confident about our negative decisions at the Choice Point. But I'm asking that we take another look at our choices. We need to realize that the Low Road puts us on the fast track to negative relating, negative feeling, negative stress, and all out negativity with our life.

Rules on the Road to Relating:

Don't Pass the Point of Prevention

One time after getting an expensive speeding ticket, I went to driving school to have my points reduced. As part of the class, the instructor taught me a very interesting lesson. He asked the class, "What is the speed limit on the major highway that intersects the city?" The answer was 65 miles per hour, yet every time someone tried to suggest this answer, he would quickly eliminate it by saying,

"Nope. Any other guesses?" Finally, after many answers were given, he said, "The correct answer is 65 miles per hour. . . when conditions permit!" You are only allowed to drive 65 miles per hour when the prevailing conditions permit it. For instance, you couldn't legally drive 65 miles per hour in a blizzard or icy conditions. He then cautioned us to learn to drive with the Point of Prevention saying, "You are only as safe as your ability to prevent an accident."

Right then it hit me! We need to learn to relate with our partner, not just any way we want to, but we must learn to relate to each other within the Point of Prevention. This can happen only when we begin to eliminate the same old accidents we've had in so many of our conversations and interactions.

Other rules along the Road to Relating also apply to driving within the Point of Prevention:

Suspend Certainty

Remember the stop sign on the Road to Relating? Staying within the Point of Prevention requires observing the stop sign and suspending our certainty. Even if we think we know all of the data, chances are there is information we are missing. Before we make a judgment or an interpretation, especially a negative one, we may want to suspend our certainty and get some further clarification. Negative interpretations bring negative feelings, and that momentum carries us all the way down to the Low Road. By suspending our mind before we make any interpretations, we allow ourself to get into our Relating Brain; the part that knows how to create a lot of clarity around interpretations.

Get Out of the Rut

Some couples take the Low Road so often that they create ruts in their relationship. These ruts are often so engrained that it becomes difficult to choose the High Road. Have you ever driven down a dirt road with ruts so deep that you can't even turn your tires?

This can be true for relationships as well. Some have continually worked out of the Reactive Brain, blown right through the stop sign, and taken the Low Road so often that it has placed us in a rut that we no longer know how to get out of. I will say again, *stopping at the stop sign is the only way to get out of the rut the two of you have created together.*

The best news of all is that it only takes one person to stop. This means that even if only one of you can keep a cool head while you begin to redirect your actions, this is enough to throw you both out of the deep ruts you've been stuck in.

The Respecting Question

There is a great traffic director who can help point you to the High Road every time you need it. This traffic director is called "The Respecting Question." This question takes you out of the rut that drives your relationship down the Low Road and lifts you right to the High Road.

> **Feeding Rule –**
> To ask the High Road question, simply ask, "Why would a (insert five positive words about the person you're discussing) do such a thing?"

For example, if the Respecting Question were asked about the husband who forgot his anniversary, the question would have been, "Why would such a loving, wonderful, decent, nice, hard-working husband ever forget our anniversary?"

Notice, I am asking *you* to ask *yourself* this question, not anyone else. Also notice how blatantly slanted the question really is. It is slanted at being positive. For some this question is powerful because it helps us figure out how to humanize the other person. I prefer to use it because it puts the other person in a respected position. That is why I call it the Respecting Question. This type of question takes us into our higher brain and allows us to create a whole new host of thinking that is not available when we position our partner in a negative light.

Good thoughts bear good fruit, bad thoughts bear bad fruit.
—James Allen

The higher brain asks this Respecting Question while the Reactive Brain asks questions that sound more like this:

What's the worst possible way I can see this?
Why is he/she so awful?
What is wrong with that idiot?
Why can't my partner be more like me?

Another example of the Respecting Question might sound like this: "Why would a beautiful, loving, caring, responsible, sweet wife buy an expensive sweater the day a tax bill is due?" Some answers might include, "Maybe she didn't know a bill was due." "Maybe she was buying the sweater for someone else." "Maybe she wanted to look good for her upcoming business Christmas Party." "Maybe she shops as an outlet for relief because of her unhappiness within our marriage."

At this point, we do not know why she bought the sweater. By taking the High Road, we choose to guess in a way that gives her the benefit of the doubt. By giving her the benefit of the doubt, we will talk differently to her and treat her more like we want to be treated. Because we are more patient, we are more likely to quickly and painlessly get to the real reason she bought the sweater.

The response to her might sound something like this: "Honey, I saw you got a new sweater. I'm sure you look beautiful in it. You probably don't realize that I'm a little concerned about our $1600 tax bill. Can we talk about this?"

What do you think her response might be? Do you think she'll react badly? I suspect she might apologize to you for the bad timing. She might also give you more data. "The sweater isn't for me; it's for your mother's birthday." Either way, by taking the High Road, you will set yourself up for a better conversation, one that has a better chance of creating better results. If it is true that optimistic people live longer, then wouldn't it make sense that a person would want to learn to find ways to take the High Road more often?

The good news is, taking the High Road doesn't just benefit your partner, but it benefits you and your relationship. Your benefit will be in the form of experiencing greater peace and optimism, and your relationship will grow in connection and commitment. The same is also true in other family relationships. Is there a benefit to taking a teenager who is rebelling on the High Road by positively interpreting his actions as normal rebellion? This doesn't mean I still can't have my rules, but there is a chance that not only will it change my thought process and I'll have more compassion for my child, but my thoughts and words are more likely to lead me to be more positive and effective with my teenager. You see, positive interpretation doesn't change the facts of my life; it just changes my view of my life.

Be careful of your thoughts, they may become words at any moment.
—Ira Gassen

We always get the final choice in how we choose to view things. In a relationship, instead of vilifying and demonizing the other person, we should try to find a way to see why a decent, caring person would do such a thing. The reason this is so important is that most likely this is the only way to ensure negative patterns will no longer continue in the future. Otherwise, the pain of our relationship will slowly drain the life out of us.

FAQ's about the High Road

Is there ever a time *not* to take the High Road? No, never! In all situations we can take the High Road or make healthy interpretations. We have all made mistakes, we have all let people down, and we owe it to ourselves to take the High Road. If everyone on earth *always* took the Low Road with one another, none of us would ever be given the opportunity to try again, and most likely all of our healthy relationships would eventually cease to exist. Second chances, or trying again, are examples of someone's willingness to try the High Road after we've given them negative data. When I am given a second chance, this means somebody is showing to me that they believe I am a wonderful, decent, caring, positive person. Because of this, I am much more likely to become this person.

Some of the most life-changing moments I've experienced with clients have been when one person who was wronged chose to take the High Road with another. I met with a woman whom I will call Brooke. When she came to see me, she felt tired and frustrated with her marriage. As she told me about her relationship with her husband, she unfolded a story of heartbreak and pain. Brooke described her husband as uncaring, rude, mean, hurtful, and two-faced. In public he was kind and compassionate, but at home, the situation was drastically different. His behavior toward her was manipulative and belittling, and she was tired of it.

I listened to her story and asked questions about their life together. During our meeting together, she realized that her husband was very different from a few years before. I agreed with her that her husband had some difficult behaviors and that we needed to gather more data to make a better interpretation. I suggested that she take him to see a specialist. After seeing a doctor, her husband was diagnosed with a rare brain disorder.

This new data was imperative for Brooke's personal High Road. It didn't negate the difficulties or pain in her life, and it didn't change the impact of his behaviors on her and her children, but it did allow her to positively interpret her husband's actions. It helped her see his behavior as a symptom of a bigger problem. It empowered her to adjust her own life, and that of her children, to deal with the symptoms and his negative behavior. It was a powerful moment when she was empowered to take the High Road with him, despite his behavior. Rather than feeling like a victim of her husband's rude behavior, she was able to reinterpret him and felt strength to take action and make decisions to improve their situation.

The greatest discovery of any generation
is that a human being can alter
his life by altering his attitude.
—William James

Now, let's consider a question: What if someone *really* is bad? What if that person *really* is mean? Should we keep being positive? In this instance, what really will change? Let's say this person has done something multiple times that was hurtful. In fact, what if this person is someone who truly destroyed our life? First, we might want to consider why a person would do this? The most positive answer to this question might be "Maybe that person is sick." Incredible. That is as healthy an interpretation as can be given for some people who end up hurting others. But possibly this is a much more understanding statement than "That person is just evil." Think about it. Could this person be evil? Sure she could, but I don't know this for sure. Therefore, if I acknowledge that she is sick, then I can let it go and move on.

Many people feel that by choosing to take the High Road in response to negative behaviors, they agree with the fact they are being treated negatively. They're afraid that if they don't retaliate or make it a point to inflict pain, they're more likely to be treated negatively again. In some ways, they may be right, because research shows that positive people actually do get walked on more often than pessimistic people. Positive people are also seen as more gullible. However, research also shows that positive people live longer, are happier, and have happier and more productive relationships than do negative people. Taking the High Road is not an excuse for another person's behavior, but it is the means by which we choose to maintain a positive attitude because of our desire to lead a longer and healthier life.

Does this mean we need to pretend that our partner isn't hurting us, even when he is? No, *and this is not what I want to convey here!* If you are in a relationship with a person who is intentionally doing things to hurt you, I am not suggesting you continue to take this or make positive excuses for his behavior. Taking the High Road does not remove the consequence of anyone's poor choices. There is a difference between making excuses and making positive interpretations. An excuse implies compliance on our part; that the behavior is okay. A positive interpretation means giving our partner the benefit of the doubt.

By one partner making the choice to hurt the other partner, the Low Road continues to be traveled, creating an even deeper rut. In real-life, what does this mean? This means the hurtful partner *will* have consequences for the behavior that he has chosen. The hurting spouse will be less trusting, feel less safety, and be less respectful. The hurtful spouse's behaviors will eventually affect all of the 7 Basic Needs. As we learned in chapter three, a long-term relationship cannot survive without meeting the 7 Basic Needs. This type of relationship will eventually suffer so much that it, most likely, will die. But for the spouse who chooses the High Road, he will have peace of mind knowing he did everything he could do to save the relationship.

Choosing to keep your head in the game, choosing to be an Empowered Communicator, and choosing to take the High Road are three very basic skills that turn the STARVED Spiral around. All three represent just the kind of character we need to make the major turnaround necessary in every long-term healthy relationship. Now that our character is tooled and ready, let's move on to the next course and learn how to communicate with our partner.

Chapter Review:

- Every personal interaction travels along the Road to Relating. The Choice Point occurs when data is gathered and it can either be interpreted on the High Road or the Low Road.
- To stop and suspend before making interpretations allows the interpretation to be made by the Relating Brain rather than the Reactive Brain.
- Taking the High Road means making a conscientious decision to positively interpret data at the Choice Point. This leads to positive feelings.
- The Low Road is problem-oriented and fosters the STARVED Spiral, while the High Road is solution-oriented and creates healthy and enduring relationships.
- Stopping at the stop sign on the Road to Relating is the only way to get out of a relationship rut.
- The Respecting Question immediately lifts from the Low Road to the High Road.

My Feeding Plan

In order to create a healthy diet that feeds your relationship, you need to have a plan. Use the "My Feeding Plan" activity to come up with some specific ideas from the last chapter that you can use to improve the health of your relationship.

Commitment to Keep Learning

What is the most important thing you learned in this chapter that, if lived consistently, would positively impact your relationship?

Commitment to Keep Changing

Based on what you have learned, what will you commit to change in your life?

Specifically, how will you do it?

Specifically, when will you do it?

The Course on Communication

Building Mutual Understanding

Chapter 10

Checking Your Partner's Vital Signs

Gaining better communication between partners is the single most sought after skill in my relationship coaching practice. But communication is only part of the equation of a healthy and enduring relationship. As mentioned earlier, an understanding of character and the skills to show character in relationships is an essential part of effective communication.

There is a reason why most people have relationship problems: Relationships are just not as easy as they appear. Having a good relationship is not innate. The skills involved must be learned and practiced, which is why couples seek extensive coaching. Just as I have trained five of my six children to understand what it feels like to balance and pedal a bicycle, I coach or "run" beside my clients—not physically, but mentally and emotionally, to assist them in learning what relating to one another really feels like. Then, as they begin to experience more effective relating, they also start to understand one another and empathy grows. This creates a new sense of confidence in their own ability to truly connect with another person.

Relationship Vital Signs

Just as taking the High Road is the key to effective relationships, communication is the vehicle that helps both partners drive down the road together, but of all of the things I teach couples, Communication is one of the most difficult skills to impart. Let's begin with an important key to knowing how and when to communicate with others: By simply checking their relationship Vital Signs. I can tell when a couple is STARVED. In the medical world, vital signs are the most effective, nonverbal method for checking the physical condition of a patient. This is also a great metaphor for checking the current emotional status of a relationship.

As a young college student, I considered studying medicine. I took a summer course in order to become an Emergency Medical Technician. Afterwards I began working for an ambulance company serving the metropolitan Salt Lake City area.

Before I could effectively treat or help any of the patients I was called to help, I first had to "get into them" by paying attention to them. I had to focus on *their* needs and where *they* were in relation to what was normal and healthy for a patient. One of the most effective ways I found to do this was to check their vital signs: blood pressure, pulse rate, number of respirations, type of breathing, level of consciousness, and temperature. If you have ever been treated by an EMT or have been in the hospital, you have probably been annoyed by the constant checking of your vital signs. You may have noticed that vital signs are always the first thing checked at each initial doctor's visit. This is so that a baseline for what is "normal for you" can be obtained. Vital signs are also checked immediately before and after any type of medical treatment. A nurse or paramedic always checks vitals prior to giving any treatment or drug and relatively soon after the treatment has been administered, so it can be determined whether or not the treatment created any change in your condition. Through all of my training, plus more than two years working with patients in the back of an ambulance, I came to appreciate the invaluable barometer of health: a person's vital signs.

Just as medical professionals gauge the health and treatment of a patient based on vital signs, we, too, can check the status of our relationship based on our partner's vital signs. Relationship Vital Signs are critical because in many ways they can tell more about what is going on with our partner than even she might be able to tell. Early on, I learned to trust relationship Vital Signs even more than I trusted what some of my clients actually said, especially when it came to relational issues or when someone felt STARVED.

When I check the relationship health of people, I look for three basic measurements:

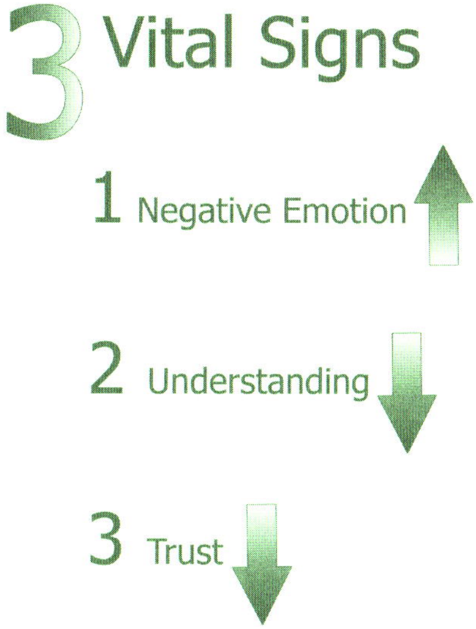

Based on these measurements, I can determine the treatment I need to administer and the follow-up necessary.

Let's explore each one separately:

Emotion

The first relationship Vital Sign is emotion. To feel and have emotion is normal. Emotions have the ability to communicate.

> *The most important thing in communication*
> *is to hear what isn't being said.*
> *—Peter F. Drucker*

The emotions I look for in a STARVED relationship are negative ones such as anger, sadness, frustration, depression, disgust, anxiousness, and feelings of being overwhelmed, plus other similar negative emotions. Each of these emotions communicates the emotional state of a person. When we tune into these emotions in our partner, we can use this information to determine exactly how to interact (or not interact) with her. Odds are we already do this because these emotions are so obvious. We know very well that our spouse needs to be in the right emotional frame of mind before we drop a bomb, such as the fact that we're going to be out of town on our anniversary, or we've just closed the garage door on his or her new car.

The act of checking our partner's relationship Vital Signs keeps us in the higher or Relating Brain, and it increases the likelihood that we won't react to our partner's emotions. Instead we will respect her Vital Signs and use them as an indicator of our partner's emotional state.

When checking for emotions, ask yourself three questions:

1. Do I sense negative emotions in my partner or others?
2. Which direction are the emotions trending—up or down?
3. What other data is available to explain these negative vitals?

If a doctor sees a patient's vital signs are dropping, she will usually alter either the treatment or the approach to how the treatment is delivered. If your partner's Vital Signs are dropping, you should stop your "treatment" altogether or alter your delivery of your treatment. By focusing on your partner's Vital Signs, your ability to feed the STARVED person increases because you're more in tune with what she is feeling. Because of this, you will know the appropriate treatment. You will also be focusing more on the "fire" than the "smoke."

Understanding

The next relationship Vital Sign is understanding. This Vital Sign measures our understanding of the situation and the context or feelings of our partner. In addition, understanding encompasses whether or not he feels understood. Do we understand *why* our partner is feeling the way she does? Or are we just assuming we understand because "she's a woman" or because "he hasn't had sex for a month"?

If we are able to really understand what is going on with our partner and can sense that she feels understood, this is a very positive sign in a relationship. However, if we notice that the more we and our partner talk about a particular issue, the more cloudy and less understandable it gets, that is *not* a good sign.

There is a direct correlation between the first Vital Sign of emotion and the second Vital Sign of understanding. If negative emotion is on the rise, this means understanding is dropping. If understanding is dropping, this is a sure sign that your "treatment" must be altered immediately.

People never care how much you know
until they know how much you care.
— John C. Maxwell

In his book *The Seven Habits of Highly Effective People®*, Dr. Stephen R. Covey explores what he refers to as "Habit 5: Seek First to Understand . . . Then to Be Understood.®" He states that this principle is the basis of the heart of any relationship. According to Dr. Covey, getting to the heart of our most important issues is accomplished by first getting to the heart of understanding. This happens by learning to listen, by reflecting on what the other person says, and by seeking to understand the other person first.

We can't be effective in our relationship if we don't understand the problem. To be effective, we need to diagnose or understand the problem before trying to fix it. How would you feel if you went to a doctor with knee pain only to have him walk into the examining room and immediately diagnose you with a kidney infection? Would you feel safe with his diagnosis? Would you trust and respect him and his diagnosis? Wouldn't you want him to be able to more thoroughly hear your side of the issue, to find out about the onset of the injury and its progression? Wouldn't you feel better if the doctor spent time showing you he understood what you were saying and could, in fact, describe the symptoms and the pain exactly how you had described them to him?

Your partner has this same desire, to be understood. For example, what if your partner just waltzed into the house, after being gone an entire Saturday, and started telling you what was wrong with you and the current situation inside your home? Would you feel safe? Would you trust and respect your partner's opinion? In this situation, as well as in so many others, thoroughly understanding your partner is a pretty good idea. Try it the way I just described and you're likely to get the proverbial frying pan smack in the back of the head, and this would hurt in more ways than one. Effectively understanding the condition of your partner, when bad Vital Signs are obvious, ensures that your relationship, like that of the doctor and the patient, will be able to survive and eventually with proper treatment, thrive.

Trust

The final Vital Sign is trust. If our partner is trusting, and this trust is growing, this shows a healthy direction and we can continue with our "treatment" during our communication. If, however, we notice trust is suffering, this is an indication that we need to stop our treatment and alter the way we are communicating with our partner. The other two Vital Signs, emotion and understanding, are also impacted by trust. People are usually much more trusting when they feel understood. The degree to which people feel understood is the same degree to which people trust.

Whenever we choose to react ineffectively to our partner's emotions, instead of trying to understand her, we actually create more mistrust. In other words, reactivity in relationships does not build trust. The important thing to remember here is that recognizing, understanding, and respecting another person's emotions builds trust.

You can't meet a need you don't understand . . . and just because you understand a need doesn't mean you need to meet it.
—Joe Thomas

A pretty typical example of Vital Signs going out of whack takes place at our house daily between 4:00 p.m. and 7:00 p.m. My wife and I affectionately call this time of day the "Killing Time." This is usually the time when our six kids are hungry, my wife is exhausted, and we have various places we need to shuttle the kids, such as piano lessons, art classes, athletic practices, and Scout meetings. To say the least, it is the most hectic time of our day.

We call this part of our day the Killing Time, not because our children's lives are in jeopardy, but because we so often feel like we are killing *ourselves* during this time of day. Can you imagine the Vital Signs that would appear in my wife if I walked into the house at 5:45 p.m., fifteen minutes before four children needed to be in three different places? Do you think her negative emotions would be going up or down during this time? If this were the case, when I walked into the house, I would see immediate signs that her negative emotions were on the rise. She would be frantically running around, calling out orders to our conveniently deaf children, or she would be trying to convince one of the children about the deadline we're trying to meet.

Whenever I walk into the house under these conditions, and after 19 years of marriage, and understanding my wife the way I do, I should still never assume I understand all of her negative emotions. Imagine what would happen if I walked into the house and said to my already strained wife, "Hey, you need to calm down. You're out of control!" This would definitely not go over well, would it? Instead,

I need to check her emotional Vital Signs the minute I walk in . . . *before* I ever begin to open my big mouth.

Yet sometimes when I enter the house in the middle of Killing Time, even though I may not be judging my wife's emotions, I don't try to understand them either. Instead, I react to her emotions and immediately try to fix the situation by taking on her same negative emotion. When this happens, I physically start rounding up the kids and emotionally try putting them in the places she wants them to be. Now you would think that by taking on her same feelings and having us team up together against our common "enemy" (the kids) that we would both feel much closer, wouldn't you? Well, this isn't the case.

My wife's Vital Signs during Killing Time alert me to her sensitive state of being. If I don't get my head in the game and show character at the Choice Point, this will most likely send her Vitals right through the roof. So when I see high negative emotions, I need to understand what all of this means without judging it or trying to fix it. My job is to simply try to understand.

Anytime you find yourself in a situation where you sense your partner's Vital Signs are rising, you must get your head in the game by suspending your need to *react* to his or her signs. Instead, get into your Relating Brain.

One great tool that helps successfully navigate a person through unstable Vital Signs is called "Get REAL." Get REAL is a four-step process that saves relationships by getting down to the real root of the problem, namely the STARVED Stuff.

Think back to all of the STARVED Stuff you wrote about in chapter two, in the "smoke" model. Look at the issues you recorded and see if you can identify the three Vital Signs associated with those issues. Do you now notice any emotions on the rise? Do you and your partner experience a lot of understanding around the smoky issues listed? How about trust? Where do you rank that? How did understanding rate? Clear as smoke? Part of the benefit of knowing how to recognize the Vital Signs in others is that you are now, most likely, on the way to more easily recognizing the smoke in the relationship. In other words, the minute you see Vital Signs on the rise, this is a sure sign that it's time to begin getting down into the STARVED Stuff.

Chapter Review:

- Vital Signs are the tools used to check the status of a relationship. Unstable Vital Signs are a sign of STARVED Stuff.
- Even though no words are spoken, emotion communicates.
- If negative emotion is rising, Vital Signs are unstable and treatment must be altered.
- If understanding is dropping, Vital Signs are unstable and treatment must be altered.
- If trust is dropping, Vital Signs are unstable and treatment must be altered.
- Vital Signs can be stabilized by not reacting to them, but by getting into the Relating Brain.

My Feeding Plan

In order to create a healthy diet that feeds your relationship, you need to have a plan. Use the "My Feeding Plan" activity to come up with some specific ideas from the last chapter that you can use to improve the health of your relationship.

Commitment to Keep Learning

What is the most important thing you learned in this chapter that, if lived consistently, would positively impact your relationship?

____

____

____

____

____

Commitment to Keep Changing

Based on what you have learned, what will you commit to change in your life?

Specifically, how will you do it?

Specifically, when will you do it?

Chapter 11

Getting REAL Communication (Part 1)

Now that we're equipped with an abundance of character and the ability to recognize our partner's Vital Signs, it's time to cut through the smoke and learn how to get down into the fire and into the STARVED Stuff.

Every conflict we run into is usually about the smoke and not the fire. Remember, smoke is defined as those things couples fight about, but that are not really the issue. Smoke is virtually any subject that gets our attention or irritates the relationship. Keep in mind that smoke is not the real problem. Smoke is just a sign that a real, larger, burning need is not being met: the fire, or the STARVED Stuff.

REAL Communication is the process we use to cut through all of the smoke and get down into the core STARVED issues, or the fire. This process helps get us through the smoke to recognize what our partner is really feeling. REAL Communication is the tool we should use whenever our partner's Vitals are becoming unstable. Remember unstable Vitals are negative emotion on the rise, understanding dropping, and trust dropping. This is typically the communication approach we should use the minute we notice the pursuer/withdrawer pattern creeping into our discussions. This is the perfect time to introduce character into the communication pattern because, if we don't Get REAL and we keep talking without effectively understanding the other person's emotion, we can pretty much predict the outcome. Their Vital Signs will continue to rise and the STARVED Stuff will never be addressed.

REAL Communication is by far the most powerful tool a couple can use as a way to reconnect the partnership and reverse the STARVED Spiral. There truly is no more powerful moment in my coaching or while teaching my "Feeding the STARVED Relationship" workshop than to be working with a couple who, for years, have been pursuing and withdrawing from each other, only to see them begin to reconnect. When they finally learn to Get REAL and start to understand each other at the STARVED level, an entirely new relationship begins to emerge.

The road to the heart is the ear.
—Voltaire

Even though the REAL Communication model is very powerful, we don't need to use it with every interaction, just those that are presenting higher Vital Signs, or on issues where there has been a history of problems, or on any issues in which a person feels STARVED.

REAL is an acronym of four basic activities that should be accomplished to have a healthy and productive conversation:

Recognize Their Emotion

Explore Their Story

Attend to Their STARVED Stuff

Lift the Conversation Upward

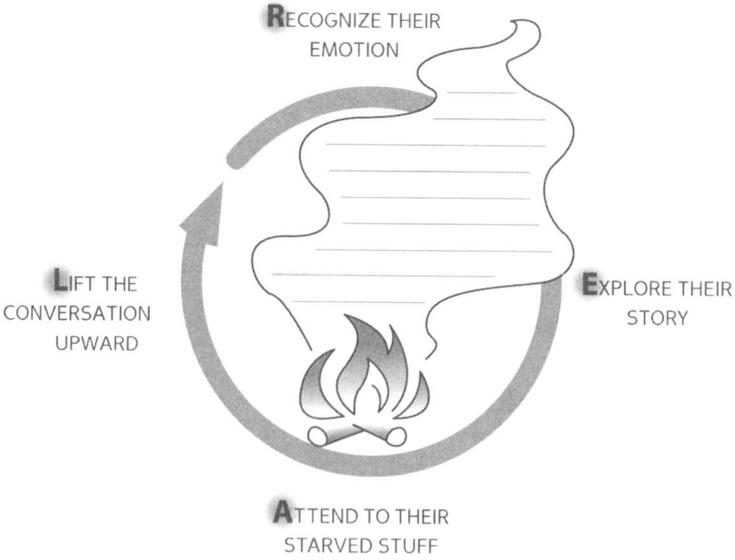

Notice the REAL model is built around the smoke and fire model we discussed in chapter two. Remember when you wrote about all of the smoky issues that tended to choke out your relationship? Each of these smoky issues carries with it elevated Vital Signs. The purpose of REAL Communication is to reverse each of these signs.

Also notice the REAL model begins in the smoke because, when it comes to communication, we've got to begin where our partner is in the conversation. Most of the people I work with are up in the smoke, fighting to be understood. Notice in the model, the smoke will be worked through to get right down into the fire, or the STARVED Stuff. How to Lift the Conversation Upward can then be taught, followed by how to build onto what your partner is saying, and how to share your own set of data and concerns.

Before I can walk in another person's shoes, I must first remove my own.
—Unknown

One more important part of the model is that three of the four areas of Get REAL all share the same word—*their*. This model is designed to help you get into "their" issues, "their" emotions, "their" stories, and "their" STARVED Stuff. The fourth section is for you. The reason for designing the model this way is so you can keep straight in your head the order of trying to influence someone. Remember, in order to influence a person, you must be willing to completely get into their head first before you try to move the conversation in any direction.

Recognize Their Emotion

One of the best skills we can learn is to immediately recognize emotion. This is the first step in the Get REAL process. When we walk into the house and find our partner is mad, scared, frustrated, upset, or just emotional, he or she is communicating with us.

Emotion is communication, in and of itself. When we see emotions on the rise, we have arrived at a Choice Point. What we do at this point is completely up to us. We can react to it and fall into the same pattern in which we have been stuck, or we can get unstuck and choose to Get REAL. In this case, we can choose not to react to the emotion of our partner and have our amygdalae go off, but instead, get into our higher brain and recognize our partner's emotion.

The most important factor in understanding another human being is to Recognize Their Emotion. If your partner slams the door as he storms out after a disagreement, this is communication. Even though we may try, emotions really cannot be held back. Let's not be afraid of emotion and see what it can teach us. Now, this is easier said than done because some of us "wear our emotions on our sleeves," while others feel an immediate need to overreact to the emotions of their partner. I am convinced that the emotional cues of others are the number one major cause of reactivity in relationships, because emotion is such an enormous trigger of the Reactive Brain's fight or flight instinct.

People who cannot feel punish those who do.
—Eleanor May Sarton

Instead of focusing too much on the negative impact emotions have on our relationships, let's focus on their never-ending benefits. Studies of interpersonal communication show that the majority of communication is nonverbal in nature and that the biggest driver of all nonverbal communications is human emotion.

Scientists have determined humans are universally hardwired to communicate their facial expressions the exact same way regardless of culture or tradition. If I induce pain or pleasure on persons in Australia, Uganda, or Singapore, they will all express the pleasure or pain with the same facial expressions. All human beings express emotion on their face. For instance, furrowed brows and a narrowing of the eyes show concern or worry. The lifting of the eyebrows and the upward turn of the lips models happiness. These outward appearances of our inward emotion are true demonstrations of our feelings regardless of our culture, language, or heritage; they are a part of our humanity. The first step to recognizing emotion is the simple task of watching for the universal signs of emotion and learning to respect the emotion, not run from it.

Conduct is more convincing than language.
—John Woolman

Let's say your partner comes home from work and vents about a problem over his latest project. As the problem is explained, he begins to get louder and begins to emote more and more about how the boss doesn't appreciate all of the extra work he put into the project. Out of frustration, your partner slams a briefcase on the table, walks down the hall to the bedroom, muttering something to himself, and then slams the door shut.

What did you just see in this scenario? Some partners might jokingly say, "I can see it's time for me to leave." But even this joke tells us something about a much bigger problem; many people just don't know what to do when their partner shows a lot of emotion. As discussed earlier in this book, some (withdrawers) might react to the emotion and leave the house. Others (pursuers) might follow this partner right into the bedroom and do whatever it takes to fix the problem and stop the hurt. Many might just sit there dumbfounded, knowing they want to help, but also keenly remembering the last time they played with this set of emotional chemicals and got seriously burned. This is exactly what this chapter of REAL Communication is all about. How do you quit using the old, ineffective communication patterns and begin to get down into the real issues?

First of all, when you find yourself confronted with a situation like this, pause for a minute before you do anything. Get into your Relating Brain and ask yourself a few questions:

What are the Vital Signs?
What emotions are being demonstrated by my partner? (Anger, exhaustion, frustration, etc.)
Is my partner trying to show me something is wrong? (In the case of the frustrated person above, didn't he just slam down his briefcase, walk away, and slam the door? For those who might need further clarification, yes, he wants it known that something is wrong, so he is communicating this through emotion.)

Remember, at this stage your goal is not to fix your partner's problem; your goal is not to get them talking either. Your goal is not even to sit there and be a listening ear. For now, your goal is simply to understand. If your partner wants space, give your partner space. If your partner wants you to come in and be with him, then be there for your partner. The only way to know what your partner wants you to do is to Get REAL and learn.

Learning to Recognize, Not React

At times, learning to recognize emotion can be difficult. To see how well you recognize emotion in yourself and your partner, run through the following test and think through how your partner would actually respond to each emotion. This test is also good to try with your children and even work associates.

Take note of your partner's tone, body position and facial expression to determine if your partner is a Pursuer or a Withdrawer. Does he or she tend to emote outwardly and publicly or inwardly and privately?

Then, ask yourself the following questions:

What does my partner do or say when he or she is mad?
What does my partner do or say when he or she is sad?
What does my partner do or say when he or she is glad?
What does my partner do or say when he or she is scared?
What does my partner do or say when he or she is embarrassed?
What does my partner do or say when he or she is physically spent?

Feeding Rule –
For the next week, practice recognizing people's emotions. Really pay attention to what your family, friends and associates appear to be feeling and how they express their feelings non-verbally. Think about learning to pause when you see their emotions rather than reacting or ignoring them. This is a skill that takes some practice, but one that reaps great benefits in all types of interactions.

Two Steps to Expressing Recognition of Emotion

Another name for recognizing someone's emotion is called *validation*. If someone is obviously mad, glad, sad, scared, embarrassed or spent and we notice and acknowledge this emotion, then the result is a genuine connection. They will feel valid and worth "noticing." This is a very powerful gift, particularly to someone who is STARVED and not feeling as if anyone cares at all, especially their partner. And the best part of validation is that it naturally lowers another person's Vital Signs, because it decreases negative emotion, increases understanding, and increases trust.

Now that our brain has been taught to recognize emotion, the next step can be addressed. There are two very basic steps when it comes to expressing recognition of another person's emotion. The first step is designed to show our partner that we are paying attention to his emotional data, which naturally builds trust. This is done by stating the exact emotion you sense from him. The second step is to solicit more data or information about the emotion by asking sincere and inviting questions. This step increases understanding about the topic at hand.

Step 1: State the emotion

In order to show you really do understand the emotions your partner expresses, you should *state the emotion your partner demonstrates*. Even though there are thousands of emotions to look for, I suggest you focus on just a few up front. Once you've learned the basic six, your horizons will be broadened and you will be able to look for a better word to express the exact emotion being expressed. Showing your partner you are paying attention is your primary goal, so it's important for you to be able to describe what you see in a way that means the most to him.

I have found it useful to note that although there are countless emotions, most are simply synonyms for the following six emotions. It would be very helpful to commit these to memory so that, in the moment of need, each of these can quickly be recalled:

1. Mad
2. Glad
3. Sad
4. Scared
5. Embarrassed
6. Spent (physical)

Within each of the above-mentioned emotions, other emotions are found:

Mad	Glad	Sad	Scared	Embarrassed	Spent
Angry	Happy	Down	Worried	Quiet	Tired
Upset	Pleased	Bummed	Startled	Uncomfortable	Exhausted
Peeved	Up	Unhappy	Nervous	Uneasy	Worn Out
Out of Control	**Hyper**	**Pathetic**	**Panicked**	**Humiliated**	**Weak**

Feeding Rule –
Warning: Avoid words that are dangerous and value-laden. These words are potential "trigger" words that carry negativity and judgment such as, "out of control," "hyper," "pathetic," "panicked," "humiliated," "spastic," "depressed," "freaked," "insecure," "weak," or "needy." These types of words can send a hurtful message, even if it's not your intention.

The key to all of this is to not get caught up in my words, but to use your own words and your own vocabulary with your partner. State your partner's emotions by simply saying, "You seem . . ." and fill in the emotion you see. Phrasing your communication in this way allows your partner to feel validated and respected. The respect comes because you aren't telling him how he is feeling. Validation comes by showing your partner that you see his emotion and that you are not going to react to it, fight it, or try to fix it. As with any rule or suggestion, customize the above words to your own situation or you run the risk of sounding like a "textbook" and not genuine.

Step 2: Invite more understanding

Once you've stated your partner's emotion and he feels understood, it's time to invite more understanding. One way to invite understanding is to ask a fairly direct question or make an inviting statement:

What's going on?
Help me understand what's happening.
What am I missing?
Fill me in.
Show me how I can help.

By putting Step 1 and Step 2 together, you *show* you are on the path to understanding your partner's emotion. By doing this, you show your partner that he can trust you with more information. This then invites more understanding. Here are a few ways to combine the two:

I can see you're upset, honey. What's going on?
You sound down, babe. Help me understand what's happening.
You seem a little tired. Show me how I can help.
"Hey, (expressing a sign of affection) . . . fill me in.
I can see you're angry. Can we Get REAL?

These suggestions are examples of rules that you and your partner could agree to practice anytime your Vitals begin to elevate and your typical pursuer/withdrawer patterns begin to emerge.

Feeding Rule –
When you recognize your partner's emotions are elevated and Vital Signs are unstable, ask your partner to Get REAL. Both partners can agree ahead of time to then follow the Get REAL process on difficult issues or any time the conversation gets escalated.

Instead of recognizing their partner's emotions, some couples start the process in reverse order by asking questions first like, "What's wrong?" or "Is there a reason why you're so quiet today?" Remember, no matter how well intentioned your questions may be, questions can inherently come off with a more judgmental tone, especially if either party has some elevated Vitals. Questions also tend to put people on the defensive, like they're being interrogated or attacked. Questions do have their place though and, in my view, they are a perfect way to get more information once you've already validated the information you've got. Remember, people want to be allowed to freely express what they feel and not have you try to fix or critique it; people just want to be understood.

Another quick rule to think about is to beware of using what I call a great counterfeit to Getting REAL, which is simply communicating words without showing any real feelings about what is being said. An example I see a lot with clients is when one person says in a somewhat frustrated tone, "I understand," or "I heard you already. You said that three minutes ago!" If you notice, each of these are signs that you're still missing the deeper STARVED issue and usually this invalidating response really is the issue. When communicating, true empathy and understanding are modeled by who you are and not just by what you say.

The best way to increase understanding is simply to increase your attention to both the verbal and nonverbal messages being sent by your partner. Listen with the goal of letting your partner express thoughts and emotions that will allow their negative energy to dissipate and understanding to take place. Trust that your partner is already communicating the messages you need to know. If you begin asking questions before you show you understand what is being said, then he will be less likely to trust you. This is why you must s*tate their emotion* before a*sking inviting questions.*

Let's practice a case study and see how effectively you can recognize and collect correct data from someone else:

Your partner comes home from work and instead of his usual call of "Hello," your partner quietly walks into the house. After you greet him, your partner immediately walks into the bedroom and shuts the door.

1. **Check the Vital Signs:** Are your partner's Vital Signs unstable? Do you see negative emotion? Is this normal behavior for him or her? ____
____
____

   What is he or she communicating to you? ________________
____
____
____

   What do you understand about why he or she is acting this way?
____
____
____
____

   Where is the level of trust between the two of you? __________
____
____
____
____

2. **State the Emotion:** "Honey, you seem (down, upset, worried, out of sorts, quiet)."
   a. What, specifically, would you say to your partner?

3. **Invite More Understanding:** "Sweetheart, you seem quiet tonight. Help me understand what's happening."
    a. How, specifically, would you invite more understanding?

Important Note

This is not the time to begin digging for more information. Restrain yourself and remember what your goal is here: You want to let your partner know you want to understand him. You want to Get REAL understanding, not get your partner to talk.

I cannot overemphasize the importance of understanding your partner. One of the most valuable lessons I've learned about understanding is that there are *never* any diminished returns on your investments to understand others. The more you try to understand, the more you will understand. When you keep your head in the game, whatever you learn will help you be able to relate better tomorrow. Your willingness to keep trying to Get REAL communicates to your partner that you really are a safe partner to talk to and that you really do want to feed their STARVED issues.

Real communication happens when people feel safe.
—Ken Blanchard

Keep in mind that no matter how badly we want to understand what our partner is going through, this information is something our partner has to give us; we can't just take it from him. Our partner always has a choice as to what he wants to share and how much he is willing to open up. This means your job is not to barge right into the room and begin pecking away and asking questions. Nor should you avoid your partner the rest of the night.

In the end, if your partner doesn't immediately want to get into the issue, then give him space and try again later. If this is a pattern you've seen over a longer period of time, then possibly set up a time to begin practicing some REAL conversations.

When you chose to get into your relationship, you promised one another that you would be there through thick and thin, through good times and bad. So maybe this is one of those bad times, but it could very easily turn into one of the good times if you practice the Get REAL process. When you recognize your partner's emotion and invite his story to be told, a spirit of inviting is created.

Explore Their Story

Every emotion has a story deep inside waiting to be told. The first step of Getting REAL has brought you to the point of recognizing and stating emotion. Inviting even more understanding is the concrete bridge that will take you to the next step of Getting REAL: Explore Their Story.

The goal of this part of the process is to help you understand the story behind the emotion your partner demonstrates. *At this point, your purpose is not to share your story. Do not steal their turn or take over their story.* There will be a perfect time to share your story once the Vital Signs are stabilized. While exploring their story, the general rule is to explore the issues that include the most emotion first. This is a simple method, similar to the medical field's method of triaging patients—where vital signs are evaluated to determine which patient needs to be treated first. The more that emotions are respected and the story is respectfully explored, the greater the effect this has on the overall mental and emotional health of the individual, as well as ensuring you are adequately dealing with the real issue.

It's so funny how we all operate. If you were standing in line at a breakfast buffet and a person walked in who was obviously starving to death and was excited to finally be able to be fed, would you make them wait for you to get your food first? Well, if you're talking to your STARVED partner and you keep interrupting their conversation, you're doing just that. And this shows that, to you, your feeding matters more than their feeding, and this will only destroy trust.

Getting to the Heart of the Matter

In order to Explore Their Story, you will need to have effective communication. Throughout this book you have learned many important skills that will each come into play while trying to Get REAL. You've learned how to keep your head in the game, take the High Road, check Vital Signs, and now how to Get REAL. While exploring your partner's story, these skills are absolutely necessary. Because of the high emotion and history of ineffective patterns in which you may both have engaged, you may have to practice these skills together until they become a habit.

Keep thy heart with all diligence; for out of it are the issues of life.
—Proverbs 4:23

Communication is at the heart of all relationships. One reason this resonates with me so much is because of my father-in-law, Dr. Michael Preece. A world-class cardiologist, my father-in-law taught me a lot about understanding the heart and the tools he used to listen to the heart. One day while we were talking, he explained that whenever he listened to the heart of his patients, he didn't just listen to the heartbeat, he also listened for what was going on between the beats and what he wasn't hearing that he should be hearing. He usually charted his healthy patients in a way that might sound something like this. "Normal rhythms and rates, no gallops, murmurs, rubs, or clicks." He told me in just one human heart there are probably about a hundred different potential variations of rhythms, murmurs, rubs or clicks, and each one is critical to understand in order to treat the heart effectively. My father-in-law ended one of our discussions with a great thought:

Anyone can hear a heartbeat, but it takes years to know what it means.
—Dr. Michael J. Preece

This statement applies perfectly to relationships as well as medicine. "Emotional hearts" can be just as complicated to diagnose as physical hearts. Just like a doctor, if you want to get to the heart of the matter and improve the Vital Signs, the right tools are needed to hear what is happening in your partner's heart. In medicine, no tool works better for understanding the heart of another than a stethoscope.

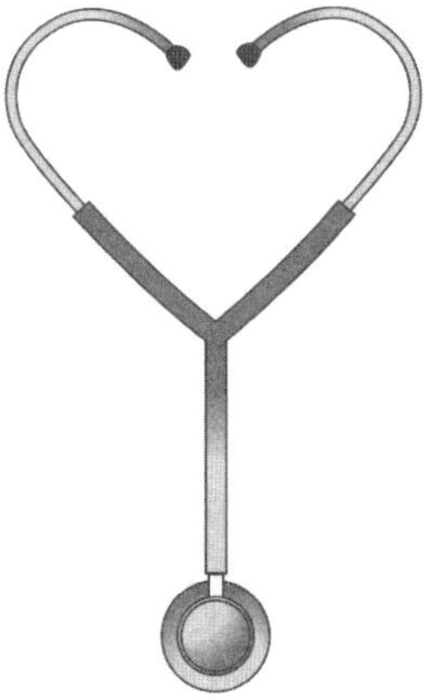

Stethoscope

One of the first things I noticed when a doctor once used a stethoscope on me (other than how freezing the darn thing was) was that he had to stop talking in order to hear my heartbeat. And then came that awkward moment when nobody spoke while the doctor focused one hundred percent on me.

There is a reason why people are born with two ears and only one mouth—so we will listen twice as much as we talk. Think about it. Do your ears have the capability of closing? No. But your mouth does. Open ears, close mouth. Listen twice as much as you speak.

Here is a simple concept with powerful results:

The reason we have two ears and only one mouth, is that we may hear more and speak less.
—Zeno of Citium
(335 BC–264 BC)

Using a "stethoscope" with each other simply means we are going to give our undivided attention to one another in order to understand what is in each of our hearts. This figurative stethoscope is utilized by the person who started the REAL process by recognizing their partner's emotion. So when you ask for more information and your partner starts downloading information onto you, begin stethoscoping this new information.

When using the stethoscope, there are two different roles to learn: the speaker and the listener. Here are a few rules for each role:

Speaker

- Look into the listener's eyes.
- Speak with love and openness from your heart, using words that are warm, soft, and friendly.
- Speak in short sentences, at a slow, steady pace so the listener can keep up with you.
- Stop every couple of sentences, to ensure understanding is taking place, so the listener can reflect back to you what he or she hears.
- Show the listener that he or she correctly understands you by either saying, "Yes and . . ."; then continue on with your next point. Or say, "No, I meant . . . ." And then clarify your position.

Listener

- Look into the speaker's eyes.
- Listen with all of your heart and mind to understand the content and intent of the speaker.
- Keep your Reactive Brain in check.
- Clarify by reflecting back to the speaker, in your own words, what you thought you heard him or her say.
- Try to find compassion for the speaker's position by not only reflecting back his or her content and feelings, but his or her STARVED Stuff as well.
- Prepare to show you've been influenced by lifting the conversation upward.

The Stethoscope in Action

My wife, Mardi, and I learned to use reflective listening, or what I call stethoscoping, about five years into our marriage. As a young couple our marriage was going pretty well, even through the first child or two, until eventually we had a major disagreement we had to Get REAL on. You see, by then, we had two kids and really never had to discipline them much because they were little. However, over time Mardi and I argued about this issue for hours as we both competed to find a way to convince the other that our way of thinking was right. She would always pursue the issue, and I would rather avoid it because it never went well.

The truest test of character is not how much we know how to do, but how we behave when we don't know what to do.
—John Holt

During this time, I was pro-spanking and my argument was based more on my habits and history than any of the latest research, or even my deepest beliefs about what was truly best for my children. I was spanked growing up and I turned out okay. On the other hand, Mardi was not spanked—maybe a few times—but somewhere down the line, she became an anti-spanker. It was probably her Bachelor's Degree in Elementary Education that cemented her thinking about the optimal ways of disciplining a child.

However, spanking a child was something we had to come to some agreement on. We couldn't keep fighting about it and we couldn't pretend it wasn't coming between us. We also couldn't compromise either because we both felt so strongly about our positions. I used to joke that we could try spanking the kids on the even days and not spanking them on the odd days, but then our kids might grow up to be nervous wrecks. Anyway, our Vitals were high, as this was definitely a STARVED issue for both of us and the smoke was starting to choke everyone in the family.

So, we pulled out the stethoscope and started to Get REAL on this monster issue. As we sat down, Mardi started as the speaker and I listened to her, prepared to paraphrase back to her what I heard her express about discipline. This is how the exchange progressed:

> Mardi: "I'm worried about how we are going to get together on this issue of disciplining the children. It really worries me."
> Matt: "So you feel very concerned about how we are going to discipline and you want to get on the same page?"
> Mardi: "Yeah, I just feel like we're coming from two different worlds, and that really worries me. We've never been so far apart."
> Matt: "So you feel that our positions are so far apart that it feels like we are in two different worlds and you're worried because we've never experienced as much discord as we have over this spanking issue?"
> Mardi: "Yeah, I just feel like spanking isn't healthy for little

kids."
Matt: "So you feel that spanking isn't good or healthy for young children."
Mardi: "Yes, I feel the most effective long-term method of discipline should be through love, respect, and the more natural price of consequences, not through force, fear, and aggression."

I paused as I listened to what my wife had just said because I understood her for the first time. Never before had she so clearly stated her position. Never before was I so far away from my Reactive Brain that I could actually hear and understand what she was really trying to say. And because her words were so clear, I was able to be in my Relating Brain, listening to her, and I could finally reflect her words back to her. She felt STARVED with the spanking idea because this concept didn't feel safe to her. She felt spanking was disrespectful and invalidating. In all actuality, it wasn't really about the spanking after all; it was about the STARVED Stuff.

Matt: "So what you're saying is that you feel spanking isn't an effective, long-term method of disciplining, but that it's better to discipline through more loving and respectful methods and not through pain and anger, right? Spanking makes you feel unsafe and feels disrespectful to our children, right?"
Mardi: "Exactly, I just don't feel good about it. I feel bad when I do it and I feel bad seeing it done."
Matt: "You don't feel good engaging in spanking or even watching it happen. It pains you and hurts you to see our kids being treated this way."
Mardi: "Yes, and seeing you hurt them that way."
Matt: "It also hurts you to see me being okay hurting them,

right?"
Mardi: "Right."

When we slowed down our conversation, this allowed us both the time and space to actually be influenced by each other. As she spoke, I normally would have started stirring up the smoke because I felt so offended by what she was saying. However, in reality, as we explored her side of the story, this simultaneously allowed me to begin to explore my side of the story. Come to find out, I actually did agree with her. I never felt good about yelling at or spanking my children either. I also came to an even more profound realization of the fire underneath my wife's position. She didn't feel safe when she saw me invalidating her position and disciplining our children. It wasn't about discipline, it wasn't about our past or who was right and who was wrong, it was about one of her 7 Basic Needs not being met.

Everything that irritates us about others can
lead us to an understanding of ourselves.
-Carl Jung

So exploring the story is doing our best to understand the story behind the emotion. My wife wasn't just trying to dominate me and fight me for no good reason. By stethoscoping with her, I found out that deep down in her heart, she was suffering. She felt unsafe because we were so far apart, she felt sad for her kids, sad for me, and sad herself that I was not able to see how she was feeling.

Now let's show you how to take the conversation to the next level and get down to what really causes all of the commotion.

Chapter Review:

- REAL Communication is the tool to use when Vital Signs become unstable. This is the most powerful way to reconnect the partnership and reverse the STARVED Spiral.
- Recognizing emotion is the first step of Getting REAL and is a Choice Point. Choose not to react to the emotion, but to recognize it.
- The first part of recognizing emotion is to state it; the second is to invite more understanding.
- Exploring the story is the second step of Getting REAL and the stethoscope is used for greater understanding.

My Feeding Plan

In order to create a healthy diet that feeds your relationship, you need to have a plan. Use the "My Feeding Plan" activity to come up with some specific ideas from the last chapter that you can use to improve the health of your relationship.

Commitment to Keep Learning

What is the most important thing you learned in this chapter that, if lived consistently, would positively impact your relationship?

Commitment to Keep Changing

Based on what you have learned, what will you commit to change in your life?

____

____

____

____

Specifically, how will you do it?

____

____

Specifically, when will you do it?

____

____

Chapter 12

Getting REAL Communication (Part 2)

Let's continue to figure out how to Get REAL Communication by focusing on the last two steps of the REAL Communication model: Attend to Their STARVED Stuff and Lift the Conversation Upward.

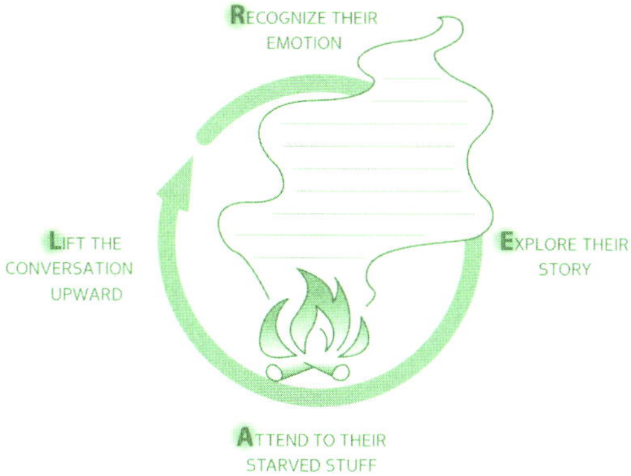

Attend to Their Starved Stuff

The third step of Get REAL is to Attend to Their STARVED Stuff, which means exactly what you just saw me do when I was stethoscoping the spanking issue. In order to Attend to Their STARVED Stuff, you have to listen for it. For a quick review, let's review the STARVED Stuff one more time:

Safety

Trust

Appreciation

Respect

Validation

Encouragement

Dedication

Behind every emotion is a story and within every story is a basic need either being met or unmet. Regardless of how beneficial the Get REAL process is for a relationship, there are a lot of reasons most couples just don't do it. I once heard of a study that explained why we might find it difficult to attend to our partner's STARVED Stuff. Simply put, most of us apparently have a pretty hard time attending to almost anything. The study, performed by some faculty of UCLA (Adler and Towne 1996), explained that throughout the semester a starting pistol was randomly fired at the back of some classrooms while professors were lecturing. When the students heard the pistol go off, they were told to immediately stop what they were doing, turn to their journals and answer questions that related to what the students were thinking about just prior to the gun going off. The conclusions were quite amazing and teach some very important lessons about people's ability to pay attention. Here are the results of the research:

- 20 percent of the students were thinking about sex.
- 20 percent of the students were thinking about food or their next meal.
- 20 percent of the students were thinking about religion or something spiritual.
- 20 percent of the students were thinking about other things, probably something like, "Hey, I wonder when that gun is going to go off?"
- 12 percent were on topic with the professor's lecture, but were not on the current point.
- Only 8 percent were actually on topic and on point with the professor's lecture.

Obviously, listening or attending to everything isn't easy for any of us. Relate this to listening to someone who is starving us or exploding with emotion, and knowing that the average attention span is about 24 seconds long. Is it any wonder we have such a hard time truly listening to others? Marketers of the world understand attention spans and typically pay for only 30-second commercials and then show dozens of them to reinforce their marketing message. If this is so successful, maybe you ought to think about abandoning the 30-minute talks in your relationship when times are tough and swap them out for sixty 30-second discussions. I can hear many of my male clients lamenting, "If only my wife would let me!"

You could see in the conversation I had with my wife about spanking how my attention could have easily been hijacked by some of the poignant and truthful things she was saying. I really wanted to react or maybe just throw myself a pity party, but the process itself helped me stay focused. Whatever the reason you're not understanding or listening to your partner, you have to find a way to overcome this barrier so you can truly get to the heart of the issues that impact your relationship. Using the Get REAL process is the way to do this.

I like Calvin Coolidge's famous statement, "No man ever listened himself out of a job." I think the same is true in a relationship, "No one ever attended themselves out of a marriage!"

I believe that attending to the needs of our partner is one of the most important things we can do for him or her. Listening to others' hearts and honoring where they feel less safe or feel less trust shows exactly how important they are to us. This act brings a true feeling of worth.

So when you are listening to somebody, completely, attentively, then you are listening not only to the words, but also to the feeling of what is being conveyed, to the whole of it, not part of it.
—Jiddu Krishnamurti

Stepping Down into the STARVED Stuff

Over the years I've listened to so many clients whom I wished would stop talking and start attending to one another's needs! Sometimes people get so caught up in the "conversation" that they no longer hear what's really being said. Instead, many people get sidetracked in the conversation and go off on some tangent as in the conversation below.

A woman shares a story and the man says, "Yeah, and?"

"Don't you get it?" And she repeats the entire story.

"So what's the big deal? What do you mean, don't I get it?"

Then they start fighting.

"You never get it. Remember last year when I told you about that one thing? You didn't get that and you don't get this. You just don't get it!"

When a tangent like this ends up taking us backward to something that happened between us in the past, I call this memory matching. There is no bigger distraction in a conversation than going back into the past to argue. If you didn't agree on it back then, what are the odds that you'll agree now?

When couples aren't going on excursions to the past or getting hijacked by their Reactive Brain, most couples do pretty well with the idea of exploring the story, but then end up fighting about the details. They miss the fact that behind all of these details or content there is so much more lying down deeper. The majority of our conversations are just the smoke, the content, or the data. Eventually though, we must take the conversation even deeper by looking for the feelings and STARVED Stuff that goes along with all of the data.

When couples go around in circles about *content,* they miss the *feelings* that surround the issue. Even more importantly, they miss the STARVED Stuff. In order to get through the smoke that abounds in relationships, couples need to cut to the chase and step down into their partner's STARVED Stuff. This means looking past the content and listening for the feelings that indicate the STARVED needs. The easiest way to get to the fire is to step down into the STARVED Stuff while stethoscoping. Either the speaker can actually walk his or her partner down from the content, through the feelings, down to where they're starving, or the listener can simply reflect their partner's words. Let's go through the steps and show how this is done.

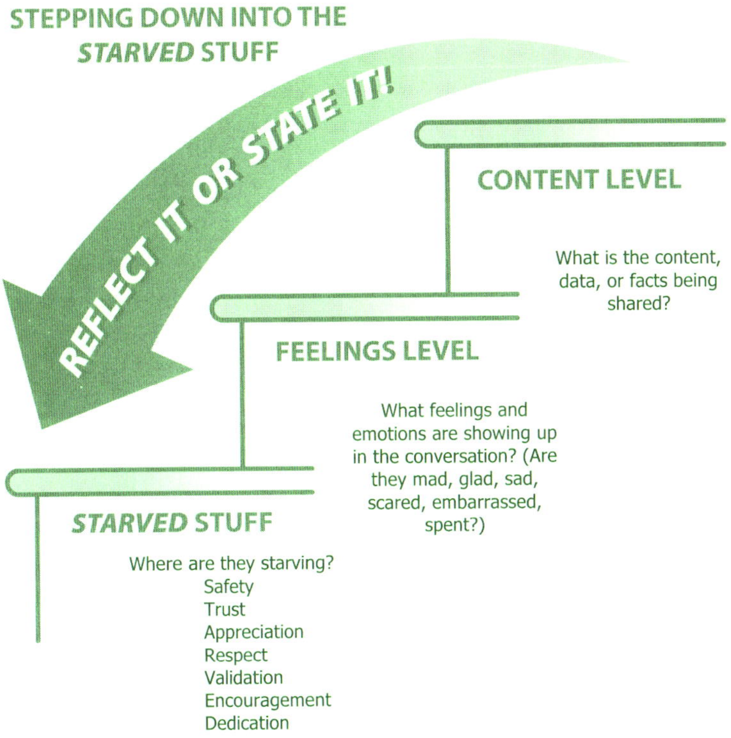

Three Levels of Conversation

Every conversation has three different levels: content, feelings, and the STARVED Stuff. Each of these levels brings some valuable information along with the answers to how we can improve our relationship. The problem is we get stuck on the top step (the content) and never take any of the other steps down into the real issues. There are two ways we can step down into the STARVED Stuff. One way is to step down and simply state our feelings and where we are starving. Another way is to use the stethoscope and reflect until there is deeper understanding.

We want people to feel with us more than to act for us.
—George Eliot

The object is to first clearly understand the content. As we progress through each turn with the stethoscope, we should focus on hearing the content. We must not give into the temptation to begin forming our response while our partner is still talking. Important data is missed when this happens. After we clearly understand the content, we can then step down into the feelings level by recognizing our partner's emotions behind her words. Emotions are identified through word choice, through body language, and by putting ourself in our partner's place and imagining how we would feel. Once we recognize our partner's emotion and state it, we can then step down into the STARVED Stuff by sincerely looking at how the data and the emotions have impacted the 7 Basic Needs. This is one of the most basic and profound methods to feed a relationship.

Read the following scenario and see if you can identify the three levels and identify the STARVED Stuff:

"I'm so tired of my husband thinking that I'm his maid and that I'm here to pick up all of his junk all day long, so that when he gets home at 6:00, the house is perfectly clean. And then he just proceeds to dump junk all over the house again. It's the same thing every day and I'm sick of it!"

Content:
- Husband thinks she is his maid.
- She picks up his stuff all day.
- The house is clean when he gets home.
- He dumps more stuff all over the house.

Feelings:
- Tired or spent
- Frustrated and angry

STARVED Stuff:
- Unappreciated
- Disrespected
- Invalidated
- Discouraged

If this husband came home and got into an argument with his wife about this subject, staying focused on content only, one can only imagine the argument that would most likely take place:

"You're a slob." (Name calling—her words come out harshly because of the level of emotion behind them.)

"No, I'm not." (Defensive—Reactive Brain)

"Yes, you are."

"No, I'm not."

"And you think I'm your slave."

"That's ridiculous. No I don't," and back and forth and back and forth.

"You never pick up after yourself."

"What do you mean I never pick anything up? I pick up every week. Last week I picked up my clothes in the bathroom and you didn't even say thank you."

Reactive Brain: Defensive, trying to prove his point while throwing some "dirt" at his wife at the same time.

Fighting about content is so easy because without anchoring it to something deeper like feelings and STARVED Stuff, content is void of roots. And notice all the reactive ruts created along the way. Anytime we dig up the past, we're usually fighting about content. Do you see how this conversation really never gets anywhere, even though this is one of the most common methods of arguing for couples?

Instead, what if the husband stethoscoped his wife and reflected the content back about her having to pick up after him all day. He could then reflect her feelings back to her by saying something like, "Sounds like when I leave my junk around the house and you have to pick it up, you really feel frustrated and upset, so much so that you feel I treat you like you're less of a person. It sounds like this makes you feel unappreciated and disrespected. I'm sure it discourages you to be treated like this."

Can't you just hear her agreeing and then continuing to share her feelings with him? Now she could have made the whole discussion a lot easier, too, if she had just stated where she was STARVED. To state where you are STARVED works like this:

Step Down into the STARVED Stuff

- When you do . . . (give the content or data)
- I feel . . . (share your feelings)
- And that . . . (share your STARVED stuff)

Examples:

"Honey, when you keep leaving your stuff around the house for me to pick up, I feel frustrated and taken advantage of, and this makes me feel like you really don't respect me."

"When you show up late from work on our date nights, I feel sad because I want to know you appreciate our time together."

The fastest way to end an argument is to get into the STARVED Stuff together. The STARVED Stuff is as deep as it goes. Your partner can't argue with your STARVED Stuff, which is one reason why so many people like to keep the fight on the content level. While you might be told that you "shouldn't feel this way," you have the right to feel whatever way you want, regardless of what other people think. If this happens, a good response might be a gentle reminder that we all have our own feelings and we have the right to have those feelings respected and acknowledged for what they are. After this happens, you can continue to move the conversation forward.

Statistically, men typically listen for content. Men use less of their brain when they communicate than women do. (Sorry, guys, it's true!) Men usually listen with just the left side of their brain. This means they're really astute at obtaining content. They usually nail the content immediately. They might say, "You did not say that. You said . . ." Then they can tell you *exactly* what you said, because they *received the content.*

The woman then says something like, "Well, that's not what I *meant*." Meaning is so much deeper than just words. When women communicate, they use both sides of their brain. In fact, research has proven that the corpus callosum, or the bridge between the right and left side of the brain, is much more developed in women and probably gives women a greater ability to receive both the content and the feelings of a conversation. We can all learn to receive both content and feelings just by learning how to "step down" into the STARVED Stuff. The more you practice, the more you'll begin to pick up not just the content, but also the feelings and the STARVED Stuff as well.

Don't assume your partner isn't hearing your feelings and the STARVED Stuff because she doesn't care. Not hearing your feelings may be a simple matter of never having had the opportunity to *learn* these principles. It is much easier to accurately pick up the content than the feelings and the intent. This is why it is so important to interpret intentions positively. Interpreting intentions helps you communicate better.

Lifting the Conversation Upward

The final step of the REAL Communication model is to Lift the Conversation Upward. This is the moment when the roles get reversed and the person who was once listening now has the opportunity to become the speaker. This is a very critical time because now more than ever, the speaker will begin to see if the listener actually understood anything they said.

Again, this is where all of the skills of character and the Empowered Communication approach come into play. Before we can actually respond to someone else, we need to be fairly clear what our goals are.

You might recall that the name of this section is "Lifting the Conversation Upward." In my relationship programs, I teach that we have the ability to take a conversation in four basic directions. Lifting the conversation upward brings the most positive results when focusing on feeding a healthy and enduring relationship, so before we respond, we should make sure we're clear as to what direction we want to go:

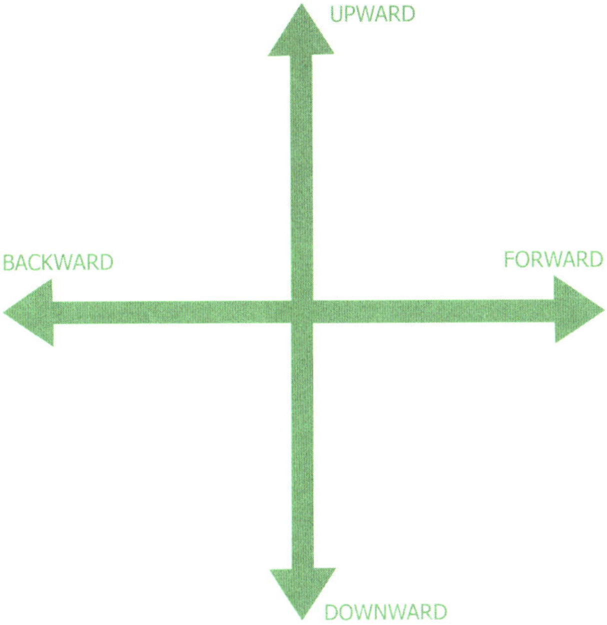

- **Upward**—healthy, selfless, proactive, unifying, positive, hopeful, and together
- **Downward**—unhealthy, selfish, reactive, polarizing, negative, hopeless, and abandoning
- **Backward**—historical, past, typical patterns approaches and methods
- **Forward**—future-oriented, solution-driven, progressive, change-minded approaches and methods

Notice that what constitutes the lifting conversation is the reverse of the Starved Spiral. If we keep taking a conversation downward, the starvation will inevitably continue. One of the biggest keys to lifting a conversation upward is to focus on areas both agree on, which is what I call the Predictable Imbalance.

Predictable Imbalance

As chaotic and difficult as life and our relationships may sometimes appear, there is an inherent order to all that takes place each day. The same is true in most of our conversations, especially our most difficult ones. Life and relationships are all about "Predictable Imbalance," or the "80/20 rule," as some people call it.

Italian economist, Vilfredo Pareto, originated the concept of the 80/20 rule around 1900. Pareto studied the distribution of wealth in a variety of countries. He discovered a common phenomenon: About 80 percent of the wealth in most countries is controlled by a consistent minority, which equals about 20 percent of the people. Pareto called this a "predictable imbalance." Pareto's rule of 80/20 has been expanded to many other areas since its first economic use.

While the accuracy of the numbers varies on the situation—for example, it might be 70/30 or 60/40, my experience has shown that this principle is just as sound in relationships as it is in economics. Check these numbers against your own experience and see if the principle applies in your life:

80/20

- 80 percent of our **disagreements** comes from 20 percent of our **issues.**
- 80 percent of our **pain** is caused by 20 percent of our **interactions.**

- 80 percent of our **time** is focused on discussing 20 percent of the things **we disagree about.**
- Generally, in society, 80 percent of **housework** is usually done by 20 percent of the **family members.**
- 80 percent of society's **problems** is usually caused by 20 percent of society.
- 80 percent of our **Safety, Trust, Appreciation, Respect, Validation, Encouragement, and Dedication** comes from 20 percent of our **activities** together.

Does the 80/20 rule resonate with you? This factor is important to understand for one reason: What usually drives couple's conversations downward is the fact that the couple continually becomes focused on the 20 percent of the conversation that keeps them distanced from one another. By allowing this divisive 20 percent to dominate the entire 100 percent of each conversation, couples set themselves up to actually create the problems they're trying to avoid.

Staying Balanced in the Practical Imbalance

One key to lifting conversations is to keep balanced in the practical imbalance. This means trying to stay balanced within the 80/20 rule by not focusing attention on the 20 percent of conflict that exists between the couple. This can be done by remembering to stay in the 80 percent zone by both "Blending" and "Building."

Blending

In every conversation with our partner, there is usually a larger percentage of what we agree on than what we disagree on. Blending is the ability to share with our partner the approximately 80 percent we agree on. Blending allows us to remove the barrier of misunderstanding and show our partner where we both agree. Typically, couples can agree on more general, principle-based ideas rather than the specifics around any given issue. When we do this, we show we buy into our partner's principles, even if we don't buy into her positions.

Blending really has two purposes: One is to reiterate to our partner that we picked up on both the content and intent of what was said. And two, Blending allows us to build a new pool of meaning that then becomes the foundation for all future change and understanding. By firmly and overtly Blending our common ground, we and our partner have defined an area of agreement with which both feel comfortable.

Building

On the other hand, Building is where the other 20 percent comes in. This 20 percent includes the things disagreed on, where there is conflict or where we need to share our unique view of the conversation. In order to build something, whether it is a house or our relationship, we must build on a stable foundation. Using the Blended 80 percent as the foundation, we can then build forward from there. The amazing realization about the 80/20 rule is that if we disagree a lot with each other, this probably means we spend the majority of our time focusing on what we *don't* have in common rather than what we *do* have in common. This type of foundation won't be able to hold the weight a relationship needs in order to survive. Make sure to look carefully at the amount of time spent on what the two partners agree upon.

Our ability to reach unity in diversity will
be the beauty and test of our civilization.
—Mahatma Gandhi

The skills of Blending and Building immediately create a sense of Safety, Trust, Appreciation, Respect, Validation, Encouragement and Dedication. By meeting the STARVED needs in their conversations, couples will gain more confidence in their ability to both agree and disagree. Let's look at some specific skills that can help.

The Steps to Blending:

- Remember to use the stethoscope on an issue to ensure both partners have heard each point of view.
- Begin the conversation by using the tools below to blend in two ways:
    - Highlight the areas of agreement.
    - Reiterate each partner's thoughts (content), feelings, and STARVED Stuff.
- Hold this as the unified stand together.

The tools to Blending are the following words and ideas. Use these to blend what you and your partner have in common as well as to show your partner that you have heard what she has just said:

- **Agree** with your partner on whatever words or ideas you can agree with.
- **Accept** your partner's beliefs, concerns, fears, stories.
- **Admit** to anything you can honestly admit to doing or feeling.
- **Acknowledge** his or her concerns and fears as valid and normal.
- **Apologize** for whatever your conscience compels you.
- **Act** in ways that communicate understanding.
- **Affirm your partner** on his or her position, your relationship and your partnership.
- **Adapt your plan** by altering ideas or perspectives you have

been influenced by and now see another or better way of doing something.

- **Aspire** for what you would like to happen in your relationship. Share with your partner your hopes, dreams, and goals.

When you are Blending, you use the data your partner has shared with you as you stethoscoped the issue. When you have effectively stethoscoped your partner and you feel you have heard what she said, it is then your opportunity to share what is going on in your mind. There may be things your partner said in your conversation that were offensive, or that you felt were rude or inaccurate or needed to be corrected. This is okay because this might be the 20 percent that exists between you and will be dealt with during the Building stage of the conversation. Just remember, before you share what you disagree on, try to blend the 80 percent that you both agree on.

You cannot antagonize and influence at the same time.
—J. S. Knox

Building Skills

Once we take our conversation through the Blending process, we will discover our common ground. Our common ground allows us to begin exploring the 20 percent of the information on which we don't agree, as well as any offensive or inaccurate information.

One of the most basic tendencies, while in the middle of any serious and stressed conversation, is the tendency to dichotomize issues. A dichotomy is an either/or position; we force a position into either option A or option B. It *has* to be just one or the other, doesn't it? Our brain wants to keep things fairly simplified and one way to do this is to minimize the options. When we share our opinions, we sometimes have the tendency to share them in a way that makes it appear that only one opinion can be right.

Our minds have the need to "know." When we don't know, we make assumption—they make us feel safer than not knowing.
—Don Miguel Ruiz

When building a blended foundation, we must open up our conversation and mind to the inevitability that the exchange of words should not lead to an either/or conclusion. Two opinions can be right simultaneously. There can be two, or multiple ways of doing things. One position doesn't have to be the ONLY correct position. Just as 1 + 1 = 2, so does ½ + ½ + ½ + ½ = 2, and other numerical combinations as well. And likewise, our spouse's position doesn't have to be the only right position. If her idea is better, this doesn't mean our idea is wrong or invalid. This simply means there is more than one way of doing things and each partner is choosing his or her way this time. There doesn't have to be a good or bad idea, or a right or wrong concept. There just has to be a choice between two good, but different ideas. Make sure each partner feels this security as both positions are discussed. As safety increases, so does trust. Continue to increase safety by maintaining respect for each partner, as well as for her ideas and opinions. As a result, we will find our safe haven increasing in size and strength.

Another dangerous word to watch out for in a conversation is the infamous word "but":

> "Reading this book is really important to me, but it's so hard to implement the skills."

Do you notice what the word "but" does to all of the words before it? The word "but" tends to erase whatever words came before it in the sentence. The reason for this is that the brain naturally categorizes sentences; thus the sentence is placed into two different phrases or sections with the word "but" immediately placing a wall between the two:

"I really love my wife, but I wish she'd take better care of the house."

The more noticeable of the two parts tends to be the second part. This tendency in your brain causes a big problem when sharing sensitive information. You don't want any walls after working so hard to create common ground. The goal is to build a bridge when you're talking with your partner and building safety. The best way to build the bridge is to use the word "and" instead of "but." Learning to use the word "and" is critical to building better and more effective conversations in your relationships:

"Reading this book is really important to me, and it's so hard to implement the skills."

"I really love my wife, and I wish she'd take better care of the house."

Below are more examples of how to use "and" instead of "but" in your conversations. Following these examples, create some "Building" sentences of your own. Check your gut as you read the difference in each sentence:

> Statement: "John, I really love you, but it bothers me when you interrupt me while I am talking."
> Rephrased: "John, I really love you and it bothers me when you interrupt me while I am talking."
> Statement: "I am usually so patient, but these kids are driving me crazy."

Rephrased: "I am usually so patient, and these kids are driving me crazy."
Statement: "Honey, I know you have had a hard day, but please don't yell at me the minute I walk in the door."
Rephrased: "Honey, I know you have had a hard day, and please don't yell at me the minute I walk in the door."

One additional tip:

Use "I" or "we" statements instead of "you" statements. For example:

"I feel we're struggling to talk" versus "You hate talking!"
"I don't feel supported in my decisions" versus "You don't support me in any decision!"
"I don't like to be late and it seems as if we have been late a lot" versus "You are always late!"

To help create even more REAL Communication, the following are rules I've found helpful in Building more positive conversations:

- Be in the conversation 100 percent.
- Have your unified common ground clearly established.
- Continue Building your conversation by sharing the 20 percent.
- Avoid dichotomizing or making something an either/or; (either you like me or hate me, either it's good or bad).
- Use "and" instead of "but."
- Use "I" instead of "you."
- Find common ground.

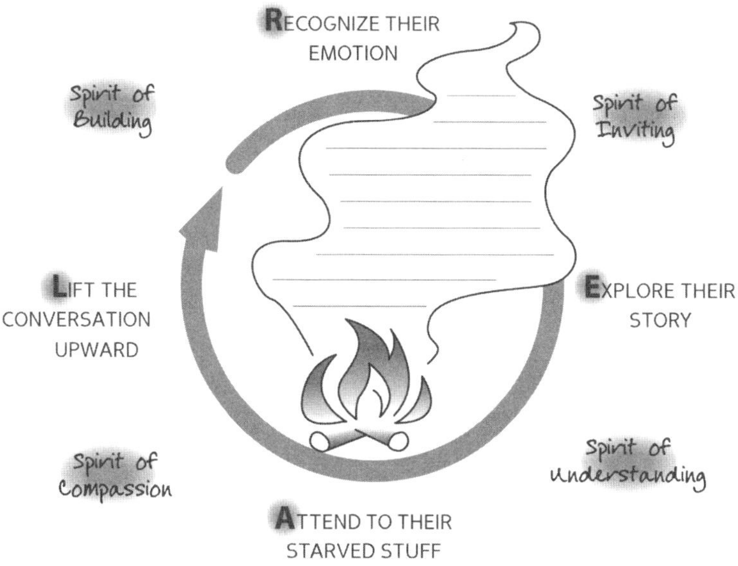

I've found a quick and easy way for you to remember the goal of each section needed to create REAL Communication:

1. Recognize Their Emotion: The Spirit of Inviting
2. Explore Their Story: The Spirit of Understanding
3. Attend to Their STARVED Stuff: The Spirit of Compassion
4. Lift the Conversation Upward: The Spirit of Building

In other words, the skill of recognizing their emotion, if done genuinely, automatically brings with it a spirit of inviting. As you use the stethoscope to Explore Their Story and begin to attend to them, a spirit of understanding fills your interaction. Attending to the STARVED Stuff and beginning to Lift the Conversation carries a spirit of compassion, and a spirit of Building continues through the lifting stage.

Can we see how having these four open, gentle spirits in our conversations helps lift us, our partner, and our relationship? We may not always agree or be able to immediately solve all our issues, which is why these four spirits are about *intent*. When our partner feels our intent of inviting, understanding, compassion, and building, doors will open to a deeper use of the Get REAL process. This may take time and dedication, but it will be worth it.

Chapter Review:

- The third step of Getting REAL, Attending to Their STARVED Stuff, involves really listening to another's heart.
- The process of Stepping Down means listening for three levels: content, feelings, and STARVED Stuff.
- The fourth step of Getting REAL is Lifting the Conversation Upward and is the reverse of the STARVED Spiral.
- Staying balanced within the 80/20 Rule requires Blending and Building.
- Blending removes the barrier of misunderstanding by focusing on the 80 percent of the discussion where there is agreement.
- Building is the tool used for the 20 percent where there is disagreement or conflict. It is important to use "and," not "but" during this step.
- The Spirit of Inviting, Understanding, Compassion and Building are the truest intent behind REAL Communication.

My Feeding Plan

In order to create a healthy diet that feeds your relationship, you need to have a plan. Use the "My Feeding Plan" activity to come up with some specific ideas from the last chapter that you can use to improve the health of your relationship.

Commitment to Keep Learning

What is the most important thing you learned in this chapter that, if lived consistently, would positively impact your relationship?

____

____

____

____

____

Commitment to Keep Changing

Based on what you have learned, what will you commit to change in your life?

Specifically, how will you do it?

Specifically, when will you do it?

The Course on Companionship

Building Mutual Benefit

Chapter 13

Holding the Love You Are Given

Companionship is the third course in our healthy relationship feast. Companionship is the desire to be with each other, as well as the desire to connect with one another on a variety of levels: physically, socially, emotionally, mentally, and spiritually. Every healthy, long-term relationship requires some sense of companionship to keep it going. Companionship is really the great motivator that helps a couple desire to show character to one another and to communicate more effectively. It is also the fuel that enables a couple to find more hope and create a stronger commitment to each other.

For many of us, the idea of creating a healthy and enduring companionship may seem like an impossible dream that we have tried to drive out of our head. Some may read this book and say, "Yeah, everything is so positive and hopeful, but Matt is not married to my partner." Others who read this book may believe in everything I've said, but don't think they have the ability or maybe even the desire to attempt to implement any of these ideas with their partner. They're just not quite sure their "companionship" is worth fighting for any more. If you have any of these feelings or you have doubt coursing through your blood, then this chapter is for you. My simple advice to you is learn what you can from this book, especially this chapter. Identify where your holes are and start fixing them before you make any final decisions about your relationship, because no matter what happens to you and your partner, you are always going to need to know how to have better character, communication, and companionship skills.

Long-Term Relationships Require Mutual Benefit

All relationships are a two-way street. I'm sure you've heard someone referring to a troubled relationship say, "Well, it takes two to tango!" One of the most common rules I use when discussing healthy long-term relationships is that they must be mutually beneficial.

The same is true if we want a long-term relationship with our partner. The relationship has to be good for both or it won't last. One of the best ways to find out if our partner feels as if he is benefiting is to communicate. Like a continuous cycle, we really can't create true companionship until we have the communication skills to understand what our partner needs. Once we understand his needs, we must exhibit the character to choose to serve these needs.

In order to take our feeding to an entirely new level—no matter where we are presently, we'll have to determine what's really happening in our relationship that might be limiting both us and that relationship. We'll have to determine if we have an issue with ***Holding***—receiving the love our partner sends, or if we have more of an issue ***Pouring***—giving our partner the love he wants and needs. And our partner will have to make the same assessment. Does he have the inability or unwillingness to hold the love we pour or pour the love we want?

The most important thing in life is to learn
how to give out love, and let it come in.
—Morrie Schwartz

Holding and Pouring

One of my favorite books is a short and simple story about a wise baker called *Jacob the Baker*, by Noah Ben Shea. In this book, he teaches a valuable lesson that sheds light on the power of feeding our relationships. One of Jacob's followers comes to Jacob looking for Jacob's insight into the purpose of life. In an effort to teach, Jacob puts his hands together in the shape of a small bowl and says,

> *"Our life is a vessel, and a vessel is formed for two functions. One is to hold"—then Jacob flattened his hands as if he was making an offering,—"and the other is to pour."*

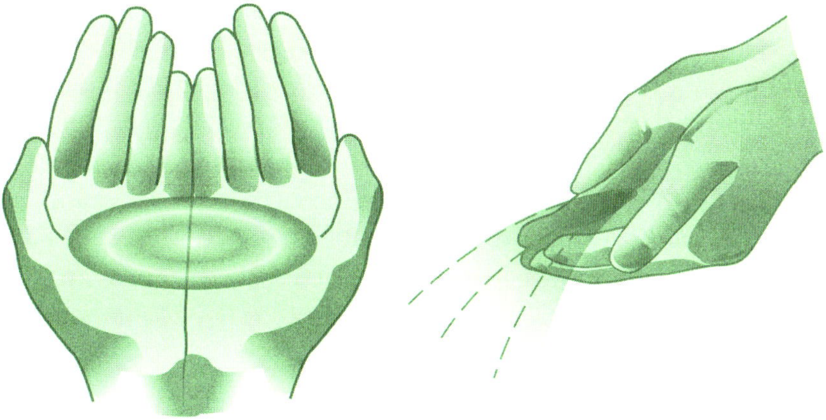

Just as Jacob demonstrates, our hands are a wonderful model for giving and receiving love from our partner. When it comes to relationships, I believe our hands have two purposes: One is to "hold" and fully receive the love our partner pours, or even attempts to pour for us. The other is to pour the love our partner longs for and needs. One purpose is to receive the food our partner feeds us; the other purpose is to feed our partner. Just as Jacob knew the principle of giving and receiving, we must also learn to give and receive love. This will not only enable more love in our relationships, but will also invigorate our relationships with a lot more life.

Holding and Pouring aren't as easy as they may appear, or couples would just do this naturally without any problems or hiccups. There are a lot of things that get in the way of a person's ability to hold the love of his partner, as well as to effectively pour the love he needs. Some relationships and individuals have very serious issues Holding the love of their partner, while others have issues Pouring love. Sometimes it's a combination of both. We will spend the rest of this chapter discussing the various ways to increase the ability to hold the love our partner pours. We will then spend all of chapter fourteen discussing how to pour the love our partner wants.

Holding Issues

Sometimes in a relationship you may feel STARVED because of a Holding problem. This is not because our partner isn't Pouring, but because we, as the holder, are unwilling or unable to receive the love we are shown or given by our partner. Sometimes our partner may actually be feeding us, but we are unable to see this because we either don't trust what our partner is doing or we don't trust the reasons behind his choice to feed us. Sometimes we may not accept this form of love because it's just "too little, too late."

Usefulness is not impaired by imperfection.
You can drink from a chipped cup.
—Greta K. Nagel

Many couples suffer with Holding issues. Generally speaking, Holding issues in a relationship can be a little more difficult to deal with than Pouring issues because they usually signify other unresolved matters that need to be dealt with. Holding issues are the equivalent of someone trying to fill a bucket that has holes in it. Can this successfully be done? Perhaps, but eventually people get tired of endlessly trying to fill this type of bucket and eventually move on to find a bucket that *will* hold their offerings.

Dealing with someone with Holding issues makes the "Pouring" partner feel like nothing will ever be enough: not good enough, not fast enough, not done for the right reasons, or never with enough care. There are many potential causes or influences of Holding issues:

- Past painful times in the relationship
- Broken trust
- Unresolved STARVED issues
- Past affairs or abuse

- Unmanaged expectations
- Gender differences
- Negative interpretations
- Physiological problems: brain traumas or disorders, etc.
- Psychological issues: depression, attachment disorders, etc.
- Addictions
- Distractions: the heart has committed to someone or something else
- Ignorance, the most common of all

Holding/Pouring Issues

Some Holding and Pouring problems are interrelated. By this I mean that people who have not been served by their partners (which is a lack of Pouring) start building up an immunity to the pain found in their relationship by either not expecting their partner to pour any love or by not accepting (which is a lack of Holding) the love of their partner. Many people believe it is better to pretend they don't care about the love their partner pours rather than admit they are starving inside.

Another pattern that occurs when Pouring has stopped is a person tends to actually stop looking for any Pouring to happen. So when his partner actually does start Pouring again, the person is unable to hold the love. This failure to hold is portrayed by the inability of the person to see the Pouring efforts of the partner.

Take a moment to think about your own situation. In your relationship, do you have problems with Holding or Pouring? Do you have problems with both? Ask yourself these questions to identify if you have a Holding/Pouring issue in your relationship. If you are in a Holding/Pouring standoff with your partner, which part of the standoff are you?

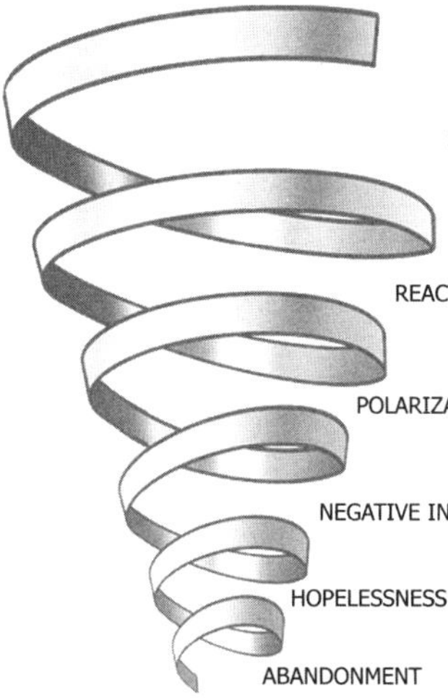

Selfishness—Do you tend to keep score on how much you are being fed?
Reactivity—Do you tend to easily reject your partner's offerings?
Polarization—Do you no longer want the same thing as your partner?
Negative Interpretation—Do you see the negative in what your partner is offering?
Hopelessness—Do you feel like it will never be good enough?
Abandonment—Do you dream about or wish for it to be over?

A Holding/Pouring standoff really is the ultimate chicken before the egg issue. In other words, which came first: your partner's lack of Pouring or your inability to hold the love offered? Remember the STARVED Standoff in which you each wait for the other partner to pour first? There are many reasons why this standoff takes place and many explanations as to why each reason is very manageable. So, before giving up on your relationship, make sure you are fully able to comprehend both Holding and Pouring the love people really do need or you risk harming your overall ability to have relationships with other people.

When it comes to Holding/Pouring, a person has absolutely no control over some issues but does have control over other issues. For example, some couples can't control the fact that their partner has sleeping problems which makes it hard for them to go to bed together. But they do have control over whether they still spend time talking and cuddling together before one of them goes to bed. Obviously, a person is significantly more empowered if he continues to focus on those things over which he can exercise some control.

The place to be happy is here. The time to be happy is now.
The way to be happy is to make others so.
—Robert G. Ingersoll

Five Common Holes

When I work with my clients, I generally see a variety of different "holes" that impact people's ability to hold the love of their partner, or their willingness to do so. Each of these five holes deserves some focus. The five holes are physiological holes, psychological holes, ignorance, addictions, and distractions. Obviously, some holes are more common than others, but in my relationship coaching practice, I have seen numerous examples of each of these areas. Just because your partner might have some of these holes does not have to mean all hope is lost. This simply means different steps need to be taken. In my practice, I have found that the principles taught in my six-week "Feeding the STARVED Relationship" workshop still apply to a relationship regardless of whether or not a partner has any holes. So don't give up, learn the principles, and see if you can influence any positive changes in your relationship. If you cannot, at least you have put yourself in a better place to understand what it takes to create a healthier relationship.

Physiological Holes

When your partner suffers from physical ailments, it eventually impacts his ability to hold the love you're sending. The following are examples of physiological issues:

- PMS
- Mononucleosis
- Fibromyalgia
- Head injuries
- Back pain
- Alzheimer's
- Schizophrenia
- Bi-polar disorders
- Chemical depression

Psychological Holes

Psychological issues in a relationship are the bread and butter for most therapists' and counselors' practices. However, I have found that these types of issues are typically not the main cause of most marital discord. The issue of trying to hold onto the love of your partner may be complicated if you've never actually had a sense of true psychological health. If you think psychological issues are affecting your relationship, I encourage you to seek the advice and counsel of a trained professional. The following are examples of psychological issues:

- Situational Depression
- Self-esteem Issues
- Attachment disorders
- Personality disorders
- Family of origin issues
- Abuse
- Narcissism

Ignorance

Lack of knowledge becomes a hole in relationships when a person just doesn't know how to connect to his or her partner. Lack of knowledge and skills become obstacles to a relationship's growing and thriving. Ignorance can also impact Holding if there is a lack of understanding about how to feed your relationship or your partner. Sometimes people just don't know any better; they have ineffective patterns because that is the only example they have ever seen.

Addictions

Addictions rob us of the most basic tool we have to help us succeed, not only in our relationships, but, maybe even more importantly, in our life. This basic tool is the ability to make choices; to manage the Choice Points of one's life. The freedom to make decisions at the Choice Points of life can have far-reaching effects. Addictions take away a person's ability to get into the Relating Brain and take the High Road. Addictions also put a person in a place where he or she has inevitably to choose between the addiction and everything and everyone else. As a result, creating long-term relationships is difficult, if not impossible, because of the addiction's overwhelming demand to come first in our life. It's hard to fully love someone who loves their addiction more.

Distractions

The last category of holes is distractions, or the things that easily distract us from our most important relationships. Do any of these found familiar?

- **Holding a grudge:** Holding a grudge against our partner is a major distraction that disables a relationship. Grudges cloud a person's ability to see clearly the present and future state of the relationship because the person is so fixated on the past and the lack of love received from his or her partner.
- **Holding court:** This is when a person takes on the role of acting as his or her partner's judge, jury, and jail warden, making all of the judgments and exacting all of the penalties for his or her partner's wrongdoings.
- **Holding patterns:** Like an airplane that is not allowed to come in for a landing and is placed in a holding pattern, too many people also place their relationship in a pattern of holding, one in which we're not committed to being actively involved, nor are we really getting closer to our goals. We just circle and circle, wondering what's actually going to happen to us. Although sometimes helpful, holding patterns most often cause partners to feel anxious and eventually get tired of not knowing what's happening.
- **Holding onto our victim stories:** Sometimes one of our biggest distractions that keep us from creating more love in our relationships is the stories we tell about our relationship.

One of the most common of all the love-busting stories is the story of being the victim. Victim stories always tend to pin the lack of happiness or the reasons for misery on someone else. Even though there are true victims in some relationships, playing the victim and being stuck in this type of story mode only prolongs the time a person remains stuck in the victim role.

- **Holding onto someone else:** The most common distraction I see with my clients is the simple distraction of someone else. Long-term, intimate and enduring relationships are best made as pairs, not trios. The minute a third person is permitted into the fold of a committed relationship or partnership, problems will arise. Any type of affair, whether sexual or just emotional, will begin to tear the relationship apart. The best way to know if we are holding onto someone else is to ask these questions:
    - Are we keeping secrets from our partner about the "other" person?
    - Are there things about this other person that we don't want our partner to know about?

  One of the problems with having "other people" in our relationship is that this adds to "the grass is greener somewhere else" mentality. But the truth is if the grass truly appears greener on the other side of the fence, this usually means that we're watering that grass more.
- **Holding onto other necessary distractions like kids, church, friends, volunteering, family, extended family, etc:** As a society, I think we are all too busy and overcommitted. We have so many other things vying for our attention. When these things tend to take over our lives, the area of our life that begins to suffer is our most important relationships. At some point, we must learn to say "No" to the distractions and "Yes" to our most important relationships. This can be incredibly complicated because the battle is not between

> "good" and "bad" choices here, but between "good" and "better" choices. Should we stay longer at work to get promoted or go home and be with our partner? Should we make a commitment to be more active in our community or keep a commitment to remain more active in our relationship? Remember, because time is limited, the only way to get more time is to make better choices.

The longer I have worked with people, the more I realize that each of us has holes. Nobody is going to get through life without some holes, and the key is to learn everything we can about every hole, build a plan and a support team, and start doing what we can today to improve our situation. If not, we or our partner will just keep losing the love that's poured when it seeps out of the holes. Eventually, the pourer will quit Pouring all together because it will seem fruitless to pour for someone who lacks the ability to hold love.

Do What We Can to Plug the Holes

If we've chosen to hold onto these holes that seep love, then we may be feeling some guilt. Guilt is usually a sign that we are doing something that is against our value system or belief system. If we don't address this guilt early enough, but instead keep holding onto other things that don't improve the relationship, the guilt tends to persist and will eventually turn into anger and frustration. Obviously the anger and frustration should be directed toward ourself because we are the cause of our problems, but all too often, in relationships, these negative feelings tend to be directed toward the partner and the stories begin to be built about why the other partner has made our lives so miserable. This lie to ourself is the product of allowing a fixable problem to get in the way of our Holding.

Do not let what you cannot do interfere with what you can do.
—John Wooden

Remember, we have the power to control some parts of each of the five holes—physiological, psychological, ignorance, addictions, and distractions. For example, we can choose to see a doctor and complete therapy or other types of treatments deemed necessary to manage many types of physiological or psychological problems we may have. We can learn new skills to increase our knowledge about relating. We can also choose to seek help through addiction groups and programs, attending meetings regularly and enlisting the help of family and friends. We can choose to manage the various distractions that impact our life and eliminate them if we truly want to work on building a long-term relationship with our partner. Eventually our priorities will be realigned. Nothing is more permanent in life and relationships than change, and over time life will create moments when Holding may be more possible than others. The only question is will we take advantage of these opportunities?

I once had a family come in to see me in order to repair a family fight that had dragged on for years. All of the family members were upset with one another. The parents and each of the six adult children continued to argue over an issue that could not be resolved. They were all waiting for someone else to have a change of heart and apologize for their lack of character. They assumed that once someone else apologized, everything would return to the way it had been. The problem was that no one was willing to see things differently and the lack of willingness to change meant that change would never take place.

I told the family that I was convinced that eventually the apologies would all come out and there would be a time when everyone would hug each other again.

"When?" the mother of the family urgently asked me. "When do you think that will take place?"

I told her, "Well, at this rate, it will probably be at someone's funeral. Funerals are final and that finality ensures a level of humility that helps people become very real, very quickly. With your family I have seen that you would rather hold a grudge, and when you hold a grudge, you have no room to hold the love someone is Pouring. By holding onto the past, the grudge is so filling that you can't hold love. *So it will all change when you all quit holding a grudge or when the time comes to hold a funeral—you decide."*

Many of my coaching clients often ask me, "So what am I supposed to do if I am married to someone who will just not hold the love I'm Pouring, or who can't get over the past? Or what if I just don't know whether or not I want to be with them anymore?"

I have found that there are a variety of reasons why a partner might be having a difficult time Holding love. We must also remember that even though we may not be able to change everything about our partner's ability to hold, *we can choose how we are going to respond.*

Five Choices to Help Us Hold the Love of Our Partner

> *A 92-year-old, poised and proud lady, who was known for being fully dressed each morning by eight o-clock—including her hair fashionably coifed and her make-up perfectly applied (even though she was legally blind), moved to a nursing home. Her husband of 70 years had recently passed away, making the move necessary. After many hours of waiting patiently in the lobby of the nursing home, she smiled sweetly when told her room was ready.*
>
> *As she maneuvered her walker to the elevator, I had the opportunity to provide her with a visual description of her tiny room, including the eyelet curtains that had been hung on her window.*
>
> *"I love it," she stated, with the enthusiasm of an eight-year-old having just received a new puppy.*
>
> *"But Mrs. Jones, you haven't even seen the room yet."*

"That doesn't have anything to do with it," she replied.
"Happiness is something you decide ahead of time. Whether I like my room or not doesn't depend on how the furniture is arranged, it's how I arrange my mind.
"I already decided to love it. . . . It's a decision I make every morning when I wake up. I have a choice: I can spend the day in bed recounting the difficulty I have with the parts of my body that no longer work, or get out of bed and be thankful for the ones that do. Each day is a gift and as long as my eyes open, I'll focus on the new day and all the happy memories I've stored away . . . just for this time in my life.
"Old age is like a bank account. You withdraw from what you've put in. So, my advice to you would be to deposit a lot of happiness in the bank account of memories. Thank you for your part in filling my Memory Bank. I am still depositing."
—Author Unknown
(http://www.fortnet.org/fapg/stories.htm)

Mrs. Jones knew how to make every day a great day no matter what her circumstance. This is a great example of what Abraham Lincoln said about attitude:

People are about as happy as they make up their minds to be.

This thought process may also be the answer to improving our own relationship. It's about choice. I've found five choices critical to creating great results in almost any relationship:

1. Relax Your Grip.
2. Risk for the Reward,
3. Change What You Can.
4. Accept What You Cannot Change.

5. Look for the Good in the Cracked Pot. (Notice I did not say "crack pot!")

Relax Your Grip

Imagine yourself getting a drink out of a stream or pond. In order to get enough water to satisfy your thirst, you don't just grab the water with your hands and squeeze a handful, because the more you squeeze, the more you lose! Instead, you open your hand, cup it, and take in as much water as you can, knowing that some will fall back into the stream. You take in as much as you can, one cupful at a time. The same holds true for Holding love. You can't control or force it. Instead, you must open yourself up, relax your grip, and let the love flow in. (I feel a song coming on!)

Relaxing your grip helps you focus less on controlling the situation with your partner and more on finding peace in the process of improvement over time.

Risk for the Reward

Two key principles to increasing closeness and intimacy in relationships are risk and commitment. Any time we want a boost in our levels of connection and closeness, we must just be willing to risk something, like being vulnerable. For example, think of the awkward first kiss of a young teenage couple where neither feels confident and yet both are curiously willing to give it a try. This kiss is a sign of their blossoming commitment to one another and yet none of it would take place if one or both parties weren't willing to risk the embarrassment, the awkwardness or potential humiliation, even if everything goes horribly wrong.

The person who risks nothing, does nothing, has nothing, is nothing, and becomes nothing. He may avoid suffering and sorrow, but he simply cannot learn and feel and change and grow and love and live.
—Leo Buscaglia

This combination of risk and commitment can create a powerful moment of intimacy that will never be forgotten. The same is also true in our relationships, no matter how long we've been at it. Risk allows us to reach new levels of closeness and commitment, and it creates the safety to foster more and more risk in the relationship. Risk acts as a primer that helps get things going in the relationship.

Risk has its rewards. For example, the wife who is willing to risk initiating intimacy when she normally doesn't, or the husband risking being vulnerable by listening to the hard-to-hear feedback from their spouse and not reacting. Both of these risks will have a potential to bring you closer together.

Change What You Can

Getting positive results together is the best way to increase the ability to see what is working and to hold the love of others. Changing what you can is a big part of this process. There is power in finding and working on the things over which you have control in the relationship. For example, if you can't rely on your partner's job skills to ensure that there will always be an abundance of money in the bank, then you can choose to work on how well you budget the money or obtain education and skills to ensure you'll always be able to make a little extra money on the side. Or, if you can't depend on your partner's reaction to certain topics you bring up, then work on finding better ways to Get REAL with his reactions instead of participating in the typical fight or flight patterns of the past. By focusing on what you can change, you increase your power to create even more change.

Accept What You Can't Change

Many individuals in relationships have Holding problems because they are mourning the loss of the relationship they thought they would have, but are not experiencing. Very few couples have the relationship they always dreamed about or thought they would have.

One common denominator to most struggling relationships, and maybe all relationships in general, is that there is always room for improvement. I have seen the frustration on the faces of a lot of my clients as they try to deal with their unmet goals. I have also seen the creation of very healthy and mutually fulfilling relationships that come from these broken dreams. Much of it is about a person's state of mind and his expectations. National statistics about divorce state that just by sticking it out for more than five years, things will improve.

> *How many unhappy couples turn their marriages around? The truth is shocking: 86 percent of unhappily married people who stick it out find that, five years later, their marriages are happier, according to an analysis of the National Survey of Families and Households. . . .*
> *The very worst marriages showed the most dramatic turnarounds: 77 percent of the stable married people who rated their marriage as very unhappy (a one on a scale of one to seven) in the late '80s said that the same marriage was either "very happy" or "quite happy" five years later.*
> (Linda J. Waite, Don Browning, William J. Doherty, Maggie Gallagher, Ye Luo, and Scott M. Stanley, *Does Divorce Make People Happy: Findings from a Study of Unhappy Marriages* [New York: Institute for American Values, 2002], 148–49.)

Things will look better as time goes on, but you've got to be willing to accept the reality of your new existence and work differently to make it better. Start smelling the flowers in your relationship! Look for the things that are working. If your relationship is about Holding love and Pouring love, how do you hold and receive love in your relationship?

One key to Holding love is to accept it. You have to be open to the way your partner loves you. You need to start receiving and accepting how your partner offers his love to you. You have to acknowledge the effort and, at the same time, encourage your partner. It is also important to hold each other accountable for doing more in the relationship instead of just rolling over and expecting the same old thing over and over again.

Look for the Good in the Cracked Pot (Not the Crack Pot!)

A water bearer in India had two large pots. Each one hung on both ends of a pole that he carried across his neck. One of the pots had a crack in it. The other pot was perfect and always delivered a full portion of water at the end of the long walk from the stream to the master's house, while the cracked pot arrived only half full. For two years this went on daily, with the bearer delivering only one and one-half pots of water to his master's house. Of course, the perfect pot was proud of its accomplishments, perfect to the end for which it was made. But the poor cracked pot was ashamed of its own imperfection, and miserable that it was able to accomplish only half of all that was expected of him. After two years of what the pot perceived to be a bitter failure, it spoke to the water bearer one day by the stream.
"I am ashamed of myself, and I want to apologize to you."
"Why?" asked the bearer. "What are you ashamed of?"
"I have been able, for these past two years, to deliver only half my load because this crack in my side causes water to leak out all the way back to your master's house. Because of my flaws, you have to do all of this work, and you don't get full value from your efforts."
The water bearer felt sorry for the old cracked pot. In his compassion he said, "As we return to the master's house, I want you to notice the beautiful flowers along the path."

Indeed, as they went up the hill, the old cracked pot took notice of the sun warming the beautiful wild flowers on the side of the path, and this cheered the pot some. But, at the end of the trail, it still felt bad because the pot had leaked out half its load, and so, again, it apologized to the bearer for its failure.

The bearer then said to the pot, "Did you notice that there were flowers only on your side of your path, but not on the other pot's side? That's because I have always known about your flaw, and I took advantage of it. I planted flower seeds on your side of the path, and every day while we walked back from the stream, you've watered them. For two years, I have been able to pick these beautiful flowers to decorate my master's table. Without you being just the way you are, he would not have had this beauty to grace his house.

—Indian Fable
(http://www.fortnet.org/fapg/stories.htm)

As was discussed in *Accepting What You Can't Change*, an interesting tool that helps a partner live with a cracked pot is to find something he does really well, and then discover new ways to enjoy and grow from this. Each of us has our own unique flaws, so what it all really boils down to is the fact that we really are *all* cracked pots! The question is, can there still be value being married to one? The answer is a resounding yes! Maybe the best thing about being married to a cracked pot is that we have to do more work, which helps us grow stronger and healthier. Perhaps this experience allows us to grow character or strengthen skills on which we wouldn't have normally worked.

Everyone has his own specific . . . mission in life. . . . Therein he cannot be replaced, nor can his life be repeated. Thus, everyone's task is as unique as is his specific opportunity to implement it.
—Viktor Frankyl

Many of us saw the public struggles of actor Christopher Reeve and his wife, Dana, as they worked through the issues of a horseback-riding accident that left him paralyzed. Dana commented regularly on how much she had grown and had come to know herself better after being able to serve him as he strived to recover from the accident. Endless benefits come from working or living with a cracked pot, and remember, if we can't see any benefits, the problem may have more to do with our perspective than our reality.

One tool that helps ensure we're finding the things that work in our relationship is the T-chart, like the one pictured on the next page.

Feeding Rule – T-Chart
Your T-chart should fill an entire page. On one side of the paper, write your name. On the other side of the paper, write your spouse's name. The goal of the T-chart is for each of you to find things your partner does every day that are positive and good—things that feed you. You don't need to talk about it, just write it down. The examples of positive activities that can make the list are endless. Things like, "You made me a plate for dinner when I was late getting home," or, "You held my hand at dinner," or, "You helped me clean up before going to bed," or, "You came home early from work on my day off."

TOWNSEND
Relationship
CENTER™
Connecting Heads, Hearts, Hands and Hopes

I felt loved when you...

Name	Name

The goal is to add three to four things to the list every day and, if possible, add them throughout the day so our partner can see what is working in the relationship. As this continues, the T-chart becomes an effective tool that increases our ability to hold the love our partner gives, because this exercise forces us to start seeing and recognizing his or her love. This list also becomes a tool of Communication because every time we write down what our partner is doing, we actually communicate to our partner our likes and dislikes. I have found that using a T-chart for a couple of months creates momentum and growth, which helps us to begin to see and hold the love our partner pours.

Where There's a Will, There's a Way

You will become as small as your controlling desire;
as great as your dominant aspiration.
—James Allen

Finally, the governing principle of being able to hold more in a relationship is, "Where there's a will, there's a way." The principle behind this phrase is a powerful truth I see operating daily in the relationships I work with. If we have the "will" to improve our relationship and to increase our ability to hold and pour more for our partner, then we will almost always be able to find a "way" to accomplish this. Even if we can't find the way, just having the will gives us the drive to keep looking until we find experts that can help. We'll talk more about this later in the course on Commitment, but for now, let's figure out if we can get some Pouring going.

Chapter Review:

- Companionship is the by-product of character and communication in a relationship. It also brings more hope to the relationship and a stronger commitment.
- Holding issues come from being unwilling or unable to receive love and result in feeling STARVED.
- Holding and Pouring issues can be interrelated. Lack of Pouring can lead to lack of Holding and vice versa.
- Holding issues generally come from five holes: physiological holes, psychological holes, ignorance, addictions, and distractions.
- Holes in the relationship can be managed with five Choice Points: Relax Your Grip, Risk for the Reward, Change What You Can, Accept What You Can't Change, and Look for the Good in the Cracked Pot.
- The T-chart is the tool to find what is working in the relationship.

My Feeding Plan

In order to create a healthy diet that feeds your relationship, you need to have a plan. Use the "My Feeding Plan" activity to come up with some specific ideas from the last chapter that you can use to improve the health of your relationship.

Commitment to Keep Learning

What is the most important thing you learned in this chapter that, if lived consistently, would positively impact your relationship?

____

____

____

____

____

Commitment to Keep Changing

Based on what you have learned, what will you commit to change in your life?

Specifically, how will you do it?

Specifically, when will you do it?

Chapter 14

Pouring the Love Your Partner Wants

Pouring love to your partner really just means feeding her and the relationship. Feeding your partner is about fulfilling the promises you made when the two of you were either married or committed to become a partnership. By now, you have learned that after the short yearning stage of love, you enter the earning stage in which you have to earn the love of your partner. Now you're going to find out how to move onto the final stage: the "enduring" stage of love.

Selflessness used to abound when you were in the yearning stage of love. Think about how many times you served your partner, sometimes to the detriment of your own needs and wants. Simply serving your loved one completed your own sense of self. This feeding and complete focus on your partner worked years ago, didn't it? You always seemed to *get* fed, without ever thinking about *being* fed.

The saying is true, "The empty vessel makes the greatest sound."
—William Shakespeare

However, over time, as the earning stage progressed, selfishness grew and the feeding gradually stopped. For some couples, this happens when couples have children, since time and resources become scarce. Others quit feeding one another when other things or people intrude—a boss, a professor, a friend, a new interest, a hobby, or any smoky issue. All of these new factors that naturally come into your life take a seat at your banquet table, moving you farther and farther away from each other. Eventually these factors make it difficult for you to continue to feed one another.

If any of this sounds like something that's happening in your relationship, know that you are normal, but don't allow it to happen. Don't just sit there—fight back! You can reclaim the love you once felt for each other, but you must do something different and you must do it now. I'm not saying you need to kick all of these other people away from your table and out of your life. What I am saying is that you need to make sure that you are always seated *next* to your partner at your relationship table—that you both have some mutual goals that you're able to communicate openly about, and that you each have the character to choose to keep your head in the relationship.

Being, not Getting

I firmly believe that no other endeavor has a bigger potential to change one's life for the better than being married. Notice that I didn't say *getting* married. After working as a divorce mediator, I have learned that getting married doesn't necessarily create a lot of long-term benefits in your life. It is in *being* married that all of the benefits are found.

If you want your relationship to last longer than your wedding bouquet, then you need to truly understand one simple concept:

Getting married is the easy part. *Being* married is the hard part.

Until you see the importance of *being* the right kind of person to your spouse, your relationship will suffer and starve. *Being* married means you are the kind of person you need to be to effectively feed your partner and meet her needs and wants. *Being* married means you are exercising enough character in your relationship to know how to satisfy and fulfill the 7 Basic Needs of your partner:

- Being a **S**afe partner (physically, socially, emotionally, spiritually, mentally, financially)
- Being a **T**rustworthy and trusting partner
- Being an **A**ppreciative partner
- Being a **R**espectful and respectable partner
- Being a **V**alidating partner

- Being an **E**ncouraging partner
- Being a **D**edicated partner

Remember, by definition, love is really no more than the seven needs you just read. Because the opposite of being STARVED is being loved, when these seven needs are met, we feel loved.

Being married means being willing to meet these needs regardless of your own mood or circumstances. *Being* married is living up to your commitment when the emotions of your commitment no longer drive you. You choose to stay committed when the commitment is most strained, just as the vows state, "through thick and through thin, in sickness and in health."

A wonderful quote by clergyman and newpaperman Jenkins Lloyd Jones (b. 1843) effectively sums this up:

> *There seems to be a superstition among many thousands of our young [men and women] who hold hands and smooch in the drive-ins that relationship is a cottage surrounded by perpetual hollyhocks to which a perpetually young and handsome husband comes home to a perpetually young and [beautiful] wife. When the hollyhocks wither and boredom and bills appear, the divorce courts are jammed.*
>
> . . .
>
> *Anyone who imagines that bliss [in marriage] is normal is going to waste a lot of time running around shouting that he has been robbed.*
>
> *[The fact is] most putts don't drop. Most beef is tough. Most children grow up to be just people. Most successful marriages require a high degree of mutual toleration. Most jobs are more often dull than otherwise. . . .*
>
> *Life is like an old-time rail journey—delays, sidetracks, smoke, dust, cinders, and jolts, interspersed only occasionally by beautiful*

vistas and thrilling bursts of speed.
The trick is to thank the Lord for letting you have the ride.
(Jenkins Lloyd Jones, qtd. in *Deseret News,* 12 June 1973, p. A4)

Being married is the ability to stay the course and stick to your commitment when times get tough in your relationship. It isn't about waiting for your partner to become the perfect partner as much as it is about your working on being the best partner you can be. *Being* married is also finding a way to enjoy the journey, even though it isn't perfect. And guess what? If you thought your partner was perfect when you were first dating, you must have overlooked a lot of things while filled with all of those yearning chemicals.

When couples come into my office and one is seriously tired of not being fed by the other, even to the point of giving up, I ask the STARVED partner one simple question. "Are you doing everything in your power to serve and feed your partner—to love her unconditionally, to positively interpret her actions, to take the High Road, to see what she is doing well, to communicate effectively your desires, and to stay committed with all of your heart, might, mind, and strength? Are you *being* the best partner you can be or are there things you aren't doing as well?"

Almost always, I'm told that they are not being the best partners they can be. They generally have specific things they can work on. Then, the other partner quickly starts talking about how the accusing partner isn't feeding them either. This happens because quite often, because when you are STARVED you don't want to improve yourself as a partner. You perhaps don't realize that by changing yourself, you will change the relationship. Instead, you want to change the relationship by changing your partner first, but you will never have as much power to change another person as you do to change yourself. This is actually a fairly typical approach for people who would rather have someone to blame than to get actual results. If both partners spent more time working on the things they knew they needed to, or the things about which their partner complains, they would see change in their relationships.

You choose whether to feed or starve those you love. But remember, you only have the power to change what *you are* doing or who *you are* in your relationship. I am one hundred percent confident that the fastest way to create a healthy relationship is to be a healthy partner.

Four Keys to Pouring the Love Your Partner Needs

Pouring love to your partner may come very naturally, or you may find that you have some difficulties giving your partner the love she wants and needs. If Pouring doesn't come very naturally to you, four suggestions might help you be successful. These suggestions are relationship tools you can use to have more love in your relationship. They should be customized to meet the specific needs of your relationship. If they are not, they will feel like just techniques or tricks, and not real life solutions that work for both of you.

Whenever I coach my clients, I constantly push them to "own" the rules and make them apply to their behaviors. The following four "feeding tools" are great ways to pour the love your partner wants:

- Learning Your Partner's Loving Style
- Cuddle Time
- Offering a Daily Special
- Creating Loving Rituals

Learning Your Partner's Loving Style

As mentioned in the preface of this book, I often find that each person and each couple I coach is as different as each snowflake that falls from the sky. This fact leads me to one of the biggest causes of starvation in relationships. The problem is not that we are all different. The fact that we are all different is the most universal truth about relationships. The problem is that we think that we are less different than we actually are! Our ignorance and the above-mentioned fact are the number one reasons why so many couples end up in the STARVED Spiral.

One of the biggest differences I've noticed about people is that we all like to learn differently. Experts in the field of learning agree that there are numerous ways of learning and understanding the world around us and that every person possesses a different learning style. For example, some people are very visual when it comes to learning and need to see something in order to learn it. Books, materials and PowerPoint's are very helpful for this type of learner. Others are auditory learners and need only to hear a new idea a few times in order to learn the concept. In this case, audio sets or lectures might do the trick. Others are kinesthetic learners and need to be actively and physically walking through something in order to connect to the concept. This type of person might play games or participate in physical activities to help the point sink in. Kinesthetic learners are "hands-on" learners, needing to touch, interact, and feel in order to understand a new idea. In my work, where I blend both learning theories and couples coaching, I've found that just as people learn differently through various senses, so too do they love and feel loved differently, probably through these same dominant learning traits.

Feeling loved from someone else is nothing more than a learning exercise. People need to learn, or come to believe, they are Safe, Trusted, Appreciated, Respected, Validated, Encouraged, and that people are Dedicated to them. So what better way to access this knowledge than through their learning style or what I call their Loving Style?

Take a quick look at your own relationship. Do the two of you want to be loved the exact same way, or do you see your differing needs and ways of accessing love? For example, one may feel more loved when she is intimate with the spouse, while the other feels more loved when the spouse makes him a good dinner. One may want to go on walks, holding hands, while the other feels most appreciated when her partner sits down and has a connected conversation. One of the most powerful ways to improve your relationship is to understand these differences and begin to learn to *communicate love in your partner's way.*

Let's explore four Loving Styles. As you review these, try to figure out how you would rank the four areas for yourself and your partner.

Touchers

Touchers need to be touched to feel loved. They use their bodies and hands as the main access point for their transfer of love. Touchers are not just sexually charged, but they touch because this is their way of showing they love you.

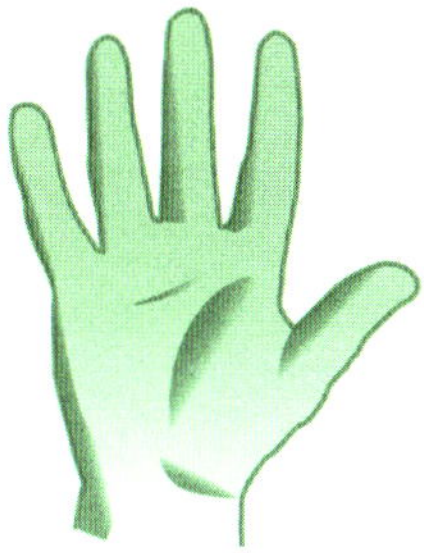

What Feeds—Initiating touch through hand-holding, kissing, hugs, caressing, cuddling, back rubs, sitting close, tickling, sex, high fives, touching as you pass.

What Starves—Avoiding each other, different bedtimes, cold shoulder, making intimacy a chore, weak hugs, lack of initiation of sex, not reaching out.

Hearers

Hearers access love through their ears. Hearers are very sensitive to tones and negativity. Words really matter to these people. Hearers are usually more talkative and tend to express their love verbally more than other Loving Styles.

What Feeds—Using positive words, complimenting, affirming, saying thank you, asking about your partner's day, sharing feelings, saying things like "I love you," or "You look hot!"
What Starves—Put-downs, raised voice, negative words, name-calling, sarcasm, questioning your partner's ability, coercive tactics, complaining, and aggressive language.

See-ers

Seers access love through their eyes. They feel love based on what they see going on around them. Seers don't really believe anything they don't see. For them, actions speak louder than words and talk is seen as cheap!

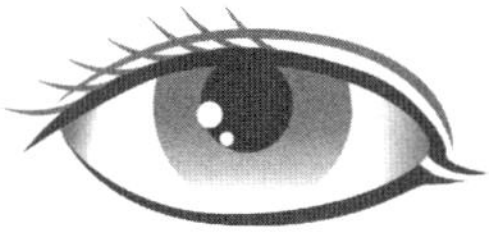

What Feeds—Service, action, making dinners, gifts, housework, helping, organizing, calling babysitters, planning the date, writing emails, letters, notes.
What Starves—Being lazy, not finishing tasks/chores, dirty house, clutter, not helping around the house, being unmotivated, complacency, not making enough effort, being unproductive, wasting time.

Sensers

Sensers are intuitive lovers. They sense if you're really into them or not. They usually gauge their love on intangibles like your time, focus, attention, energy and presence. They feel loved just knowing you are really with them or present in the moment and connected.

What Feeds—Taking time off, being a homebody, being "present," being early, maintaining eye contact, paying attention,

having positive energy, making time together.
What Starves—Ignoring your partner, inattentiveness, multitasking instead of paying attention to them, being preoccupied, no downtime, never home, avoiding your partner, being too busy, disconnected, unfocused.

Now, perform the following exercise to see exactly how you and your partner rank each of these four areas:

Instructions

1. Put your names in the appropriate place at the top of the assessment.
2. Under your partner's name, rank your guesses about your partner's Loving Styles from their favorite (1) to least favorite (4) and write your answers in the corresponding boxes.
3. Have your partner record his or her guesses in the column under your name.
4. Now have your partner write his or her actual ranking from 1–4 in the column under his or her name.
5. Complete this activity by doing the same thing in the column under your name.
6. Once you have finished, compare the results. Circle any differences of more than two points. For example, if your #1 Loving Style is third or fourth on your partner's list, circle it.
7. Spend some time discussing what you learned about each other.

Woman			Man		
	His Guess	Her Ranking	His Ranking	Her Guess	
Touchers: Holding hands, hugs, kisses, sex					**Touchers:** Holding hands, hugs, kisses, sex
Hearers: Positive words, compliments, "I love you's"					**Hearers:** Positive words, compliments, "I love you's"
Seers: Service, gifts, notes, emails, housecleaning					**Seers:** Service, gifts, notes, emails, housecleaning
Sensers: Attention, focus, time and presence					**Sensers:** Attention, focus, time and presence

Interestingly enough, only 15 percent of my clients have the same Loving Style, which I find ironic because remember when the yearning stage was filled with all of the Loving Styles? Just remember that gaps arc absolutely normal, so don't be alarmed if your scores had some gaps where your number 1 was his number 3 or 4, or vice versa. Being different isn't the problem. Now, take a quick look down the columns where you guessed your partner's Loving Style. Were your guesses pretty close to his or her answers? If not, you've been working on some pretty bad assumptions lately that could be the cause of some problems.

If you see a big difference in your answers and your partner's answers, this might tell you a lot about how little you actually understand one another. Many times relationship pain comes when we have high expectations that something is going to happen and then nothing does. Usually the gap between expectations and delivery needs to be dealt with and, as long as the two of you are misaligned, you're going to keep feeling pain in your relationship. This is when you begin to feel STARVED. Understanding your partner's Loving Style can create a lot of new opportunities to pour the love your partner wants, as well as give you a better understanding as to why your partner might not naturally love you the way you want to be loved.

Again, just as we all have different or more preferred ways of learning in our lives, so too do we all have different ways or preferred ways of loving. If you assume you both love the same way, then you're going to choose to love your partner the way you want to be loved. Based on the numbers you posted above, this might create problems for both of you. By not learning and adapting to how you both like to be loved, not only will this ensure you are going to starve your partner, you are also ensuring you're not going to be looking for what your partner is doing to love you your way.

Making a Difference with Our Differences

When it comes to Loving Styles, a person would be hard-pressed to find two people more different than my wife and me! My Loving Style tends to be more through hearing and touching while my wife Mardi's style is found in seeing and sensing. Over the years these differences have sometimes been exaggerated. When these differences were not understood and we were both expecting each other to love the same way, factors such as expectations created some pretty damaging effects to our relationship. Now that we understand our individual Loving Styles, a lot of the love Mardi gives me is now noticed and felt. Before we understood each other's Loving Style, Mardi would always make me great meals and make sure we always had dinnertime as a family. She loves giving me presents for my birthday or Christmas. She makes sure we go on trips together, whether with the family or alone. She gets me involved in the family and, when I'm gaining weight or looking frumpy, she's quick to help me improve. Before, I was waiting to be loved my way with more touch and words and now that I understand how she works, I can give her more credit.

When we build, let us think that we build forever.
—John Ruskin

Now remember, I sense love in a completely different way from Mardi—through touching and talking. Even though I love a good meal and a clean house and family vacations, these things didn't make me feel loved in the way Mardi intended. Because of this, in the past, she never got credit for all of the work she was doing.

I personally prefer to *hear* that I'm loved. I love to hear positive words from my wife, like affirmations and compliments. I love to "hear" the love of my wife! Because I am a hearer, I was the first person to say "I love you" to her when we were dating. I'll never forget that day because it was the first time I ever noticed that Mardi and I had different Loving Styles. I looked deep into her eyes, then nervously said, "I love you," and just by saying this, I felt it even deeper. A quiet moment followed, and then she didn't say anything. There was just a long quiet pause. Then, she just smiled and said nothing. I swear I actually heard crickets chirping in the background. "Huh?" I thought to myself. This was definitely not going the way I had mentally planned, and I was devastated! Why couldn't she just say it back? Later I found out that words just weren't her way of expressing how she felt. Instead, she made me homemade doughnuts and wrote me a letter in which she eventually expressed the same feelings. I used words—she used doughnuts. That's how not recognizing the differences can sometimes starve us.

Knowing that my wife needs to "see" me loving her has put an entirely different slant on how I show my love to her. For example, as you can imagine with six kids, we have a ton of housework to get done every day just to keep our heads above water. Mardi, who is an amazing mom and partner, usually has most of it done by the time I get home every evening, so I made a deal with her to leave all of the dishes in the sink for me to take care of when I get home. She knows that I don't do this because I *like* to! And, it's not even because they just need to be done. If it were up to me, I would just use paper plates that we could throw away when we're done! However, that just doesn't "look" right to Mardi. So every night—well *almost* every night—when I get home, I do the dishes and whatever else I can to help clean up the house to show my wife how much I love her. Mardi interprets this service as me loving her—her way.

The same is true for how Mardi shows me love. My Loving Style is hearing and touching. I feel most loved when we talk to each other positively, when we compliment each other, and when we hold hands or touch one another. My way of feeling loved is not my wife's way and my wife's way of feeling loved is not my way, and the good news is it's okay! When I come home and do the dishes, usually Mardi will stand around the kitchen and talk to me, making a great effort to connect with me in my way. When I notice her asking me about my day, I see she is trying to feed me and when she sees me vacuuming or changing diapers, she knows I love her. When I bring her home a gift or a treat, she "sees" I'm thinking about her. I am Pouring the love she wants. But if I'm watching TV, the kids are screaming, there's a stinky diaper around, the house is a mess, it's 9 p.m. and all of the children are up, she's not feeling the love. Mardi pours the love I want when she grabs my hand in public or touches my back or smacks my behind when we're crossing in the halls in the house. When this happens, I know I'm loved and I know she's trying.

Your goal with learning the Loving Styles of your partner should be to learn to understand how she feels loved, and then pour that love by finding ways to meet those needs. This newfound understanding of how your partner wants and needs to be loved unleashes an amazing amount of love and goodwill in your relationship. You must learn to not only love your partner the way she wants to be loved, but maybe even more importantly, you need to learn to accept the love your partner gives and start noticing her efforts.

Cuddle Time

One of the best ways I've found to help couples refill their reserves in the relationship, and pour love, is to find time to connect with each other every day, in the style that each person in the relationship prefers. Over the years, I have found there is one activity that can meet all four Loving Styles at once: Cuddle Time! In one half-hour of Cuddle Time per day, you give and receive a 30-minute dose of touching, hearing, seeing, and sensing. In fact, this step is key to keeping a balanced diet of love in your relationship.

That which we persist in doing becomes easier, not that the task itself has become easier, but that our ability to perform it has improved.
—Ralph Waldo Emerson

For many, this is a fairly difficult task because each partner's styles can be so different, or the couple just doesn't have time, or the kids are always around. When helping get couples back into the habit of connecting, I ask them to think of a time in their relationship when they truly felt like they were connecting on a regular basis. One particular time seems to be brought up most often: the old days when they used to cuddle together every night—snuggling, kissing, touching, talking, and holding each other. Even though they may have been running on high chemicals and low clarity during that stage of love, there is still something very important to learn from this.

Now, before either of you start rolling your eyes and running away, let me describe what Cuddle Time is and what it isn't.

Cuddle Time is—

- An opportunity for holding, touching, talking, and connecting
- A chance to talk about positive feelings, memories, hopes, and things you appreciate about each other
- A chance to look into each other's eyes and see a partner who wants to be with you
- Uninterrupted time and space to be present, focused, and attentive to each other

Cuddle Time is not—

- Foreplay, or a grope fest, is not a precursor to sexual intimacy and should not be directly connected to sex. Too many couples have learned not to even touch each other because touch leads to sex. Cuddle Time is where touch is essential and sex is not a question. If you are going to have sex, I believe in adding it—after Cuddle Time is over. This way you know when it's happening.
- A place to talk about kids, family, money, business, schedules, activities, or work, or to deal with conflicts, fights, problems, or carpool schedules.
- Watching television together, although cuddling during activities like this is also recommended.

  Cuddle Time is a wonderful winding down activity when

your partner sees and feels you fully paying attention. Eye-to-eye contact should be a critical part of the connection process. Even though back rubs and massages are great, make sure there is some eye-to-eye contact.

Cuddle Time's Two Hard Fast Rules:

1. **No Groping!**
2. **No Griping!**

Cuddle Time challenge: I challenge you and your partner to take the Cuddle Time challenge and spend the next month going through the following process:

Week 1—10 minutes a night of uninterrupted Cuddle Time
Week 2—15 minutes a night
Week 3—20 minutes a night
Week 4—30 minutes a night

Start slow and begin to build a Loving Ritual of feeding each other every night. See what happens when you commit to loving your partner every single night. If nights don't work, try mornings. Some couples who work opposite shifts have to do this in the middle of the day. Others break it up, half and half, with some time in the morning and some at night. Remember, the practice is Cuddle Time, but the main objective is to show our love by finding some time to love your partner *her way* every day.

Cuddle Time can heal your relationship! In my workshops, I've always joked about the childish things we do to each other when we go to bed angry. Have you ever gone to bed mad at each other, accidentally rubbed your feet up against each other and then quickly pulled your feet away? How dumb is that? I guess you were hoping your partner didn't *notice*? By having Cuddle Time every night, you're really performing a "health check-up" on your relationship that forces you to evaluate the condition of your relationship. If you agree right now that no matter what mood you're in or what arguments you've had that night, you will always have Cuddle Time, you are committing to something bigger than either of you. You're committing to your relationship working, regardless of your mood or emotion.

It is better to sleep on things beforehand than
lie awake about them afterward.
—Baltasar Gracian

I'm not saying you should never go to bed angry, because quite honestly, I believe that sometimes a good night's sleep takes a lot of energy out of what seemed like a big problem the night before. What I am saying, however, is that even when you don't feel like holding each other and cuddling, you agree to do this because you've made a commitment to do so. In essence, Cuddle Time is a Choice Point to start feeding your relationship every day because cuddling, even when you don't want to, strengthens your resolve to exercise character in your relationship. Sometimes you may not feel like being married, but the habit or desire should be there to honor the commitments and behaviors you both believe in, regardless of what you're feeling. Test this out for one month and see what impact this has on your relationship. I promise, you will see some powerful results. I have seen this one activity reconnect relationships more than any other activity I suggest.

Offering a Daily Special

Now that you know your partner's Loving Style, I want you to put your new information to work by intentionally finding a creative way to pour love and feed your partner every single day. This should be something you've uniquely created just for her, just for that day. I call this important offering your "Daily Special." Have you ever been to a restaurant where they had a Daily Special? At a restaurant, the chef chooses a Daily Special to add variety to the menu, test new items, and draw people in. Or, it could simply be because the "special" is a favorite of the chef.

One of the fastest ways to begin feeding the STARVED relationship is to start offering your partner a Daily Special. The Daily Special is created by walking through three partner-focused steps every day which will ensure the constant feeding, creativity, and connectivity in your relationship.

For many, the need to do the Daily Special will seem obvious. The problem is actually creating the time to do it. Imagine the impact on your relationship if you found five minutes a day to focus uninterrupted, positive thoughts toward your partner. Imagine how much more powerful it would be if you actually acted upon these thoughts. The habit of doing a Daily Special for your partner can have a profound effect on your relationship.

One way I've found works well is to create the Daily Special while you're doing one of your daily routines. For example, you might create your Daily Special while in the shower every morning, or on your daily jog, or during your drive to work. The obvious goal is to come up with something you can offer to your partner that shows your partner you are thinking about her. I feel confident that if you practice offering the Daily Special for the next two months, you'll begin creating a habit of Pouring love and feeding your partner the love she wants, just as you did when the two of you were dating.

3 Steps to the Daily Special

In order to offer the Daily Special, you need to follow three very simple steps:

1. Connect to your spouse's needs.
2. Ask the Loving Question.
3. Deliver the Daily Special and learn.

Let's look at each step in more detail. The following are some specific things to look for and questions you can ask yourself as you prepare your Daily Special:

1. Connect to your partner's needs, Loving Style, and STARVED Stuff.
    a. Needs: What does his or her day look like today? Is it likely to be hectic and overly stressful? What is his or her schedule like today? What kind of mood is he or she in today?
    b. Loving Style: Does he or she feel most loved by hearing, touching, seeing, or sensing? Remember, this isn't about you, but about your partner and how he or she likes to be loved.
    c. STARVED Stuff: What does he or she need most: Safety, Trust, Appreciation, Respect, Validation, Encouragement, or Dedication?

2. Ask yourself the loving question: "What is the most important thing I can do today to love my partner his or her way?" Again, remember to think of this from your partner's perspective, not yours.

3. Deliver the Daily Special and learn: Offer your Daily Special to your spouse, then watch how your spouse responds. If you are the receiver, receive what your partner gives with the spirit in which his or her offering was given. This is a *learning* process for both of you. Neither one of you may hit it right on the mark each time, but as long as you learn and grow together, you are on the right track.

Examples of Daily Specials

For Touchers:

- Gently stroke a sensitive place without leading to sex.
- Give a foot massage or back rub.
- Hold hands while walking together in public.
- Sit on the same side of the booth, rather than across from each other, when you go out to eat.

For Hearers:

- Leave a loving voice mail.
- Say "I love you" without expecting a response in return.
- Express verbal appreciation.
- Share a happy memory together.
- Have a chat about something important to your partner.

For Seers:

- Fill up your partner's car with gas.
- Surprise him with a favorite lunch or dinner.
- Leave a note in her car, planner, pocket, lunch box, or purse.
- Buy a favorite treat and leave it in the car so he will find it in the morning.
- Clean a part of the house.

For Sensers:

- Notice when your partner has a unique need or desire, and then do something about it.
- Give your complete attention to your partner.
- Pick up on a mood without having to be told.
- Take the afternoon off and spend time together.
- Go on a walk together.
- Give lots of eye-to-eye time.

Delivering the Daily Special could easily become mundane and part of the "same old, same old," so add some spontaneity and variety and keep things fresh. Think outside the box, so to speak. No one wants chicken noodle soup every day; add in a spicy taco, some warm Apple Crisp, or creamy hot cocoa once in awhile. Be creative and come up with new things that will surprise and delight your partner. The more thought and effort you put into it, the more meaningful this will become for both of you.

As one who tends to travel a lot, delivering speeches and workshops around the country, I'm not home as much as I used to be in the past, so I've needed to find more creative ways to offer my partner the Daily Special. An excellent example of someone going out of her way to pour love and serve the Daily Special was when Mardi found a way to celebrate my birthday with me while I was three states away. I was on a trip teaching a workshop in Carlsbad, New Mexico, alone in my hotel room after a difficult day. I remember getting a call from my wife and talking with her on the phone for a few moments. She wished me Happy Birthday and had the entire family around the phone so they could all wish me a Happy Birthday, too. At the same time, I heard a knock on my door and while still talking to her, I answered the door. Standing there was a couple of the housekeeping staff with a card and a small Hostess cupcake from the vending machine. A match was stuck into it that was quickly burning out. The housekeepers began singing along with my family on the phone.

It could not have been better choreographed. My wife had somehow put together a plan to serve me a Daily Special hundreds of miles away from my house. She had contacted the hotel—which was really more of a motel than a hotel—and had somehow talked the staff into finding me a card, a cake, a candle, and then coming to my room to sing Happy Birthday to me, which by the looks on the two housekeepers' faces was something neither of them were excited to do or had done very often for their guests! The long and the short of this is, that night I knew my wife loved me and she couldn't have picked a better way to serve me when I was away on my birthday than to let me "hear" the voice of my family on my special day.

When I give, I give myself.
—Walt Whitman

Your goal with the Daily Special is not to overcomplicate your life or add more "to do's" to your list. The purpose of the Daily Special is to make your partner feel "special" daily. These specials should be delivered with a simple and loving feeling and should reinforce your love for your partner. As these add up over time, they will create a bigger and bigger menu of loving acts you and your partner perform for each other. With time, you will create a menu so abundant and fulfilling that your partner will never have to look elsewhere to be fed.

Loving Rituals

When I was little, I had a long-term relationship with a very loving friend named Buddy. Buddy was a Maltese poodle who taught me one of the most important lessons I have ever learned about relationships: the importance of consistency. Because my parents were divorced, I was a latchkey kid. When I was old enough to stay by myself, I would come home from school and have a lot of time alone waiting for my sisters to get home, or my mom to come home from work. During that time, my best friend, Buddy, was always there. The two of us shared a lot of wonderful traditions that helped us both have fun and feel loved.

Without fail, when I came home, I would go to the backdoor and Buddy would be there to lovingly greet me. Every single day it was the same ritual of him yelping while I tried to unlock the door. Then we'd see each other and connect right on the floor by the backdoor. He would seem so excited that his front lips would actually curl up like he was smiling. He would then lick me and run around in circles and I would sit down and hug and kiss him. After we greeted, I would then deliver Buddy's favorite tradition, which was to have me put peanut butter on the roof of his mouth and then I would watch as he would try for about five minutes to lick it all off. We did that every day for years. I always knew he would be there and he always knew he'd get peanut butter. Even if we had a falling out before I went to school, Buddy would be there when I got home.

Buddy had other rituals with other family members too. Whenever my mom would play the piano, Buddy would sit by her side, howling out a tune. If she started to play the piano without him, he would sprint from wherever he was in the house and come to the side of the piano, howling on the run. My sisters also had a ritual with Buddy. Every time they wore pink fuzzy slippers, Buddy thought each one was a furry girlfriend and he would begin attacking my sister's feet. Each of these traditions brought us closer together and each tradition made our relationship feel safer and more predictable. There is a reason a dog is considered man's best friend: consistency and ritualistic behavior.

To keep the lamp burning we have to keep putting oil in it.
—Mother Teresa

Many of the things we cherish most in our lives are the Loving Rituals we had growing up as children. There are also many traditions or rituals we experience in our lives and each has distinct and special meaning. Many of them are sacred for various reasons. For this reason, they are not to be messed with. For example, we have all experienced the patriotic traditions that surround our flag. When we're in a public setting and the flag is being presented, we all tend to stand, place our hands over our hearts, and sing the national anthem. Everyone knows what flag ceremonies look like because we've been through them. They become predictable experiences that unite us in pursuit of a common goal. In the case of the Pledge of Allegiance, unification and patriotism are usually the result. Just as we have traditions around patriotism, we also have religious traditions or rituals that happen every time we attend church, as well as traffic rituals like waving to thank the person who let us merge in front of him or her on the road.

Just as it is important to have all of these traditions in our lives, it is equally important to create Loving Rituals in our own relationships to ensure that we will habitually find time to both pour love consistently for our partner and to ensure our partner sees the love we've actually been sending.

It is one of the most beautiful compensations of life that no man can sincerely try to help another without helping himself.
—Ralph Waldo Emerson

Relationship experts and family researchers have found great importance in creating rituals in relationships. Loving Rituals set up consistent times to be loved by a partner and these become healing moments. These are the habitual times we spend feeding our spouse. Loving Rituals are beneficial because they are profound feeders of the STARVED relationship and ensure the feeding will be pleasurable, permanent, and a priority. Like the food pyramid, we need to make sure we get a balanced diet of love in our relationship, that our Recommended Daily Allowance of love is always met.

You might be thinking that Loving rituals and Daily Specials sound similar, but there is a difference. Loving Rituals are permanent fixtures in healthy and enduring relationships. They take place the exact same way, every single day, every single week, every single month, and every single year for the rest of your relationship. Daily

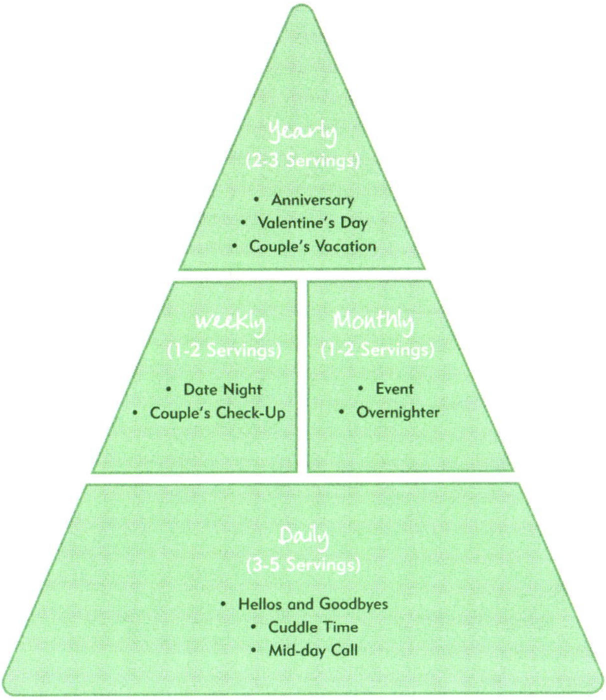

Specials however, will change every day and, at times, might not even always be noticed or fully recognized.

Some examples of Loving Rituals:

- Waking up together and cuddling in the morning before you get up
- Hello and good-bye kisses
- An afternoon phone call or text message
- A welcome home hug and kiss
- Cuddling on the couch while watching the late night news
- Reading the Bible or other books together
- Date nights every week
- Anniversary trips every year
- Inside jokes or nicknames

Benefits of Loving Rituals

There are many benefits to Loving Rituals, but in our most personal and intimate relationships, one of the greatest benefits of traditions are that they act as a barometer of where our relationship stands. In my own relationship with my wife, when I see that traditions or rituals aren't being delivered, I worry about the health of our relationship. I recognize that we are not Pouring love like we need to in order to have a healthy relationship.

Mardi and I have a ritual where if either of us catches our partner's stomach growling, we will ask the other out loud, "What did you say?" and the other person is supposed to answer, "You heard me." And then we usually laugh to ourselves a bit. I know it's a dumb thing, but we've been doing it for more than 20 years and it matters to us and only us. That's what is so powerful about Loving Rituals. We all have them! In fact, we've forged them over years of living together, and in many cases, they're our fondest memories of the relationship. At times these moments feel sacred because only we share them. However, on the occasions where tension exists between Mardi and me, or we've been fighting, I have noticed that one or the other of us won't respond with the typical, "What did you say?"

When rituals thrive, the relationship tends to thrive as well. To have a healthy relationship, each of us needs to not only eat the right food—like the Daily Special, but we must also eat the right food *consistently*. This is the purpose of Loving Rituals.

Get Your Recommended Daily Allowance

Marriage is like vitamins: we supplement
each other's minimum daily requirements.
—Kathy Mohnke

As important as the food pyramid is to your physical health, the Loving Rituals pyramid is just as important to your relationship health. In order to have a balanced diet, I suggest you have three to five daily servings of Loving Rituals, with one to two weekly and monthly servings, and two to three annual servings of love.

I had a couple I worked with who would wake up every morning and say, "Good morning." Then they would get up and get ready. I have other clients who get up every morning and pray together. I have clients who don't go to bed until they hold hands. The ideas for Loving Rituals are endless!

Fill in some of your own ideas for your Loving Rituals pyramid and then share them with your partner.

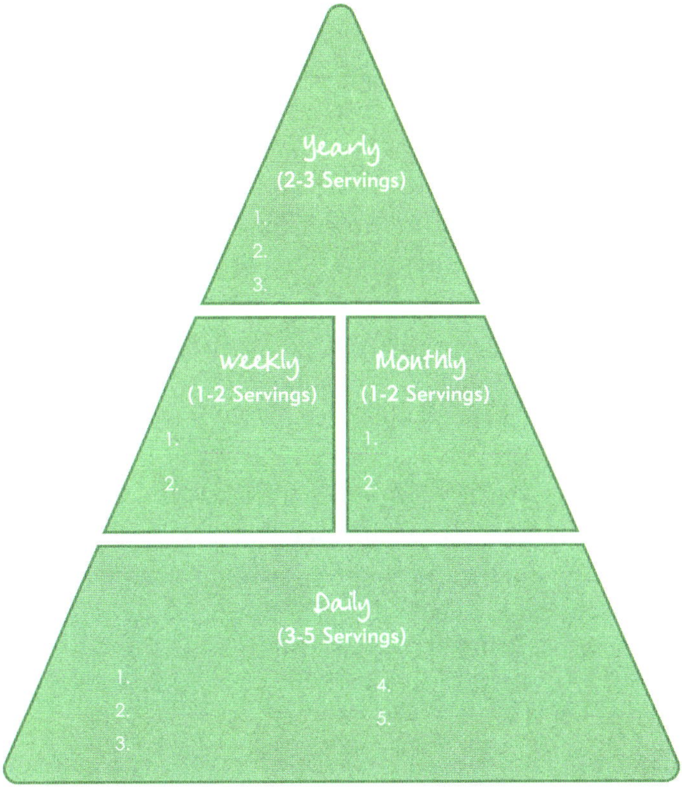

One of the fastest ways to figure out Loving Rituals is to think back to the early days of your relationship and see if there weren't some things you used to do for each other that made a big difference every day. It's never too late to start Loving Rituals. You just have to find a way to make formal what you're already doing casually in your relationship. Don't wait because you may find that Loving Rituals are what you'll miss most when your partner is no longer around.

Loving Rituals Tie Us to Our Partner

Remember back to the first chapter of this book when the three stages of love were discussed and how my grandfather-in-law reached the level of Enduring Love with his wife? One of the things he missed most when she passed away was their Loving Ritual of cuddling in bed every night. A week after the death of Margaret, one of the most comforting things he recounted was how he "could still feel her presence" when he was alone in bed. The power of rituals gives us hope when life is difficult.

What's great about these traditions is that when you get in a fight and have a ritual you both have exercised often, a moment of choice appears. Are you going to choose to keep the tradition alive or are you going to choose to be right? This Choice Point gives you the chance to reboot your love multiple times a day and to create a healthy and lasting relationship. There is nothing more important than Pouring love through a consistent diet of loving connections. Most couples can clearly see how they have let their relationship get to a point of starvation. The reality of creating a healthy relationship is not just improving the communication and reaction problems that exist, but at some point also learning to pour love and to feed the relationship what it needs to survive and thrive.

Loving Is about "Creating Ties"

The numerous ways you can actually pour more love into the life of your relationship has been reviewed. The fact that relationships are about Pouring the love your partner needs, not just the love that's easy for you to pour, has also been explored. We've covered many tools that can be used to love a partner the way she wants to be loved, by learning her Loving Styles. We reviewed the rules of Cuddle Time and the importance of delivering a "Daily Special" for your partner—some little act of love or kindness customized to their needs that day. We've also talked about the importance of the Loving Rituals that create a steady and consistent diet of love that feed the relationship and ensure you're getting all of the nutrients you need to sustain you through the tests of life.

All of these ideas remind me of a chapter in the book *The Little Prince* by St. Exupery. There is a wonderful lesson taught about the power of serving your partner, or as he called it, "Creating Ties." In the book, the Little Prince is a tiny man who rules over a tiny planet up in the heavens. The Prince lived on his planet with a lone rose that he spent much of his time nurturing and serving and listening to as it complained about things. Eventually he became bored with his life and left his planet to explore the other planets. He wanted to see what they had to offer him. He eventually found his way down to Earth, where he saw many of the beauties this earth had to offer, like expansive rows of rose bushes that overwhelmed his senses with their beauty and at times made him forget the one rose he so faithfully served back on his home planet. When the Little Prince was about to return home to his planet, he learned a very important lesson from a fox he had befriended. The lesson was about the difference between his rose that he left back home and the other flowers found here on the earth. The lesson he learned was so important that he wanted to go visit the beautiful rose bushes that swept him off of his feet when he arrived to earth and convey to them his newest learning. This is what he taught them:

He told them, "You're not like my rose. You're nothing like it at all. . . . You're the way my fox was. He was just a fox like a hundred of thousands of others. But I've made him my friend and now he's the only fox in the world that I know."
And the roses were humbled.
"Roses, you're lovely but you're empty." And he went on. "One couldn't die for you. Of course, an ordinary passerby might think that my rose looked just like yours, but my rose, all on her own, is more important than all of you together. Since she's the rose that I've watered. Since she's the one that I put under glass. Since she's the one that I sheltered behind the screen. Since she's the one for whom I killed the caterpillars. Since she's the one I listened to when she complained or when she boasted or even sometimes when she said nothing at all. Since she's my rose."

One of the most powerful lessons about loving, serving and Pouring for our partner is the power our Pouring has to help us fall in love. There will always be more beautiful partners, who, at first glance, under the fog of our more superficial Yearning Love, we might be enamored with, but remember as was discussed in the beginning of this chapter, the goal should not just be to have the right partner, but maybe, more importantly, to focus on being the right partner. Being the right partner is just as the Little Prince learned. The only thing that truly matters is our ability to make our partner feel Safety, Trust, Appreciation, Respect, Validation, Encouragement, and our Dedication. The more we love our partner through the Loving Styles, Cuddle Time, "Daily Special," and Loving Rituals, the more this love will tie us to that person and the more love we will feel for our mate.

Chapter Review:

- Pouring love into the relationship happens when giving love to a partner. It is all about open communication and Mutual Goals.
- There is a difference between getting the right partner and being the right partner. Being the right partner is the ability to stick to the commitment when relationship times get tough.
- Understanding the four Loving Styles helps identify unique ways of feeling loved as well as how best to express love.
- The best way to pour love into the relationship is to find a time every day to connect. Cuddle Time can fill that need and will satisfy all four Loving Styles.
- The "Daily Special" is a creative way to pour love every single day. Knowing what to offer for the "Daily Special" comes from asking, "What is the most important thing I can do today to love my partner his or her way?"
- Loving Rituals provide set times and events weekly, monthly, and yearly to pour love into the relationship. Loving Rituals are profound feeders of the STARVED relationship because they ensure consistent feeding.

My Feeding Plan

In order to create a healthy diet that feeds your relationship, you need to have a plan. Use the "My Feeding Plan" activity to come up with some specific ideas from the last chapter that you can use to improve the health of your relationship.

Commitment to Keep Learning

What is the most important thing you learned in this chapter that, if lived consistently, would positively impact your relationship?

____

____

____

____

____

Commitment to Keep Changing

Based on what you have learned, what will you commit to change in your life?

Specifically, how will you do it?

Specifically, when will you do it?

The Course on Commitment

Building Mutual Growth

Chapter 15

The Commitment to Learn and Change

So far, in **The Solutions** section of this book, we have learned about three of the Four Courses that feed healthy and enduring relationships, namely the courses on Character, Communication, and Companionship. The final course we will cover is the course on Commitment. The course on Commitment is really the course that ties the rest of the courses together. One would naturally expect the topic of commitment to come up in a book on relationships. However, the commitment we're talking about here might be a little different than the one you're used to.

Many couples view the topic of commitment simply as living up to the promise they made at the altar to always "love, honor, and cherish . . . until death do you part." I hope that after reading the previous chapters in this book, you can see the obvious importance of loving, honoring, and cherishing your partner to help ensure your partner never feels STARVED within the relationship. To me, this kind of commitment is invaluable when it comes to the long-term health of your relationship. For the remainder of the book, two more commitments will be presented that can make an even bigger difference than almost any other commitment you have made so far in your relationship. These two commitments are hardly, if ever, mentioned by any officiator at a wedding ceremony or by any partners who proclaim their love to one another.

- The commitment to keep learning
- The commitment to keep changing

For me, the commitments to keep learning and changing are maybe even more important to a healthy and enduring relationship than virtually anything else we commit ourself to, because how else do we create a healthy and enduring relationship without continuous improvement?

As discussed at the beginning of this book, during the yearning stage of love it is difficult to really know our partner because we are both so caught up in the drive to be together and the yearning chemicals toward each other. Yearning sometimes overrides our best screening processes for recognizing a healthy relationship. This is why character and commitment are vital to a relationship. Once the chemicals and drive wear off, it is our character to act on our promises and our commitment to keep learning and changing that ensures we will stay in the game with our partner and keep earning the love we desire.

Learning and changing ensure growth and improvement, which is the foundation for the hope we desire to have in life and our relationships. Hope in life comes when we see that we are capable, or will soon be capable, to handle all of the various changes life will throw at us.

Having commitment in a relationship is not just a blind promise, or a silver bullet, or a magic potion. It doesn't guarantee success, but it does increase the likelihood of success. Commitment means we're not going to keep living our relationship on autopilot; we're going to become intentional about making it better, and we will commit to learning and changing in order to be healthier and more effective together. Henry David Thoreau describes this form of commitment perfectly:

> *I know of no more encouraging fact than the unquestioned ability of a man to elevate his life by conscious endeavor.*

The key to Thoreau's quote is two words: conscious and endeavor. The word *conscious* means mentally awake or intentional, and *endeavor* means to try or attempt. According to Thoreau, one's ability to elevate one's life—and I would add relationships—is always possible, but the elevation won't take place without an intentional or conscientious attempt. We have to *want* the elevation to take place.

We have to want it to be better and improve. Improved relationships won't take place unconsciously or accidentally. A healthy, whole, fulfilling, long-term relationship is inevitably a choice and, in a lasting relationship, this must be a *mutual* choice. Part of the commitment I am hoping you will begin to make is to improve your relationship through "conscious endeavor."

The Will Paves the Way

When two people are genuinely committed to each other and to the improvement of their relationship, there is nothing they cannot accomplish. As mentioned in the chapter about Holding, the phrase I drill into the hearts and minds of couples who are worried about the future of their relationship is "Where there's a will, there's a way." I believe wholeheartedly in this statement.

Where there is a will, or a commitment, to truly learn to improve a relationship, there is actually a way to make this dream become a reality. Having the "will" is the drive, the purpose that fuels the search for the skills, tools, principles, and methods to improve things, and it paves the way to improvement. As long as we have the will, it's just a matter of time until we find the right answers, and we've got plenty of time because we did take a vow that we're in this "until death do you part," right?

So, in order to discuss the two parts of commitment, I want to go more into depth on both the need to learn and the need to change. Obviously there is an inherent order to the two commitments because you really need to learn before you can change, right? So, for the remaining pages of this chapter, we will learn how to turn on the lights in our relationship, meaning we are going to learn how to really tap into what we need to do to improve our relationship. The final chapter of commitment will be about changing, actually doing what we have learned, so we can really make a difference.

Learning Is about Turning on the Lights

Nothing in life is to be feared, it is only to be understood.
—Marie Curie

During the September 11th terrorist attack on New York City's World Trade Center, I remember hearing stories about people who were trapped in the underground subways or in dark buildings near the site of the attack. The victims, caught in the catastrophe, discussed how disoriented they were, not being able to see through the dust and darkness. They felt hopeless in the dark, unsure of what to do; sure they couldn't stay where they were, yet confused which direction to go because they couldn't "see" any way out. Through trial and error, many eventually discovered that their best friend in that darkness turned out to be their cell phones. Although their phones were useless as telephones because they were inoperable underground, each phone provided a tiny bit of hope for the people in the form of light. Their phones emitted enough light to help them maneuver through their dark, hopeless surroundings and eventually led them to more light, which then led them to daylight. Sometimes even one small cell phone ended up creating enough light for two or three people to follow. Those shaken New Yorkers united around their tiny borrowed light and together made their way out of traumatic darkness.

This is such a powerful metaphor for couples. So many times, couples also end up in traumatic darkness. Afraid, alone, and not sure how much longer they can stay in their relationships, they are just as unsure about which direction to go. They don't want to make a mistake and yet they feel that by doing nothing they are already making a mistake. These same couples often ask me, how much longer do I need to stay with this person? How much more of this do I have to take before I can just move on? My suggestion to them is, before they make any decision to move on, they must first turn on some lights. Here are what I like to refer to as "The Four Lights of Learning" that I think can make all the difference in taking a relationship out of darkness and into the light:

- **Self-awareness:** The ability to see personal strengths and weaknesses and understand the impact these have upon others.
- **Empathy:** The ability to clearly see, feel, and understand the feelings and needs of others.
- **Vision:** The ability to clearly see one's future with all of its potential hopes and dreams.
- **Conscience:** The ability to personally see what is healthy and what is unhealthy in relation to our deepest values, principles, and beliefs.

Each of these lights is a powerful tool that helps us to act more humane. These same lights are what separate humans from the rest of the animal kingdom. To me, they are amazing gifts that possess the unique ability to bring a person out of the deepest darkness in his relationship and into the light of a healthy and enduring relationship. The Four Lights of Learning, when used together, ensure the "brightest and clearest" path for both individual and relationship growth.

Why do these Four Lights play such a powerful role in creating healthy relationships? Simply put, they are the essential conditions of all personal growth and development. I am convinced that before anyone can ever grow or develop their relationship, they must first continually be growing and developing themselves. The Four Lights will always lead us to our partner's STARVED issues, yet they are also the source of understanding ourself, our purpose, others, and truth. You have probably noticed the Four Lights of Learning being turned on throughout the reading of this book:

- **Self-awareness:** Have you noticed you've become more self-aware about the part you play in helping or hindering your relationships?
- **Empathy:** Have you had a greater sense of empathy or feeling for your partner?
- **Vision:** Have you had a clearer vision of what your future can look like and what you want most out of your future with your partner?
- **Conscience:** Has your conscience prompted you to go and practice specific learnings from this book with your partner?

Can you see how all of the growth and development that happens within us comes from these lights and that these lights are what will help us decide the changes we need to make in our life, or whether we are on-course or off-course toward our goals? In other words, we cannot build a lasting, loving, caring, and mutually beneficial relationship in the dark. We must strive to increase the light, or understanding, that we have of ourself and our partner and make use of this light to improve how we relate to one another. These Four Lights will enable us to turn on more light in our life and illuminate the sometimes dark surroundings we experience.

We cannot hold a torch to light another's
path without brightening our own.
—Ben Sweetland

To further emphasize this point; have you ever met people who weren't self-aware? Have you recognized how these people have no idea how they impact their relationships or conversations? Have you ever met those who have no empathy for others or who have no vision for who they are or what they could give back to the world? Have you ever met someone who has no conscience? You've probably run into many people who lack these lights. Most likely, they are people you do not like being around. Their lack of light inevitably starves people, because their ignorance to these Four Lights makes people feel unsafe, mistrusted, unappreciated, disrespected, invalidated, discouraged, and uncommitted.

Turning on the lights is a very personal endeavor. The best way I've ever found to get into the high brain, where the lights all work, is by learning to ask ourself certain questions; questions that will direct us into learning at higher levels, questions that will take us on a journey as to where we need to improve and will teach us how to make these changes. Each of the Four Lights has a different question we can ask ourself that will create more light.

Let's take a deeper look into the Four Lights of Learning and show how we and our partner can use these lights to continue learning and changing in our relationship. Remember, these Four Lights are like muscles that must be exercised or they will shrink. Now, let's start working them out and turn on a few lights!

Self-Awareness

As a visual person, I love cartoons. One of my all-time favorite cartoon artists is Gary Larson, the creator of the Far-Side Collection. Picture a boat floating on the top of the water with the typical funny-looking "Far Side" character standing up in the boat, looking over the side, down into the water. Deep in the water, underneath the boat, is this underachiever's partner, suited up in his diving attire, with his bell helmet firmly connected to a hose that rises to the surface and into the boat with his partner. Looking closer at the cartoon, we can see the diver's face is obviously stressed; his eyes are bulging and something is definitely wrong. Unbeknownst to the ignorant partner, who is clumsily standing in the boat, his feet are on the air hose of his partner, pinching his friend's lifeline. What makes this so amusing is the fact that the clueless partner—all warm and dry—is completely oblivious to the impact he is having on his partner. He doesn't respond, he doesn't move, he just keeps suffocating his partner.

How symbolic is this cartoon when it comes to many of our most important relationships? At some time or another, how many of us pinch off our partners' lifeline, taking from them the much-needed supply of air that fills them up? Sometimes this happens when we're simply too preoccupied to pay attention to one another and one or both of us are left hanging without any hope of catching our breath. Other times, we intentionally "kink the hose" in an effort to hurt one another as badly as we feel we've been hurt. The important thing to remember is: *why* the hose is kinked is irrelevant. The reality is, someone is suffocating and he must get air immediately! Excuses never compensate for a partner's lack of air.

Self-awareness is the ability to gain a clearer understanding of our impact on others—not just our weaknesses, but also our strengths. This is where we begin to learn how we tend to starve others and how we actually starve ourself as well. This is also where we realize and understand our own feelings about being STARVED by others. Self-awareness helps us recognize where we generally react, as well as recognize our deepest pains and fears. To be truly self-aware, we must also know what we do well and where we struggle to be effective. Some questions that might help us become more self-aware arc

- What am I most afraid of?
- Where do I tend to react most often?
- What are my biggest STARVED needs?
- How do I react when I feel STARVED?
- Am I ever the cause of others feeling STARVED?

For many therapists, self-awareness is the most important light a person can illuminate, and so this is where counselors tend to focus much of their attention. However, this can be too much of a good thing. Many people become so focused on the "whys" of their problems that they begin to suffer from "analysis paralysis" and are thus unable to move on because of their imperfections. Another stumbling block to self-awareness is the unwillingness a person may have in seeing the impact he has on his partner, always finding ways to blame the other person for his problems. I see this with couples every day in my office.

One person says something like, "I really just wish you would show me that you care about me more. I don't feel you do."

To which the other person usually responds, "What do you mean I don't show you I care? Don't be silly. You're so needy it makes me sick. I always show you I care! Didn't I spend my whole weekend helping you when you were sick in bed?"

To which the partner responds, "Yeah, you helped me one day in the last year . . . big deal!"

And off they go, arguing, demeaning, ignoring, avoiding, and name-calling while trying to convince the other that they actually do care and do show love for each other.

Self-awareness comes as we learn to quiet our inner dialogue so we can listen and learn from what others are telling us. This can take place only when we put the stories away, lower our defenses, and begin to accept responsibility for our actions and impact on others. Eventually, we will learn our strengths and weaknesses. The opportunity for self-awareness is always going to be there. The only question is whether or not we are going to become self-aware the hard way or the easy way.

Empathy

The Light of Empathy is where we begin to actually feel for

and understand the needs and wants of another person. The word *empathy* comes from the root words "em," which means "within," and "pathos," which means "feelings." *Empathy* then, by definition, means that a person is *within the feelings* of another person. Empathy is different from sympathy, because sympathy means a person has experienced *similar* feelings to what another person feels. For example, if my dog died last year and your dog just recently died, then I can have sympathy for you, because we've had similar feelings about our dogs. Empathy, however, is a higher state of understanding. Because we might lack a similar experience, we are forced to get "into" the other person and understand from his frame of reference. One of the most effective tools to dealing with other human beings is the ability to get into their frame of reference—to get in their shoes and walk a mile in their world. Empathy is the light that allows us to see the STARVED needs of another person. This new light can open up an entire new world with our partner and can give us ideas about how to feed the needs of others.

Don't judge any man until you have walked two moons in his moccasins.
— Indian Proverb

In many regards, current trends in our society seem to run counter to the critical call to empathize with one another. We live in a time of efficiency, fast food establishments, and arenas, where we no longer need to relate with one another. In fact, we don't even have to have a conversation—even with the people who serve our food at restaurants! These days, we place an order by simply giving a number for a combo meal and a "Yes" or "No" if we "want fries with that." Historically, connecting with others was critical to survival, but today it's not uncommon to hear of the death of someone who was completely alone, to the point where no one realized he or she had died until the bills were no longer being paid.

People used to gather at town squares, stores, barbershops, or churches to talk, connect, and bond. Now, instead of connecting face-to-face with friends, many choose to sit alone, surfing the Internet for hours on end. Where we used to access each other's souls through the eyes, now we sit alone for hours chatting online with people we know and don't know, oftentimes purporting to be people we aren't. For ages, we were forced to read the same news and hear the same stories everyone else in the community heard. We used to have to deal with people and try to understand them from their perspective. Now, with so many choices of media and entertainment, we can choose the news we like and bond and cling to the ideas that make us feel most comfortable.

Dr. Stephen Covey once said, "In order to influence someone else, you must first be influenced by them." Think about this for a moment. In order to influence someone else—or, in other words, in order to have power with someone else—we must first receive power from them. This means that in order to influence someone, we must receive *their* permission and *their* insights, so we can know how to influence them. It's as if the other person will tell us the combination to the lock we desire to unlock, but we must first pay attention to them. This means we need to turn off all of the "sending" parts of our brain and turn on all of the "receiving" parts of our brain.

Thousands of candles can be lit from a single candle, and the life of the candle will not be shortened. Happiness never decreases by being shared.
—Buddha

One key to empathy is learning to silence one's self. Silencing ourself is when we suspend all of our thoughts and agendas in order to remain open to our partner's influence—open to what our partner is communicating. Test this out sometime. Just sit and wait to be influenced by your partner before you haul off trying to change them.

You'll be amazed at the impact this can have.

Many times in our relationships, we tend to favor listening to useless noise over awkward silence and then we stop to complain that our relationship lacks depth. How can we expect a relationship to grow when we never really make any space for it? This space may mean we need to find time or the desire to improve the relationship. It may also mean we need to find energy or just more concentration. Most importantly, we need to find silence in our head, where we can be influenced by our partner before we ever try to influence them, as was discussed through the keys of Getting REAL.

Here are some powerful questions we can ask ourself in order to turn on the Light of Empathy and to get into the heart of our partner:

- What is it like to be my partner?
- What would it be like to be in a relationship with me?
- What would it be like to be my best friend?
- What are my partner's needs and wants?
- What are my partner's biggest fears and concerns?
- What is my partner's STARVED Stuff?

Vision

The third light is vision—our vision of our potential, and our future together with our partner. *Vision* is the ability to clearly see our goals, dreams, and potential. The mental creation of goals usually precedes the actual physical completion of these goals. The Light of Vision comes by having a "bigger perspective," or a more complete view of the situation. This vision is invaluable in helping us recognize what is most important in our relationships. Vision helps us prioritize and manage multiple expectations simultaneously. Vision also shows us what a healthy, well-fed relationship actually looks like. Without this vision, feeding the STARVED relationship is not going to happen.

The following are some questions to help us create more vision in our relationship:

- What do we both want most in our relationship?
- What are our biggest goals and dreams together?
- What is the ultimate goal for our relationship?
- If we had a healthy, enduring relationship, what would this look like?

One of the leading causes of divorce is lack of vision. Remember the yearning stage, when you both spent a lot of time dreaming about the future together and talking about these dreams? Often, as years go by, less and less time is spent "creating the vision," with more time spent on being busy, trying to "live" the vision or making the dreams come true. Couples get so caught up running around, working, and living in the moment that sometimes they quit dreaming or imagining a different, brighter future together.

To accomplish great things, we must dream as well as act.
—Anatole France

Many couples have come to me with one partner having completely lost the vision of what their relationship is all about. They have replaced their old vision with a completely new vision, a vision that no longer includes their partner. Many times, couples let their vision settle for the status quo and they stop seeking to create the amazing results their imagination tries to muster.

I learned an excellent example of how our vision evolves and changes after ring shopping with my wife before we got married. Like many couples who choose a diamond ring to symbolize their engagement and marriage, Mardi and I went in search of the perfect diamond on our not-so-perfect budget. To be honest, the process of ring shopping was quite overwhelming. I was overwhelmed by the prices, the sizes, my lack of experience as a gemologist—basically everything about the whole decision. I was ignorant about what was possible and affordable, but I wanted so badly for the ring to show my commitment to my fiancée to symbolize my love for her. At first, all of the rings and the diamonds looked alike. There were big ones, little ones, different cuts and on and on. Soon I realized that no two diamonds really looked alike. There were important features like cut, clarity, and color that I had to understand. After seeing dozens of diamonds, I finally made the decision and bought my soon-to-be wife a beautiful, glowing, relatively small diamond ring. It felt good to have stretched for my loving bride. I really couldn't have imagined anything more beautiful. In fact, in more ways than one, it still remains the most valuable piece of jewelry we own.

Destiny is no matter of chance. It is a matter of choice.
It is not a thing to be waited for, it is a thing to be achieved.
—William Jennings Bryan

After spending all of that time studying diamonds for this big decision, I was now paying much more attention to all of the diamonds people were wearing. I started to notice more and more diamonds on people's hands. I noticed ¾ carat or 1 carat diamonds, some of lesser quality and others of nicer quality. Seeing all these rings blew me away! How could anyone ever afford such a ring? Where did they ever find such big diamonds?

Then one day I heard about the Hope Diamond. The Hope Diamond is kept in the Smithsonian National Museum of Natural History. It is known to be the most perfect blue diamond in the world. This gem weighs in at an amazing 45 ½ carats and is valued as high as a quarter of a billion dollars.

Wow! Before, I thought a ½ carat diamond was a lot, and then I thought the bigger diamonds, like the 1 or 2 carat diamonds were pretty amazing, but I never imagined a gigantic 45 ½ carat diamond! From this I learned that my vision of what a diamond was or could become was seriously limited. Luckily, my wife's view of what a diamond could be was also limited.

So many of our dreams at first seem impossible,
then they seem improbable, and then, when we
summon the will, they soon become inevitable.
—Christopher Reeve

Later, my vision of what a diamond could become was stretched to an even more mind-blowing proportion. This happened while reading a news story about a new discovery in space. Did you know there is a star called BPM 37093, and it is still floating through space even as you read this? BPM 37093 is actually the burnt out core of a sun. After millions of years of life, the sun burns out, leaving nothing but crystallized carbon core, or a diamond. However, this diamond is unlike any other diamond we have ever seen. It is roughly 2,500 miles across and has a carat weight of ten billion, trillion, trillion carats. That's a ten with 34 zeros behind it. Now *that* is one crazy diamond! This diamond measures roughly the width of the United States of America!

I began to think about how my vision of diamonds has changed over the years from that first diamond I purchased to symbolize the love I had for my wife. I don't think the size of a diamond is the great indicator of how much love partners feel for one another, but where I once thought I knew diamonds, I now know there is much more to them than I could ever imagine.

Go confidently in the direction of your dreams.
Live the life you have imagined.
—Henry David Thoreau

I was convinced that if my vision of diamonds was fairly limited, then so was my vision of my relationship. In the beginning, I knew our relationship could be great, but my vision of greatness in a relationship was limited. In the beginning, my vision was a ½ carat vision. I knew my wife and I would have a happy life. We'd have fun and my wife was beautiful and life would be great. Since that time, my vision has expanded to a 45½ carat vision. We have children who are doing well, friends, a wonderful house, neighbors; we've made it together through some tough tests; we share our own language and our own personal set of nonverbal communications; we have traveled the world together; and someday we'll even have grandchildren! My vision of our relationship is bigger than I ever imagined 15 years ago. Then I ask myself, "If all of this adds up to a 45½ carat marriage, then how much more can my relationship become if I stretch my vision to the same level of a diamond that is 2,500 miles across in size? What is the equivalent of having a BPM 37093 relationship? How amazing can my relationship really become?"

What is your vision of how great your relationship can become? Is it a ½ carat relationship? Does it have the hope of the 45½ carat Hope Diamond? Or can it become bigger and better than either of you could ever imagine? What would this look like? I dare you to begin dreaming about it and create your own BPR or "Best Possible Relationship."

I like the saying, "It is better to aim for the stars and drag your feet in the treetops than aim for the treetops and drag your feet in the mud." Use your third Light of Vision to begin imagining the unimaginable about how amazing your relationship can be.

Conscience: What Am I Being Prompted to Do in This Relationship?

The final and most powerful light is the Light of Conscience. Conscience is the light that helps us live up to what we know and believe to be true and good. This is one of the most powerful tools in creating a long-term and mutually beneficial relationship, because this is the most basic motivator of all healthy choices, especially when combined with the other learning lights. This light allows good things to happen, as the conscience is truly the source of all that is good in humanity.

An excellent example of conscience happened when Jim and Jane came into my office. Jim and Jane had completely different styles of interaction. Jim was fairly sensitive and caring and Jane was more bombastic and hardened. As a couple, they had been through a lot of very difficult business situations. They were completely worn down by some of the business decisions made by Jim that resulted in lawsuits and other financial strains. On about their third visit, the two of them were in my office when they again started arguing about his fears and then her fears.

In a heated exchange, Jane began to cry as the STARVED fire began to surface. Where traditionally Jim would have dismissed her, he instead stopped. He got very quiet, reached out, and held Jane's hand. He then showed her how much he understood by paraphrasing back to Jane what he heard her say. She felt understood and they just laughed at each other and the moment went away. A while later I asked Jim what happened. Why did he choose to be silent? Why did he reach out to touch Jane in that moment? His answer was perfect.

"It just felt right. (Conscience) I could sense that she just needed me to touch her and to love her and so I did."(Empathy)

This was Jim's conscience at work. This same conscience is what will drive you to get it right. Conscience is an amazing guide to help you exercise and strengthen your character, if you will just follow the light your conscience gives you.

Another excellent example of how conscience prompts character is the story of King Louis the VIII. This story also shows the power of all of the lights being put together in one situation:

> *King Louis had been taken from his throne and imprisoned. His young son, the prince, was taken by those who dethroned the king. They thought that inasmuch as the king's son was heir to the throne, if they could destroy him morally, he would never realize the great and grand destiny that life had bestowed upon him. They took him to a community far away and there they exposed the lad to every filthy and vile thing that life could offer. They exposed him to foods the richness of which would quickly make him a slave to appetite. They used vile language around him constantly. They exposed him to lewd and lusting women. They exposed him to dishonor and distrust. He was surrounded 24 hours a day by everything that could drag the soul of many as low as one could slip.*
>
> *For over six months he had this treatment, but not once did the young lad buckle under pressure. Finally, after intensive temptation, they questioned him. Why had he not submitted himself to these things—why had he not partaken? These things would provide pleasure, satisfy his lusts, and were desirable; they were all his. The boy said, "I cannot do what you ask, for I was born to be a king."*
>
> *(Vaughn J. Featherstone, "The King's Son," New Era, Nov. 1975, 35.)*

Obviously, this boy had a clear vision of what he was called to be and he had the self-awareness to know and understand his own weaknesses. He also had the empathy or understanding about the motives and needs of those who were holding him captive. The greatest tool he had, however, was his conscience, which empowered him and guided him to know what was healthy and good for him, what would help him reach his vision. Conscience tells us what is right and what is wrong. I believe it is our conscience that makes us reach to be better. Our conscience can be anything that leads us to do better or to feel more love for another person. Once engaged, I have seen it change more relationships than almost any of the other lights because it is our highest self, our truest core of who we are.

Here are some excellent questions you can ask to ignite your conscience:

- What is the most important thing I can do right now to feed my partner their way?
- What do I need to change to make my relationship better?
- What is my heart telling me I need to do right now?

For me, the single most important light we need to turn on is our conscience. The word *science* means "knowledge" and the word *con* means "with." Together, the word *conscience* means that we make a decision "with knowledge." What knowledge are we talking about here? The knowledge between what is right and wrong, what is healthy and unhealthy. The knowledge of what our values and principles would have us do. This is why conscience is the single most important light we can turn on and is what will eventually lead us to have character and integrity in our relationships.

Four Lights Combined

Whenever a couple comes into my office frustrated with each other, in a moment where they have both either shown a lack of character, communication, or companionship, I simply run them through the Four Lights to help them, and me, gain clarity. Giving them each a piece of paper, we run through the Four Lights. I ask them to answer the Four Lights questions for themselves, in their own heads and in their own hearts:

- **Self Awareness:** What part of the problem in the breakdown did you play?

- **Empathy:** What were your partner's needs and wants during the episode? What was his or her STARVED Stuff?
- **Vision:** What are your long-term goals and dreams when it comes to this particular relationship? What do you want most together?
- **Conscience:** Review the previous three lights and ask, what is the most important thing you need to do right now to fix the problem you co-created?

As a result of these Four Light questions, a solution has been created that now needs to be acted upon, a new light that will lift the relationship if character is engaged. Without fail, one or all of these questions generate learning that is critical to experiencing a successful outcome the next time a couple comes upon a similar situation.

We really cannot create lasting growth until we learn and incorporate this learning into our lives. Without the Four Lights of Learning, we are doomed to keep living the same problems. Here is why . . .

- **Without self-awareness, we lack humility.** We see only the faults of everyone around us and how these people pull down our relationship.
- **Without empathy, we lack compassion.** We might intellectually understand where someone is hurting, but we don't feel for their pain so we don't act to make it better.
- **Without vision, we lack hope.** We are without a plan and instead of leading our relationship to a mutually prescribed end, we are led by the whims of our own moods, circumstances and STARVED Stuff.
- **Without conscience, we lack character.** Without the prompting of what is good and healthy to do, we have nothing to exercise character against and we fall back to our weakest self, doing what is easiest and most self-serving.

Using the Four Lights of Learning provides us with that extra push, and learning is really the answer to all of the other critical areas we've discussed throughout the book. This form of learning helps us to correct our approach and drives us into the higher brain and into taking the High Road.

We cannot become what we need to be, remaining what we are.
—Max De Pree

The most powerful use of the Four Lights comes when we're in the middle of a difficult subject we've traditionally fought about, but now we've learned to Get REAL, and we see that we are actually creating a different relationship, a learn relationship. Learning decreases regrets, so couples don't let so many precious minutes together slip by, leaving regrets that they really could have done more or been better. Learning together is what eventually turns the hearts of even the most STARVED couples into two loving, caring, and promising people. Learning builds humility, compassion, hope and character, but only if couples actually change because of the things they have chosen to learn.

Chapter Review:

- The commitment to keep learning and the commitment to keep changing are the most important commitments in a healthy and enduring relationship.
- The Four Lights of Learning bring clarification to relationships. Self-awareness, empathy, vision, and conscience are essential to personal growth and development.
- The Light of Self-awareness is the ability to understand one's negative and positive impact on others.
- The Light of Empathy allows one to actually feel for and understand the needs and wants of another person. Empathy illuminates the STARVED Stuff of others.
- The Light of Vision shows the potential in the relationship. It is made from clearly seeing the goals, dreams, and possibilities of the future together.
- The Light of Conscience inspires one to live up to what he or she believes to be good and true. It is the basic motivator of all healthy choices.

My Feeding Plan

In order to create a healthy diet that feeds your relationship, you need to have a plan. Use the "My Feeding Plan" activity to come up with some specific ideas from the last chapter that you can use to improve the health of your relationship.

Commitment to Keep Learning

What is the most important thing you learned in this chapter that, if lived consistently, would positively impact your relationship?

Commitment to Keep Changing

Based on what you have learned, what will you commit to change in your life?

____

____

____

____

Specifically, how will you do it?

____

____

____

Specifically, when will you do it?

____

____

____

Chapter 16

Becoming the Change You Seek in Others

Finally, we've made it to the last chapter of this book, and I'm sure your relationships are bordering near perfect by now, aren't they? In reality, healthy and enduring relationships aren't about reaching a level of perfection any more than having a healthy body is about having a perfect body. Health is a state of being and a state of mind, not a state of perfection. Remember **The Goal** of this book, as stated in the preface, is to help us learn how to create healthy and enduring relationships. Now, 16 chapters later, we have reviewed many wonderful tools and ideas that have changed the lives of thousands of people. Yet, none of this really matters unless we choose to incorporate into our own relationship some of what we've learned.

The position you're now in, here at the end of this book—with your head full of so many new ideas—reminds me of a fun riddle used in my workshops. Here we go, see if you can figure this out:

> *Two frogs are sitting on a log and one decides to jump in.*
> *Now how many frogs are sitting on the log?*

If you answered, "One" to the question, then you are just like the majority of people with whom this riddle has been shared. Most of us assume that when someone decides, or learns, they need to do something, then that action automatically takes place. In my years as a coach, I have learned a person's knowledge about what he or she *wants* to do means very little until they actually *choose* to act upon their decision. Therefore, two frogs sitting on a log, with one deciding to jump in, might mean the one actually decided, in the end, not to jump in; therefore two frogs may still be sitting on the log. So, too, with couples: Unless you both decide to actually make the changes contained in this book and then actually change, you may both remain on the lifeless log of your relationship.

Just as we all know the foods that are not healthy for us, we also know the bad habits we need to break in order to obtain good health, yet we still don't act on either of these facts. In other words, it's one thing to talk about not eating cake or vow to not eat cake, but the real moment of truth comes when we are faced with that delicious warm cake, dripping with pure milk chocolate. What then? What will our call to action be?

Knowing junk food is unhealthy for you but eating it anyway is an example of learning a principle in order to change, but not having made the decision yet to actually change. The way we know change is actually occurring won't be by what we or our partners say, as much as by what we or our partners do. Changing is the ultimate sign of your commitment to your relationship and, in the end, is a sure method to feed the STARVED relationship.

Learning and Changing Helps Feed the Four Courses

In the previous chapter, we learned nothing is more important to creating a healthy and enduring relationship than the sincere commitment of two people, and for these two people to put continuous learning and intentional changing before all of the other goals in their relationship. I've found that most people assume that they've outgrown or completed their formal learning and changing when they've graduated or completed their last class in high school or college, but nothing could be further from the truth.

Remember, most of us operate out of our Reactive Brains or amygdalae, and this part of our brain is more worried about learning to "stay alive" than it is about learning how to create healthy and enduring relationships. In essence, because of our Reactive Brains, we've actually learned and changed in to living the STARVED Spiral. Instead of turning on the Four Lights that make us more human, we've actually learned to decrease the light by mastering the darker arts of being selfish, reactive, polarizing, negative, and hopeless. This is why our commitment to learning and changing is so critical, because these traits will take us in a completely different direction in our relationship.

If a man's education is finished, he is finished.
—E.A. Filene

The commitment we're talking about here is a commitment to learning and change that ends up producing healthier relationships. This is the constant and steady relationship diet that produces more character, communication, companionship, and commitment. A commitment to learning and changing how to live these four principles together ensures that we don't have to keep reliving our own "Groundhog" day over and over, but instead we can create a new life and a new relationship.

We Can Improve Our Ways

Learning and changing also means we don't need to keep making the same mistakes day after day after day. This means that, although we will be challenged by our relationships, we don't need to be challenged by the exact same thing in the exact same way, day after day. The only way to ensure that we avoid this is to stay committed to learning and changing. This is the foundation of growth and development and the foundation of healthy and enduring relationships.

An excellent example of how the power of learning and changing affects our lives is found in a five-chapter book written by Portia Nelson:

Autobiography
From *There's a Hole in my Sidewalk*
by
Portia Nelson

Chapter I
I walk down the street.

There is a deep hole in the sidewalk.
I fall in.
I am lost . . . I am helpless.
It isn't my fault.
It takes forever to find a way out.

Chapter II
I walk down the same street.
There is a deep hole in the sidewalk.
I pretend I don't see it.
I fall in again.
I can't believe I am in the same place.
But, it isn't my fault.
It still takes a long time to get out.

Chapter III
I walk down the same street.
There is a deep hole in the sidewalk.
I see it is there.
I still fall in. It's a habit.
My eyes are open.
I know where I am.
It is my fault. I get out immediately.

Chapter IV
I walk down the same street.
There is a deep hole in the sidewalk.
I walk around it.

Chapter V
I walk down another street.

Understanding we will always deal with holes in our sidewalks, or relationships, as was discussed in chapter thirteen, does not mean we need to keep falling into them. Learning and changing together ensures we'll get somewhere in our journey with one another. If we consistently fall into the same relationship holes, neither of us will ever get anywhere in our relationship. However, when we learn and make adjustments, we will make progress and see new ways around the holes. As a result, we will travel streets we've never explored before.

As was also discussed in earlier chapters of this book, it seems to me that too many people are convinced, after they have fallen into the same hole time after time, that it's their partner's fault. However, as pointed out in *Autobiography*, it takes both the hole and someone choosing to fall into it to create a problem.

The turning point of *Autobiography* is in chapter three, when the author says, "My eyes are open." At this moment, the passerby becomes a force or "empowered" in her own life. She is no longer the victim of the holes in her life. She learns to maneuver through the holes, to work around them, to bridge them and to create better results in her life. The same is true in our relationships. Have you learned to "open your eyes"? Do you fully understand how to choose a different path, not just away from your partner, but more importantly, to choose a different path with your partner? You no longer need to be the victim of your relationship or your partner. You can learn to maneuver through the holes, to work around them, to bridge them, and to create better results together.

Learning and Changing Isn't Just a Relationship Issue

Another reason why people need to learn to change together is that learning and changing is an issue much bigger than the relationship. Change is constant or, as others say, "change is inevitable." On an even bigger scale, life is going to change around you and your partner. Your children will change; they will grow up and move out of the house (some days this might sound like a welcomed event!). Your job will eventually change; you might get better work hours or have better opportunities or you may also receive more pay. These changes will create not only benefits, but stresses as well. The physical health of both you and your partner could improve or worsen, or even the health of one of your children or grandchildren, which in turn could deeply change the relationship.

Many of the things that starve you today will change naturally and could be a source of feeding you tomorrow. Change could also bring challenges that might alter your views of the world, or there could be a shift in your collective paradigm that could eventually bring you closer together. Your great power does not come in trying to avoid change, but instead in how you learn to respond and manage change in your life. Only things that are alive can grow and change, which should come as good news for all of us. Because we are alive, we have the opportunity to grow and change. Change is not something we "make" our partners do to help us feel more fed; change is something we all must master in order to make it through the endless trials that come with being alive. The more we are able to stay committed to living with character, and committed to learning and changing, the more hope we will see, not only in our relationships, but in our life as well.

How We Handle Change Is Important

In working with my clients, I have noticed that every person has a different way of dealing with change. This reminds me of a story I once read by Vicki and Don Hale. This story shows the difference between how cattle and buffalo handle the exact same trials of life:

> *On the great plains of the Midwest, buffalo roam the fields with the cattle. The cattle and buffalo live on these plains and eat from*

the same fields. There is, however, a big difference between the two. When storms come to these plains with thunder, lightning, and forceful winds, the cattle turn and run in the same direction the storm is going. However, buffalo, turn, face the storm, and, with all their energy, run into the storm. Cattle spend all their time and energy running from a storm, which they cannot outrun, prolonging their agony, and even their terror. By facing the storm, the buffalo find themselves quickly passing through it. We have a choice in life, with all of the storms we encounter: we can be like the cattle, spending our time and energy running from our trials, or we can be like the buffalo, facing life's trials, and passing quickly through them. Either way, trials in life are ours; it is how we face them that make us who we are. (As told to Vicky and Don Hale)(http://www.fortnet.org/fapg/stories.htm)

It is important to remember that change is about choice and that while you and your partner will not be able to choose what trials you are going to face, you will always be able to choose if you turn and face them, using your gifts and strengths to deal with them, or if you will continue to outrun them. In the end, staying committed to learning from your choices and changing your life will automatically align you with life's healthiest learning.

Be Committed to Change Together

There is nothing more disheartening in a relationship than to see one partner who is incredibly motivated to build a healthy and enduring relationship, while the other seems disinterested in even trying. People in their frustration always end up asking me, "How much longer do I have to keep working on this alone? When can this commitment end?" There really is no good answer for such a tough question. However, what I usually say is, "Not quite yet!

Don't give up until you're effectively living all Four Courses of this book, especially the course on Commitment." What I mean by this is, don't give up on your partner until you have successfully learned, and then changed yourself, based on the Four Courses in this book. Have you learned and changed your character, communication, and companionship skills with your partner?

Again, there are good reasons to end a marriage or long-term relationship with another person. If you are being abused in any way, if your partner has a severe addiction, or if the two of you are continuously arguing with each other, it may be time to make the change. No matter what the situation, I have found that by strengthening your own character, communication, companionship, and commitment to growth, the changes you make only make you stronger.

Your Commitment to Learning and Changing Is Not Dependent on Others

Even if your partner is not living the commitment of learning and changing, this does not mean you can't or don't need to. Your individual growth and development is not based upon your partner's efforts, but instead on your efforts. Just as with all of the other principles you've learned—character, communication, and companionship—commitment to learning and changing is still critical regardless of what your partner is doing or the current state of the relationship. You will need every one of these skills and tools whether you choose to stay together, separate, or divorce. So don't tie your improvement to the work of another person.

Either way, commitment to learning and changing will increase the likelihood that your relationship will improve. If the relationship doesn't improve, you will be more prepared, better skilled, and much more able to see the healthiest way to move forward. When principles become part of your value system, your character will shine through and your influence in your relationship will increase. By being on the High Road, you will have a much better view of the matters at hand than if you remain on the Low Road.

Individual growth is dependent only on *your* willingness to learn. Growth, as a couple or partnership, depends on the level of commitment to mutual learning and changing, but it must be a choice that you both make individually. You can't force, coerce, or manipulate your partner into wanting to learn and change. And in the end, she won't be able to coerce or force you into staying in a relationship where mutual commitment to learning and changing is nonexistent.

If you find your partner is resisting learning and changing, there are some real consequences that exist for those who are unable or unwilling to learn and change. The consequences come from not following the principles. No one can take away the consequences; we can only live the principles. My advice to you is to keep trying to create optimal conditions for effective learning and growth. Be bold in your desire to learn. Try to implement everything you learn and maintain hope that your partner will eventually see the light.

Learning and Changing Brings Hope

For me, the greatest reason we should be learning and changing is the fact that it brings hope into our relationships and into our lives. I think of the cancer patient who, when first diagnosed felt a cold, hopeless feeling overcome her. In her ignorance about the disease, she had only fear. However, as she began to see her character and her faith being awakened, she began to feel hope. As her understanding and awareness about the disease and its myriad of solutions was explored and the roads were opened, she felt hope. As her friends and family warmly encircled her, she felt hope. All of this hope is a by-product of her willingness to learn and be open to all of the information and energy around her, and her willingness to change when her eyes were opened and she saw a healthier way.

Where there is great love, there are always miracles.
—Willa Sibert Cather

The same is true in our own relationships. Hope isn't knowing everything there is to know about our partner, or always feeling warm and close with one another, or always having profoundly deep and intimate experiences. Hope doesn't come from the ability to avoid pain and struggles in our lives or relationships, but instead hope in a relationship comes from commitment and confidence in our character to do the right thing and the competency that we can do things the right way. Hope really is a by-product of knowing we are competent enough to effectively handle the struggles and trials we will inevitably face. Hope is the confidence felt in knowing how to handle a conflict and how to communicate through the difficult issues in the relationship. Hope is the result of seeing consistent patterns and traditions of love at play in the relationship. Hope flows from the fact that together we are committed to each other and the promises we made to each other when we were first married. The hope that comes from learning and changing reminds me of a quote by Victor Hugo:

> *Be like the bird that, passing in her flight awhile on boughs too slight, feels them give way beneath her, and yet sings, knowing that she hath wings.*

We really must learn to have the hope and confidence of this bird who feels the limb give way beneath her, yet she sings. Why is this bird able to sing? What helps her to be so happy and hopeful? The bird knows she has wings. The wings to fly in our relationships do not come from the boughs or branches on which we choose to land. Our confidence and hope should come from our ability to fly in our relationship, no matter what Birds know the principles of flight, and now after learning the Four Courses, we know the principles of healthy and enduring relationships. We just need to gain more confidence in them by incorporating them more fully into our life.

Take These Principles and Fly

Throughout this book, we have increased our skill set with some basic tools and practices, as well as some foundational principles. However, the work is still not done. Now we need to implement these principles, along with our partner, and customize our own set of practices and solutions based on the principles of character, communication, companionship, and commitment. We've also got to determine how to ensure Safety, Trust, Appreciation, Respect, Validation, Encouragement and Dedication for one another. Along our journey though this book we have had the opportunity to create our plan for how to implement what we have learned by filling out "My Feeding Plan" at the end of each chapter.

These Plans, complete with our commitment to keep learning and our commitment to keep changing, can now serve as our recipe for how to feed our relationship. We can use each Plan as a step-by-step instruction sheet to a healthy and enduring relationship. If we feel overwhelmed, we can just pick one or two of our Plans and start living the commitments we have made. Our Plan and our Commitments will bring positive progress in our relationship.

And again, remember the words of Gandhi:

You must be the change you want to see in the world.

You must be willing to put forth the effort to make more of your relationship, and the change starts with you.

- If you want more Safety, then be more safe.
- If you want more Trust, then be more trustworthy.
- If you want more Appreciation, then be more appreciative.
- If you want more Respect, then be more respectful.
- If you want more Validation, then learn to validate.
- If you want more Encouragement, then be more encouraging.
- If you want more Dedication, then be more dedicated.

Don't wait for your partner. Start feeding today!

Chapter Review:

- Knowledge about what is wanted in the relationship means very little until action is taken in the Choice Point to implement the knowledge and change the relationship.
- A commitment to learning and changing produces a healthier relationship by increasing character, communication, companionship, and commitment.
- Power comes not in trying to avoid change, but in learning how to effectively respond and manage change in life. This brings hope to relationships.
- Individual growth and development is not based on someone else's efforts. It is the outcome of one's personal efforts.
- Each "My Feeding Plan" is a step-by-step instruction sheet to a healthy and enduring relationship.

My Feeding Plan

In order to create a healthy diet that feeds your relationship, you need to have a plan. Use the "My Feeding Plan" activity to come up with some specific ideas from the last chapter that you can use to improve the health of your relationship.

Commitment to Keep Learning

What is the most important thing you learned in this chapter that, if lived consistently, would positively impact your relationship?

Commitment to Keep Changing

Based on what you have learned, what will you commit to change in your life?

Specifically, how will you do it?

Specifically, when will you do it?

About the Author

Matt Townsend, MA

For over 15 years, Matt Townsend has been energizing and involving audiences large and small with his unique approach to building and maintaining successful personal and business relationships. Matt has the perfect mix of cutting-edge research in communication and human relationships combined with the skill of a top-notch humorist. This blend ensures that audiences are entertained as well as enlightened and leave with practical information that can be immediately applied to their life.

Having dedicated his life to the study of communication and interpersonal relationships, Matt has worked extensively in the areas of results-oriented communication, conflict resolution, and leadership training. He has experience with speaking and training hundreds of Fortune 500 companies, such as CNN, Cox Communications, and Lockheed Martin. Other past clients include AT&T, American Express, Dupont, General Mills, Hewlett Packard, Honda, IBM, Nike, Panasonic, and the US Navy.

"The Matt Townsend Show" is broadcast each week to thousands of radio listeners in the Intermountain West. Matt earned his bachelor's and master's degrees in Communication as well as a master's degree in Human Development and is presently pursuing his doctoral degree in Human Development. His greatest joy and measure of success come from his marriage to his wife, Mardi, and from raising their six children.

Testimonials

Workshop

I have attended private sessions with Matt, along with a six-week workshop, and have come away each time feeling more empowered to make my life better. The tools that he gives and the principles he teaches are simple and truly have had a positive effect in my life. The way Matt teaches makes it fun and makes so much sense. I wish I would have had this knowledge many years ago. It has helped in my relationships in all aspects of my life and has made me a better mother, a better friend, and a more confident person. Matt and what he teaches are truly AWESOME!!!

—JC

I just have to tell you that you have made an amazing difference in our family. Because of what you taught us, we totally changed the way we spend time together and turned it from a time that we dreaded into a time that was unique and special for all of us. You are a miracle worker.

—CH

The things we have learned from you have totally changed our lives. We have revamped every aspect of our relationship and our pattern of living. Just the couple of [workshop sessions] we've had has helped a TON!

—RG

We have only been in the class for two weeks, but it has made a dramatic difference in our relationship. This workshop is the most remarkable thing I have experienced in my entire life.

—CF

Coaching

I'm coming out a changed man.

—DP

Thanks, Matt, for everything. Like most, I never intended on ending my marriage. I think that this will help both of us move forward into healthy relationships with our kids and most of all, each other. You're an awesome coach and offer an incredible service; wish we could have met you 15 years ago.

—CS

Matt has made a huge difference in our relationship. Our relationship is like night and day difference. It has been better in the last 5 days than it has been in 10 years. We just need to keep being reminded about what Matt teaches.

—RL

He's great. I feel completely different from when I came here. We are so lucky we found him. I can't wait for the workshop.

—CM

My husband and I highly recommend Matt. We feel confident in sharing his name with our closest friends and family, knowing that they too will receive the skills to make their own marriages stronger and happier.

—A and DY

I've learned more in this 6-hour workshop about how I relate than I have in 50 years of marriage.

—SC

Products by Matt Townsend
Available at www.StarvedStuff.com

Feeding the STARVED Marriage Workshop on DVD and CD!

Feeding the STARVED Marriage
12-disc DVD program and two 100-page workbooks

This 12-disc set allows you to benefit from Matt Townsend's *Feeding the STARVED Marriage* workshop as if you were attending it in person. Matt's dynamic workshop is featured in its entirety as well as two complete 100-page workbooks. In this DVD set, Matt takes you through the principles needed to strengthen and reenergize your relationship and identifies the skills and tools to implement your new knowledge.

Feeding the STARVED Marriage
6-CD Audio Program and 20-page workbook

This 6-CD audio set features a condensed version of Matt Townsend's *Feeding the STARVED Marriage* workshop. With his humorous and entertaining style, Matt explores the fundamental principles of relating in a step-by-step process that is divided into six sections. Each section includes learning activities as well as goals for improvement. The 20-page workbook provides a visual image of Matt's principles and activities.

5 Keys to a Happy and Healthy Marriage CD

In this one-hour disc, Matt Townsend examines the keys to a healthy long-term relationship. The first step is to learn about what starves a marriage. Then Matt teaches five keys that can feed and nourish a relationship into a vibrant and strong companionship. These principles can be applied to any type of relationship—marriage or otherwise. Even better, they can help a relationship in any stage, whether it is STARVED or just has the munchies.

www.FeedingRelationships.com

Visit Matt's blog at www.FeedingRelationships.com and join the worldwide conversation or look into our Relationship Coaching Program to receive ongoing support, information, and training about how to feed a STARVED relationship.

Find out more about Matt and his services at

www.StarvedStuff.com

or call

1(877) 5 RELATE